LEADING

MANAGING FROM A DISTANCE

VIRTUAL

DURING THE CORONAVIRUS

TEAMS

WRITTEN BY

CATHERINE MATTISKE

A separate
Official Companion Workbook
is available for this title.

Please visit the website for details:

www.id9intelligentdesign.com/books

Also by Catherine Mattiske

Train for Results

Training Activities that Work

LEARNING SHORT-TAKE SERIES:

Adult Learning Principles 1

Adult Learning Principles 2

Adult Learning Principles 3

Confident Facilitation Skills

Creative Business Thinking

Customer Service Excellence

Debrief and Feedback Strategies

Effective Time Management

Fast-track Instructional Design

Influencing for Opportunity

Internal Performance Consulting

Leading the Training Team

Listen and Be Listened To

Making Meetings Work

Managing for Performance

Managing Organizational Change

Negotiating for Success

Negotiating for Success - The Next Step

Negotiating the Million Dollar Deal

Persuasive Presentation Skills

Recruiting for Results

Sales Force Leadership

Successful Project Management

The Effective Leader

Understanding and Managing Diversity

Understanding Customer Motivation

Understanding Relationship Selling

TPC - The Performance Company Pty Ltd
PO Box 639
Rozelle NSW 2039
Sydney, Australia
ACN 077 455 273
email: tpc@tpc.net.au
Website: www.tpc.net.au

National Library of Australia
Cataloguing-in-Publication data

Mattiske, C
Copyright © 2020 By Catherine Mattiske

Leading Virtual Teams: Managing from a distance during the coronavirus
ISBN 978-1-921547-99-7
1. Occupational training. 2. Learning. I. Title.
Dewey class no: 658.4022
Printed in USA
Distributed by TPC - The Performance Company - www.tpc.net.au

For further information contact TPC - The Performance Company, Sydney Australia phone +61 9555 1953 or TPC - The Performance Company, California on +1 818-227-5052, or email info@tpc.net.au

Further information on the author can be found at www.id9intelligentdesign.com

Dedication

This book is dedicated to the
global network of talented,
empathetic, and successful business
leaders working every day in
challenging situations to create,
grow, and lead brilliant virtual
teams who are impacted by the
COVID-19, coronavirus
pandemic.

Catherine Mattiske

About the author

Catherine Mattiske
CEO and Founder
TPC - The Performance Company

Australia

Catherine Mattiske is a leading training professional, author, and publisher, with an internationally acclaimed career spanning 30 years across an array of industries including banking, insurance, pharmaceutical, biotechnology, and retail.

Mattiske established 'The Performance Company,' a leading-edge training and consulting organization, in 1994. The Performance Company has offices in Sydney, Los Angeles, New York, and London.

Catherine Mattiske has earned a reputation for helping clients achieve their personal and business goals across Australia, the USA, United Kingdom, Europe, Africa, New Zealand, and Asia.

Mattiske's client list has a global reach, including high profile Fortune 100 and 500 companies.

Catherine Mattiske is an accomplished author and publisher. The best-selling, '*Train for Results*' *(Allen and Unwin)*, is on academic reading lists worldwide. In 2014, she authored '*Training Activities that Work*' with a group of her Certified ID9 Professionals. Catherine Mattiske released the 27 part 'Learning Short-takes®' series of books.

Recognized globally for her achievements in business, Catherine Mattiske was a member of the US Congressional Business Advisory Council. Mattiske has been awarded for her influence to US business and has also been nominated on several occasions for the prestigious Australian Business Woman of the Year.

Since expanding her Australian business to the US and Europe in 2001, Catherine has worked with her team remotely and built a global virtual organization. Catherine knows the highs and lows of leading virtual teams, and she is passionate about helping leaders overcome their barriers to success when leading virtual teams.

When the coronavirus was announced as a pandemic, Catherine fast-tracked this book to ensure that it was available to help leaders globally.

.

Acknowledgments

The world is a better place thanks to people who want to develop and lead others, especially at this time during the coronavirus crisis. What makes it even better are leaders who share the gift of their time. Thank you to everyone who takes the time to grow and help others grow, and keeps teams engaged and motivated during what history will undoubtedly show as one of the most challenging times for humanity.

To all of the leaders, who shared their challenges and victories as personal stories included in the book, thank you. While I've changed your names and unable to publicly acknowledge you individually, thank you for meeting with me at such short notice. Your accounts will indeed benefit others who are experiencing similar situations.

Thank you to my husband and family, who provided me with endless cups of coffee and quiet space so that I could write this book so quickly.

I would like to recognize and thank all who have reviewed *Leading Virtual Teams*.

All of the testimonials are by senior leaders, at the highest level of management, leading their teams during the COVID-19 pandemic.

In some cases, as global leaders, they were mobilizing thousands of employees to work from home in a matter of days, juggling technology, processes, and the needs of their people, and yet they generously offered to read *Leading Virtual Teams* and provide their thoughts.

During this global crisis and unprecedented operational change for many organizations, my sincere appreciation goes to each person who took the time to read and review *Leading Virtual Teams*.

To everyone involved, your collaboration and contribution are invaluable.

Thank you!

Catherine Mattiske

Praise for Leading Virtual Teams

"With virtual working becoming the new normal for companies large and small, this book is very timely. For anyone struggling with issues either managing or working in, a virtual team, this book provides a wealth of great information. There are lots of useful suggestions throughout and good exercises to assess each area covered. I particularly like some of the tips around building a virtual team culture that provides strong ideas for building team engagement remotely. The tech side of working virtually is only one small aspect of making a virtual team successful, and this book helps you ensure success."

**Dr Andrée Bates, CEO Eularis,
London, UK**

"Unchartered times demand progressive leaders who are prepared to learn and adapt with new leadership skills of their own. It's never too late to pivot and learn new ways to lead. [Leading Virtual Teams] is so timely and urgently needed"

**Greg Creed, retired Yum! Brands CEO,
Dallas, USA**

"The COVID-19 crash course in virtual working has suddenly changed almost everyone into a digital worker for at least some of their job.

The world has changed forever, in a matter of weeks, the adoption of technologies into business meeting culture that has been resisted for years are suddenly completely mainstream. Cameras that had been stubbornly kept switched off are now on. Meetings that had to be in-person are turning out to be just as much of a success when run virtually with the appropriate active facilitation. Although the technology works well, the dynamics of virtual work and leadership require new skills, and many executives have been left scrambling to apply their skills in new ways.

Responding to the crisis, Catherine Mattiske has rapidly drawn on her years of experience to provide an excellent guide for leaders trying to navigate this challenging new world."

**Robert Hillard, Chief Strategy & Innovation Officer, Deloitte Australia
Chairman, Australian Information Industry Association,
Melbourne, Australia**

"The learnings and insights that Catherine generously shares in her book are instrumental in elevating leadership and results that is now driven in this virtual world. [Leading Virtual Teams] is required reading for any leader looking to ensure that their business survives in this new reality of the virtual world. Catherine has developed proven, thoughtful communication methodologies that help leaders succeed in their every day and defining moments. What surprised me is how extensive and comprehensive the book is… full of highly valuable purposeful information that readers can apply straight away in their business."

Boaz Fischer, CEO of CommsNet Group and MyBizSecurity, Canberra, Australia

"Most organisations have now been suddenly forced into a virtual world, without necessarily having the guidance or direction to do that effectively. What a wonderful and timely resource "Leading Virtual Teams" is for all those caught short! Our organisation had a great business continuity plan developed, which we implemented with ease. However, I hadn't considered the changes that I would need to make to now lead and manage in a completely virtual world. This book has allowed me to quickly focus on the requirements of the here and now, and to challenge my staff around what is needed in our brave new world. I loved the content and set out of the book. It really covered off all of the essential subjects required to ensure that any business or organisation can seize the opportunities and become bigger, stronger and fit for purpose.

The timing and foresight of this book are incredible. It has helped me to focus on the requirements of the here and now, and to think about the future in positive and innovative ways."

Lucinda Nolan, CEO of the Ovarian Cancer Research Foundation. Melbourne, Australia

"This book is all about giving you options, for increasing yours and your virtual team's cohesion, performance, and results. This book is an arsenal of straight forward tools, insights, and real-world practices for upping your "Virtual Team Leader" game. It will help you avoid being blindsided by common and uncommon virtual team derails, so you spend your time building instead of recovering your team from a misstep (yours and theirs).

Under COVID-19 conditions, the timing of the book could not be better. Local leaders are becoming virtual team leaders, who are realizing there's a ton of things they don't know about leading their team in a virtual environment. This book will help leaders see quickly what they don't know and avoid problems onsite leaders rarely face."

John St. John, MBA, PHR, CoachTrains.com, Washington DC, USA.

This book provides a practical model for leaders creating and modifying virtual team environments. The model accommodates a range of team environments - local to virtual - that are typically found throughout organisations.

It also provides specific advice to leaders (like me) who are adjusting and supporting their people with a rapid transition to a completely virtual team environment. The self-assessments and case studies add practical substance to this model guidance.

When many of us have been cast into a virtual team environment without notice, this book is my chart for navigating the organisation through rapidly-changing weather that seems the new norm.

Catherine covers the spectrum of team development and management methods applied to virtual environments, providing a refreshing perspective to how we can effectively lead in a dispersed and physically distant context.

I was pleasantly surprised to receive advice on who to give effective virtual presentations. In a role that frequently draws on presentation skills, I find the guidance most valuable for translating what I do from the physical to the virtual field.

Leading Virtual Teams is becoming my #1 leadership guide!

Peter Morison, CEO, VicWater - the Victorian Water Industry Association, Melbourne, Australia

I have had the honor and privilege of leading virtual global teams in various organizations for the past eighteen years. *Leading Virtual Teams* provides practical, real-world applications, guides and checklists, and recommendations that will help any manager/leader successfully lead virtual teams.

The future of the workplace will require almost every organization to have manager/leaders that can successfully lead and manage virtual teams. The content within *Leading Virtual Teams* reaches a large global audience. I am confident that after reading the book, everyone from the most inexperienced manager/leader to a manager/leader with years of experience will benefit equally from Catherine's masterful understanding of leading virtual teams.

The topic of leading virtually fascinates me. Even as an experienced virtual leader, I'm always looking for ways to be more effective as a manager/leader, so I felt a sense of excitement and positive energy as I read the book. Now my goal is to implement a few tips and recommendations with my team. If you want to be an effective leader, lead virtual teams successfully, empower your team, continue to build successful relationships, and leave a legacy - I would highly recommend you read *Leading Virtual Teams*.

Dr. Samuel C. Rindell, Head of Talent Management Strategy & Operations, Cigna, & Professor of Leadership & Management, Connecticut, USA

Leading Virtual Teams is a timely resource to help leaders manage anxiety and build resilience in individuals and teams to 'keep the lights on and stay open for business' during these challenging times.

Also, it is an essential "how-to' playbook" for managers and leaders to find a way to resolve, reimagine, reform, and return to business and customer service in a new world of remote virtual working.

This book is a very comprehensive commentary of what it takes to be a successful leader in managing virtually through building engagement, building trust, EQ, and creating a productive virtual team culture.

There is not much that this book does not cover, and it will be a valuable resource, even for those who have already been operating in a remote work environment.

The chapters on culture, performance, communication, leadership skills, and social media, all highlight the need that leading virtual teams is a delicate balance between success and failure. Fortunately, this book helps the reader understand and succeed in this new way of working.

I was very surprised that this book not only addressed the role of leaders and managers, and helping others to succeed but also emphasised the focus on the leader, and how to develop ongoing sustainability through building connected networks, building a personal brand and planning a way forwards.

The tools and worksheets are very thought provoking and insightful in bringing a better understanding of the virtual workplace.

Leading Virtual Teams discusses the essentials of virtual team management and leadership. It's easy to read cover to cover and have available as a reference guide.

Jay Patel, Head of Digital Learning, National Australia Bank, Melbourne, Australia

Leading Virtual Teams is a very pragmatic book with a lot of cases on how to become a better virtual leader and with specific examples of the current COVID-19 crisis. It's one of the first books you can find that specifically addresses how to manage our new virtual reality since COVID-19 changed (most likely forever) our lives. The language is very direct, and the structure is very straightforward. I also liked the combination of definitions, examples, activities, and statements of real people.

I particularly enjoyed two sections: the concept of High Performance Virtual Teams, a natural evolution of the so-called HPTs, and the development of skills, abilities, and competences of a successful virtual leader.

Juan Jose Piedra, CFO, Sandoz Industrial Products S.A., Barcelona, Spain

World Health Organization

Excerpt from: Mental health and psychosocial considerations during the COVID-19 outbreak[1]

18 March 2020

Messages for people in isolation

28. **Stay connected and maintain your social networks**. Try as much as possible to keep your personal daily routines or create new routines if circumstances change. If health authorities have recommended limiting your physical, social contact to contain the outbreak, you can stay connected via telephone, e-mail, social media, or video conference.

29. **During times of stress, pay attention to your own needs and feelings**. Engage in healthy activities that you enjoy and find relaxing. Exercise regularly, keep regular sleep routines and eat healthy food. Keep things in perspective. Public health agencies and experts in all countries are working on the outbreak to ensure the availability of the best care to those affected

---

[1] Source: https://www.who.int/docs/default-source/coronaviruse/mental-health-considerations.pdf?sfvrsn=6d3578af_2

Contents

List of Activities

A-Z Case Studies

Introduction

Is the virtual team you are leading
functioning at full capacity?

Are all your virtual team members
confident, productive, and positive
even though the coronavirus is
impacting the way they work?

Are all your virtual team members
engaged, involved, and a team-
oriented player?

Do you always know how to deal with
multi-cultural team members
sensitively?

If you answered NO to one or more of these questions, you need to read this book.

International business educator, Catherine Mattiske set up her first global virtual team in 2001. After years of leading virtual teams internationally, she has written this book to help you be the best virtual leader that you can be. With the impact of the coronavirus, this book is essential for all leaders who are changing how they work, and how their teams come to grips with working in a very different physical and emotional environment.

This comprehensive book will answer many virtual team member questions you have, including how to:

- Understand different leadership types – local, virtual and hybrid
- Know what makes a robust virtual team leader
- Build virtual teams
- Create a virtual team culture
- Communicate for peak performance
- Know which communication method to use in which situation
- Manage global and cultural adaptability
- Tap into potential cultural intelligence
- Manage up virtually – when your boss isn't in the same office as you

- Improve your presentation skills
- Avoid the seven deadly presentation mistakes
- Get to yes faster using virtual negotiation skills
- Monitor and value your self-worth
- Build your online presence via social media
- Efficiently and productively build your internal and virtual networks
- Plan your career development

If you are serious about being a strong and successful virtual leader and leading the way for more virtual team leaders in your organization, this book is a must-read for you.

PART 1
VIRTUAL LEADERSHIP
FOUNDATIONS

Virtual Management Skill Set

Distance managing and virtual leadership is an essential competency for leading in a global environment. Now, with the coronavirus, leaders who were office-bound with teams that they could meet within the office have faced a new reality – becoming instant virtual leaders. Distanced from their usual workplace with organizations working from home is a new challenge that some never thought they would need to face.

This book provides practical information and tools to help virtual leaders' bridge the communication gaps created by geographical separation and develop peak performance from employees they rarely see in person. Filled with need-to-know advice and practical tips, this book shows virtual leaders how to successfully build, maintain, and manage global, virtual, and cross-cultural teams.

> At the end of this chapter, you should be able to distinguish the needs of virtual leaders and virtual team members in various virtual team settings and compare this to your work environment.

We will discuss the elements of successful virtual leadership and assess the current and potential skill set for virtual leaders and team members.

> The benefit of this chapter is that you should be able to identify foundational behaviors contributing to success as a virtual leader.
>
> You should also recognize behaviors in virtual team members that contribute to success in a virtual team, allowing you to apply this to your own team environment.

At the end of each chapter, a critical point summary is included for a fast-track review of this book.

Activity 1 - Virtual Leadership Foundations Assessment

Understanding how to manage and assess virtual teams is critical to global business success. This assessment looks at the key skills in managing virtual teams to improve individual and group performance.

It is designed for you to assess your current skills in this area personally. This assessment is for your personal use to help you determine your existing strengths and areas of development.

For each question on the following page, rate yourself on each of the techniques.

Virtual Leadership Foundations	1	2	3	4	5
	Never	Rarely	Sometimes	Most of the time	Always
I can define the difference between a local leader, a virtual leader, and a hybrid leader.					
I ensure that I manage virtual team members differently.					
I enjoy working independently in an isolated environment with little face-to-face interaction with others.					
I am focused on my ability to stay in control of the project, contract, or team, to keep things on track, and to know the current status of single and multiple projects.					
I consider that I successfully control emotions, manage prejudice in the workplace, and inspire others.					
I practice integrity without compromise.					
I exhibit calm professionalism within my country and across borders to maintain team cohesiveness and open communication.					
I understand the cultural background, biases, and traits of virtual team members.					
I give others the authority to make decisions, take responsibility, and be accountable.					
I have a formal process for assessing the suitability of potential virtual team members when I form a new virtual team or take over the management of an established virtual team.					
TOTAL					

Please total your scores for Never, Rarely, Sometimes, Most of the time, and Always.

Reflecting on your answers

All of the skills above are necessary to lead virtual teams and will be explored in this and later chapters.

Congratulations on all the statements that you answered, 'Most of the time' and 'Always.' Please don't worry, though, if you scored high on the 'Never,' 'Rarely', or 'Sometimes' columns.

This book will guide you through the maze of virtual leadership and give you strategies to significantly improve the skills you have identified.

The Benefits of Virtual Management

The need for virtual management and geographically dispersed teams continues to benefit organizations for many reasons:

- **Financial considerations** - From an economic perspective, it makes sound business sense for many companies to take a decentralized approach to organizational structures.

- **Geographical diversity** - A workforce that is geographically diverse can be a huge business benefit in less tangible ways. With employees worldwide who are natives of those countries or speak the local language fluently, many companies have a keen competitive edge in those countries, over single country based competitors.

- **Faster time to market** - Moving into new and emerging markets is also much more manageable when a company has someone local who understands the political, financial, and corporate landscape.

- **Pressures of the global marketplace and economy** - Globalization has increased the need for virtual management. Even though conducting international business has become technologically accessible, new strains have emerged when working with cross-cultural teams and the need to understand and overcome cultural and language difficulties.

- And in 2020, with the onset of coronavirus – **Employee health and safety** - The instruction to safeguard the health of populations globally has brought *benefits* that some teams may be currently experiencing – the ability to focus, reduced travel time, increased family connection. However, as we will look at later, the challenges for some are, and will become, overwhelming.

Leadership types – local, virtual and hybrid

Determining where a local company structure ends, and a virtual company structure begins are often blurred.

Local companies are those who have employees conducting their work collectively at the same location each day. They may be in the same building or located in several buildings close enough to walk (or shuttle) to project meetings or work together physically where necessary.

Those employees who ONLY communicate with others in their building or on the same campus are working under the **local company structure**.

If employees need to communicate and collaborate across locations that are not close enough to walk (or shuttle) to the company would be considered a **virtual company**.

It has been common practice for companies to locate certain groups, such as accounting and other administrative departments, in different locations from the main office. These companies are NOT considered virtual since regular participation in interdepartmental meetings is not critical to the success of most projects.

> Therefore, a **virtual company** has at least one worker NOT in the same physical location each day as co-workers on the same team or project. In many organizations today, team members are NEVER physically in the same room or office locations.

Any combination of local and virtual is considered a **hybrid model**.

The Virtual Leader Defined

Depending on the company structure, there are three types of Leaders: The Local Leader, the 100% Virtual Leader, and the Hybrid Leader.

The **Local Leader** is defined as someone who works in the same physical office as his or her team members.

Local Leaders may use virtual tools such as email, instant messaging, and the internet; however, it's the LOCATION OF THE EMPLOYEES that defines whether the team is local or virtual, not the technology used.

The **100% Virtual Leader** works with team members who are not in the same location as him or her.

The **HYBRID Leader** has a team that is a combination of LOCAL team members and VIRTUAL team members.

Whether you are a 100% Virtual Leader or a Hybrid Leader you are faced with the challenges of being a Virtual Leader. Your skills as a Virtual Leader are different than a Local Leader.

Core Competencies of Effective Virtual leaders

> Leader – someone who can create and communicate a vision and inspire others to achieve the vision.

The workplace has changed and evolved into a complex environment of various team structures, both formal and informal. Successful virtual teams and their virtual leaders navigate between locations, time zones, cultures, and teams to achieve their goals.

Virtual management can be a challenge, especially if you've never met your team members face to face! Virtual management can be especially challenging for virtual leaders whose natural leadership style is to lead to a higher degree through relationships than their counterparts. Managing people whom you hardly ever see in person adds more complexity to the role of a leader.

If you are moving into or have been thrust into a virtual management role, you'll need new tools, skills, knowledge, and processes for daily virtual management.

> If you are an existing virtual leader, you'll know that the biggest mistake you can make is to do everything the same way you did when you managed a local team.

Patty: I've been a manager in a construction company for five years based in Los Angeles. Three months ago, my company acquired a company that had offices in Florida and also overseas.

Overnight my role changed from managing my local team to have my team work from home. On the announcement that California was going into lockdown, my team members went into panic. We are far from paper-less, so we needed to think about how we'd work remotely. It sounds ridiculous now, but we'd never considered this before. To add to the challenge, we also have team members in Florida and Hong Kong all working from legacy systems making team communication difficult on the prospect of working remotely.

Once we'd packed boxes of files, organized laptops with the right software, and purchased new hardware for everyone: monitors, keyboards, cameras, and printers, I thought we were done with the challenges. I hoped that once I could get my team members safely working from home that it would be straightforward. That was only the beginning.

It's been a challenge for me to adapt my leadership style. I'm used to looking across the office to see who's at their desk, being able to talk to team members when I need to, and knowing the projects are on track via our archaic whiteboard in the office.

In the first week, I set up apps to communicate, share files, and video-conference. My team members are home-schooling kids, but getting their work done. I've entirely changed my leadership style within weeks to one of 'imperfection is okay'! Some days I question, "what am I doing?" however, all my team are virus-free and generally coping pretty well....most days!

> The biggest mistake you can make is
> to do everything the same way you did
> when you managed a local team.

Virtual management requires a high level of commitment to personal communication with EACH team member. Virtual managing needs LESS directive and MORE guiding and advising.

Introducing the Core Virtual Leadership Model

Throughout this book, we will explore the core attributes, skills, and knowledge of virtual leaders, in detail. For each part, you will be able to assess your skills and think through areas of development.

In a fast-paced virtual world, leadership is a never-ending growth opportunity, always having to deal with new challenges and opportunities. *Therefore, there is no such thing as the 'perfect leader,' and all leaders* are wise to have an action plan on which they are working for continuous development

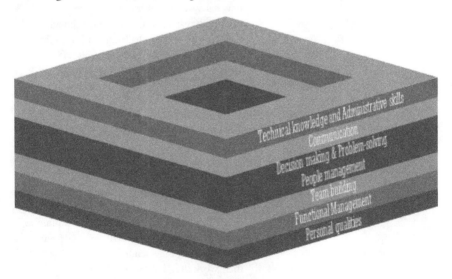

Figure 1 - Core Virtual Leadership Model

The Virtual Leader requires focus in seven core areas:

1. Personal qualities

2. Functional Management

3. Team building

4. People management

5. Decision making & Problem-solving

6. Communication

7. Technical knowledge and Administrative skills

As we explore each of these core areas, individual assessments will be available for you to complete and reflect on your strengths and areas of development.

KEY POINTS SUMMARY

- Distance managing and virtual leadership are essential competencies for leading in a global environment.

- You can be a highly successful virtual leader by bridging the communication gaps created by geographical separation and get peak performance from employees whom you rarely see.

- By understanding your role as either a local, virtual, or hybrid leader, you can best determine the style of day-to-day leadership that is appropriate for each situation.

PART 2
VIRTUAL LEADER
PERSONAL QUALITIES

What makes a strong Virtual Leader?

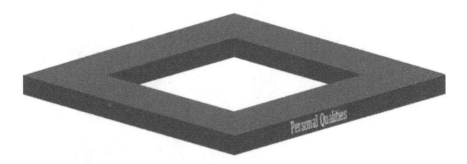

Personal Qualities for Virtual Leadership

In this chapter, you will be able to assess your skills, attributes, and knowledge regarding Virtual Leadership.

Some people are very well-suited to working on a virtual team. Generally, these people possess certain personal qualities that are highly desirable in virtual leaders.

Activity 2 -   Virtual Leadership Personal Qualities

Your perception of the top ten ideal personal qualities and characteristics for virtual leaders

Virtual Leadership IDEAL virtual leader qualities		My Perception: 1 – list top ten ideal personal qualities and characteristics for virtual leaders 2 – prioritize them 1-10
1	6	
2	7	
3	8	
4	9	
5	10	

Ideal personal qualities and characteristics for virtual leaders

There is no absolute answer – just your opinion of what's essential in your role as a virtual leader.

Some suggested qualities and characteristics include being:

Accessible

Action-based

Articulate

Communicative

Considerate

Courageous

Demonstrates Integrity

Expressive

Fair-minded

Honest

Independent

Intuitive

Objective

Passionate

Proactive

Self-Motivated

Straightforward

Trustworthy

Activity 3 - Your Prioritized List – Personal Qualities

Comparing the list that you created with ours above, create your prioritized list of which personal qualities that you consider are essential for virtual leaders.

The prioritized list of Virtual Leader qualities	My Perception: My revised prioritized list
1	
2	
3	
4	
5	
6	
7	
8	
9	
10	

Remember, there is no correct answer – just your opinion of what's essential in your role as a virtual leader within your organization.

Functional Management Skills

As discussed, the virtual leader requires many skill sets.

The skills of **Functional Management** include the ability to stay in control of the project or team, to keep things on track, and to know the current status of single and multiple projects.

Specifically, this subset includes the following:

- Scheduling tasks
- Organization
- Time management
- Leadership
- Prioritization
- Goal setting (manager and team)
- Tracking and reporting progress
- Managing change
- Budgets and finance

Shimi: I work at an International Business School in Dubai. I have a genuine interest in people, and my team is located throughout the UAE and UK.

The biggest hurdle for me as a virtual leader, especially in these challenging times, is time management.

Initially, I thought I could be 'all things to all people,' and then I realized that my natural style of managing every last detail wasn't going to work.

Then, in March 2020, we were all ordered to work remotely in light of the virus outbreak.

I had to increase the trust in my team, set the goals with them, prioritize projects, and then delegate responsibility to them to do the work.

This was a significant growth step for me. I'm used to being in detail, but now with my team spread across many different locations in Dubai and also some administrative team members in London, all working from home, everything has become more pronounced.

I realize that I need to be the manager to check on their progress and remove barriers for my team when they need me to step in, but not in detail anymore.

Quickly I could see the impact of changing my style. Since taking a much more helicopter approach, my team is happier, more productive, and I'm focused on the operationalization of the strategic plan.

The team has pulled together to get through this crisis as a united team.

Activity 4 - Personal Assessment - Functional Virtual Management Skills

The following activity will allow you the opportunity to assess at an in-depth level of your current and potential skills.

This assessment is for your personal use to help you determine your existing strengths and areas of development.

For each question, rate yourself on each of the techniques and then total each column.

Functional Management Skills		1	2	3	4	5
Skill	Measure	Never	Rarely	Some-times	Most of the time	Always
Scheduling Tasks	I have the ability to plan and schedule tasks, milestones, and deliverables across a geographically diverse team.					
Organization	I have a high level of organizational skill. I have the ability to plan and organize management and team tasks and events.					
Time Management	I have the ability to manage time and tasks across time zones. I understand how cultural differences affect an individual's concept of time.					
Leadership	I have the ability to lead by influence rather than authority. I establish and maintain trust with diverse team members across cultures, time zones, and functional units. I am accountable for decisions and outcomes for the virtual team.					
Prioritization	I can prioritize work for self and team members. I maintain ownership for setting, changing, and communicating team and individual priorities for local and remote team members.					
Goal Setting (manager and team)	I have the ability to set clear, measurable goals and objectives for myself and the team as a whole. I have the ability to accurately measure and verify results and effectively communicate results to senior management.					
Budgets and finance	I can work with team members to set, manage, and control budgets, costs, and revenues. I can use a virtual reporting system to maintain the appropriate level of control and understanding of the financial status at all times.					
	TOTAL					

Reflecting on your answers

All of the skills above are necessary to lead virtual teams and will be explored in this and later chapters.

Congratulations on all the statements that you answered, 'Most of the time' and 'Always.' Please don't worry, though, if you scored high on the 'Never,' 'Rarely,' or 'Sometimes' columns. This book will guide you through the maze of virtual leadership and give you strategies to significantly improve the skills you have identified.

Skills to become a successful virtual leader

In addition to well-matched personal qualities and excellence in functional management, successful virtual leaders require other skills and attributes.

These are:

1. Managing professional integrity

2. Maintaining professionalism across borders

3. Virtual EQ – controlling emotions

4. Prejudice in the workplace – intentional and unintentional

5. Inspiring others

1 - Managing professional integrity

A successful virtual leader will practice integrity without compromise. Integrity is being true to yourself and others.

> integrity [ɪnˈtɛgrɪtɪ][2]
>
> 1. adherence to moral principles; honesty
>
> 2. the quality of being unimpaired; soundness
>
> 3. unity; wholeness

---

[2] Collins English Dictionary = Complete and Unabridged © HarperCollins Publishers 1991, 1994, 1998, 2000, 2003

15 Integrity Keys for Success

These 15 Keys for Success may assist you in **maintaining integrity** in your day to day virtual leadership role.

1. Be authentic and trustworthy

2. Be genuine

3. Do what you say and say what you do

4. Take responsibility for your own decisions and actions

5. Do not blame others for your mistakes

6. Be honest

7. Follow the company rules

8. Be considerate of others

9. Do the right thing

10. Demonstrate integrity and encourage and value it in others

11. Create and maintain minimum standards

12. Establish expectations

13. Establish consequences of need meeting your expectations

14. Be consistent

15. Practice what you preach!

> "The glue that holds all relationships
> together -- including the relationship
> between the leader and the led is trust,
> and trust is based on integrity."
> -- Brian Tracy

Being a virtual leader ensures that you are **authentic, trustworthy**, and **genuine**. That means doing what you'll say you'll do.

For the virtual leader, integrity means taking responsibility for your own decisions or actions, and NOT blaming others for your mistakes.

Having **integrity** means being honest, following the company's rules, having a good work ethic, being considerate of others, and doing the right thing.

As the leader of a virtual team, your team members will be guided and influenced by you and your actions. You need to demonstrate integrity, and you need to encourage and value it in others.

> You cannot change the fundamental
> beliefs of any of your team members,
> but you can insist that they maintain
> minimum standards of behavior while
> they are part of your team.

You have a responsibility as a leader to establish expectations and consequences for not meeting these expectations. Remember, practice what you preach – you also need to meet the same standards consistently.

Maintaining professionalism across borders

Many virtual leaders only address professional integrity when things go wrong.

One of the challenges of establishing and managing high levels of professional integrity is forming with the team from the outset of your expectations and standards.

The key to success is to draw out the opinions and existing standards around professional integrity within your new or established virtual team.

Virtual Team Professional Integrity Code

It's never too late to create a virtual team professional integrity code.

An ideal time is when a virtual team is formed. However, creating the code is a perfect team meeting or virtual conference agenda item that can be implemented at any time.

Once created, your team is accountable to the standard and has discussed the consequences of not living up to the code, making your job as a manager more comfortable, if and when things go astray!

A virtual team professional integrity code outlines the shared responsibilities of virtual team members in ensuring professionalism, honesty, and integrity when dealing with each other, internal and external clients, suppliers and others with whom they interact.

Case Study A - Example Virtual Team Professional Integrity Code

Example 1 = A Virtual Team Professional Integrity Code

Each of us is responsible for our behavior, and we all need to take accountability for the behavioral choices we make. This Code is in place to help our team make informed choices about team behavior and to communicate our core values of teamwork, honesty, and performances.

Some examples of the way we achieve honesty and integrity in our actions include:

- We do not tolerate dishonest behavior by our colleagues and subordinates

- We will respect different cultures, time zones and act with integrity and empathy at virtual team meetings

- We give accurate, honest and complete information to fellow team members and other parties

- We do not use funds, information or property of the Company or its customers for our benefit, nor do we assist others in such behavior

- We Act With Honesty and Integrity

Example 2 = A Virtual Team Professional Integrity Code

We are always judged by how we act. Our reputation will earn the respect it deserves if we work with honesty and integrity in all our dealings and do what we think is right at all times, within the legitimate role of the business.

Examples of the way we achieve this principle include:

- We comply with our internal standards, which help us meet our ethical, legal, and regulatory obligations and minimize risk to ourselves and the company.

- We respect the customs and business practices of the counties in which we operate and do not compromise the principles embodied in this code.

- We discharge authority (if any) to sign documents on behalf of the company responsibly. Our signature indicates that we have received and understood the nature of the document being signed and that it has been properly authorized.

- We do not act outside our authority.

- We notify the relevant senior leader of any breach of the law by a colleague, a member of this team, or subordinates.

How to create a Virtual Team Professional Integrity Code

As a first step to building a **Virtual Team Professional Integrity Code,** might be by conducting a brainstorming meeting with your team.

It may be tempting to simply write the code yourself and distribute it to your virtual team. This approach will most likely have little team ownership and may be viewed as being autocratic rather than collaborative.

To begin, ensure that all of your team members have reviewed the Code of Conduct.

Then, schedule a meeting, either face-to-face or a Zoom (or similar web conferencing platform), where teams can contribute, and you can create visuals for everyone to see.

Ensure that your whole team is present and facilitate a discussion with them by asking these questions:

- What does professional integrity mean to you?
- How can this be reflected in our virtual team?
- As a team, what will be the result of our professional integrity?
- What will we do?
- What won't we do?

Dominic: Working as the Sales Director for a pharmaceutical company in Latin America is a fast-paced environment. My team of 26 managers is across the region. Each of these managers has local teams.

My management team and I get together only once per year, so our time together is very precious. Now with the COVID-19 situation, this year's conference was canceled.

I decided that we would do a virtual session for the entire 3-day conference event. We all set-aside our calendars, just as if we're at the conference, but everyone was working from home.

As part of this, we created a Virtual Team Professional Integrity Code. Some of my team questioned what it was; others requested that we work on projects and initiatives instead. We started our virtual conference with this activity. It was excellent! My team's commitment, engagement, attitude, and ability to highlight their strengths and weaknesses came out. By 10 am on Day 1, we were done! However, for the rest of the time, our Code became the basis of our discussions and like a secret language between us.

What I was most thrilled about it that so far, 10 of my managers took it back to their local teams, and created their own Professional Integrity Code with their teams.

We've been posting the Code on our intranet space for all the other teams to view. Now, I've noticed other managers jumping on board.

I'm looking forward to the day when each local team has its own Code, that maps into the Regional Code! What took only 2 hours to complete, has had a fantastic follow-on impact.

How do we create accountability for Professional Integrity?

Working virtually, share your screen or use the whiteboard feature in your virtual meeting (Zoom has this feature, as do many other similar products) and record their answers. Make sure that you, or another team member, record *exactly* what is said, not an interpretation of a team member's contribution.

Make sure that all team members contribute.

Either within the same meeting or outside of the meeting create a document that is an exact copy of what was written on the flipchart or whiteboard.

Consolidate the outcomes of the brainstorming session into a team code. This may be a lengthy process of 'wordsmithing' and negotiating over inclusions and exclusions. This task of consolidation may be complted at a second meeting, or at least after a break of 30-60 minutes.

Once again, create an electronic document of the first draft of the **Virtual Team Professional Integrity Code.**

At a follow-up meeting, refine the code.

Once the **Virtual Team Professional Integrity Code** is finalized, distribute it to each team member, your manager, and communicate it widely.

Once your team's **Virtual Team Professional Integrity Code** has been written, refined, and communicated, there are several things that you can do on an on-going basis to maintain professional integrity.

Review the list of tips shown here.

- Find out the acceptable/common behaviors related to work at your organization's locations.

- Use people's names correctly. Ensure that you use the correct pronunciation, do not shorten without permission.

- Ask how a team member would like you to use his or her titles, e.g., Doctor, Ms., or Miss.

- Learn about each team member and the cultures they come from to determine cultural norms.

- Be careful not to stereotype.

- Demonstrate respect at all times, regardless of how stressful the situation.

Your first step: Conduct a brainstorming meeting with your team.

- Step 1 = Review the Code of Conduct, focusing on the areas around Professional Integrity.

- Step 2 = Schedule a team meeting

- Step 3 = Ask these questions:

  - What does Professional Integrity mean to you?
  - How can this be reflected in our virtual team?
  - As a team, what will be the result of our Professional Integrity?
  - What will we do?
  - What won't we do?
  - How do we create accountability for Professional Integrity?

- Step 4 - Consolidate the outcomes of your brainstorming session.

- Step 5 = At the next meeting refine the code

- Step 6 = Distribute your Virtual Team Professional Integrity Code to each virtual team member and communicate it widely.

Virtual Emotional Intelligence (vEQ) – Controlling Emotions

Groups generally perform better when they can establish a high level of group cohesion.

> "The ability of a group to accomplish its purpose depends largely on the capability of its members to communicate with each other effectively. Interpersonal communications are the cornerstone for effective team planning, problem-solving, action, reflection, and evaluation."[3]

This status can be reached by establishing group emotional intelligence.

Group emotional intelligence is reached via interactions among members. In a virtual team setting group emotional intelligence is formed by using different patterns to local teams.

Virtual groups take longer to develop norms and social relationships, and that technology may block social talks of the virtual members. This

---

[3] Duarte, D & Snyder, N, 1999, Mastering Virtual Teams: Strategies, Tools and Techniques that Succeed

distancing may lead to the establishment of lower levels of emotional intelligence in virtual groups.

In this chapter, we will focus on controlling emotions as an attribute of an active virtual leader.

There are times when things get stressful, and sometimes frustration leads to emotional, angry outbursts, stonewalling, or silence. As a virtual leader, calm professionalism will maintain team cohesiveness and open communication, leading to higher productivity and achievement of goals.

Albert Mehrabian is known best by his publications on the relative importance of verbal and nonverbal messages. His findings on inconsistent messages of feelings and attitudes have been quoted throughout human communication seminars worldwide, and have also become known as the 7%-38%-55% rule.

Mehrabian's studies maintain relevance today, especially for the virtual leader. According to the study, **only 7% of communication is via the words we use**. 38% of communication is via our tone of voice, leaving 55% of communication via body language.[4]

Given that much of the virtual discussion is via email, telephone, and video conferencing, Zoom's or similar, it is hardly surprising that communication gets misinterpreted, jumbled, or evokes an emotional reaction.

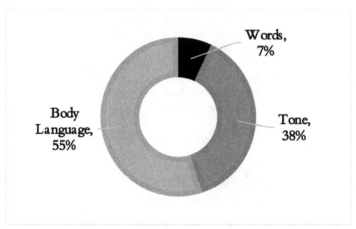

Figure 2 - Albert Mehrabian: Mixed Messages of Communication

---

[4] Mehrabian, A, Nonverbal communication, first published 1972. Source: Communication without Words" – Psychology Today – 1968

To add further possibilities of miscommunication, **we listen faster than we speak.** The average person **speaks** at a rate of 100-200 words per minute. Let's say that's an average of 150 words per minute, for example. The average person **listens** at a rate of 500 words per minute.

Therefore, when you are listening to someone speak, your brain could process a further 350 words per minute.

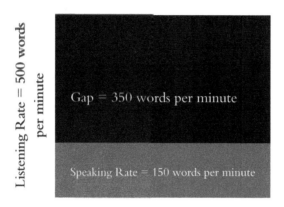

Figure 3 - Gap in speed between speaking rate and listening rate

Therefore, we have a lot of time to think about other things – not necessarily what the speaker is saying! Think about the types of occasions that you have tuned out, either accidentally or on purpose.

Elements of Successful Virtual Leadership

- Staying calm and unemotional are the keys to successfully managing conflict and highly emotional situations.

- When everyone else is stressed, angry, and frustrated, it takes just one person remaining calm and being the voice of reason to bring everyone else back to resembling regular, healthy team members.

- You are not required to agree with everyone, and you must maintain professional integrity at all times.

The most widely used communication method of the virtual team is email. When someone riles you, and it is not possible to immediately meet in person, you need to call, email, or video conference. However, ensure that you have waited until you are calm before doing any of these.

Review the list of NEVERs:

Email NEVERs:

- Send angry emails.

- Send accusatory emails.

- Reprimand anyone via email.

- Copy others into an email that contains anything that might make the recipient look bad or feel humiliated.

- The first choice is to meet face-to-face. With today's technology, this is easily possible; however, time zones may make this problematic.

- If face-to-face or phone communication is not possible, then carefully craft a professional email.

The first choice:

- Speak to them face-to-face via video call.

- When sending a reply email, write it, then wait, reread it (or have someone else read it), then edit and then press 'send'.

Prejudice in The Workplace – Intentional and Unintentional

Bias in the workplace has two forms: intentional and unintentional.

Intentional prejudice is:

- Premeditated discrimination

- Intolerance

- Unfairness

- Narrow-mindedness

- Bigotry

For example, when working with a virtual team, it is not appropriate for assignments to be made according to the manager's personal favorites, favoring one gender, nationality, or race over another. This may appear on the surface as unintentional prejudice. It is not. The manager's actions were intentional and based on discrimination. Most international organizations do not tolerate deliberate intolerance.

Unintentional prejudice is when someone says or does something unintentionally that offends another person in some way.

Our values and beliefs drive our behavior. We all have prejudices.

Be aware of your motivations, attitudes, and opinions. Try to understand your prejudices and strive to make decisions about people based on facts and observations, not on bias and general assumptions.

- Knowing about culture and cultural biases/traits is not stereotyping an individual or demonstrating prejudice
- Using that knowledge solely to make decisions and ignoring other information may be prejudice

Be aware of language patterns – using **them or us** signifies a difference, for example, us (co-located team members) vs. them (virtual team members)

An example of enlightened companies who respect their multicultural workforce may follow the following basic principles:

Most organizations do not tolerate any form of workplace discrimination based on gender, race, age, skin color, religion, marital status, sexual preference, heritage, or physical or mental disability. Most organizations have printed guidelines stating that they will not tolerate any other forms of discrimination prohibited by law or regulation in the countries or localities where they operate.

Most organizations do not tolerate any form of psychological, physical or sexual harassment or any other violation of the dignity and respect of employees in the workplace. Should an employee be subjected to harassment, his or her supervisor or manager has to ensure that it ceases immediately. Employees are requested to report incidents of harassment to their manager or human resources department at once.

Ali: I had no idea that I'd upset Ashley during our last teleconference.

I'm based in London and was brimming with pride about how my British team members had calmly and smoothly relocated their work to their homes during the coronavirus pandemic.

I said to my American virtual team members, "you know, us Brits are a bit hesitant about these things before they happen, wondering 'can we deliver the goods.' Not like you American's, always confident regardless whether you think something will work or not!"

During the call, I didn't notice that Ashley had put herself on mute and hadn't contributed to the rest of the conversation.

There were nine of us on the line, so I didn't even realize. Pilar, in Spain, told me later that Ashley was furious with my comment.

I was caught entirely unawares. Ashley thought that I was putting American's down, saying that they fake confidence all of the time.

This is not what I was thinking at all! In my mind, I was actually saying how resiliant American's are at rallying towards their goals with a positive attitude.

I guess that's not what I actually said.

Prejudice in the workplace – IN PRACTICE

- Discuss the elements of successful virtual leadership.

- Knowing about culture and cultural biases/traits is not stereotyping an individual or demonstrating prejudice.

- Using that knowledge solely to make decisions and ignoring other information may be prejudice.

- Be aware of language patterns – using **them or us** signifies a difference, for example, us (co-located team members) vs. them (virtual team members)

Inspiring Others – Finding their passion!

- If your actions speak louder than your words and reflect impeccable personal integrity, others will aspire to be like you.

- If you encourage and praise, rather than bully and reprimand, you will make others feel good about themselves.

If you give others the authority to make decisions, take responsibility, and be accountable, you are giving your team the tools they need to be successful in business.

You cannot control or direct people. You can only inspire them. The rest, they have to do for themselves.

A real virtual leader will influence and inspire others to reach for success.

KEY POINTS SUMMARY

- Ensure that you maintain professional integrity and uphold the value of Integrity at all times

- Maintain professionalism across borders by controlling emotions and ensuring that you avoid unintentional workplace prejudice

- Inspire others by leading by example

PART 3
BUILDING A VIRTUAL
TEAM

What skills do virtual team members need?

Team member attributes, skills, and knowledge

So far, we have focused on what it takes to be a virtual leader. Now we'd like to shift focus to the virtual team member. What is the most appropriate skill set for a virtual team member?

Introducing the Core Virtual Team Member Model

In the previous chapter, the Core Virtual Leader Model was introduced. Being part of a successful virtual team also requires a core set of skills, attributes, and knowledge. The following model depicts these.

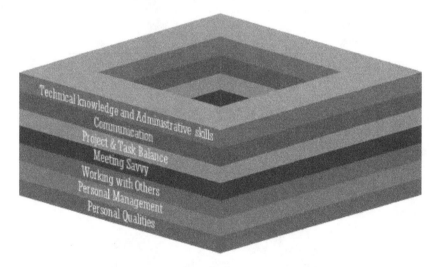

Figure 4 - Core Virtual Team Member Model

The Virtual Team Member requires focus in seven core areas:

1. **Personal Qualities**
2. **Personal Management**
3. **Working with Others**
4. **Meeting Savvy**
5. **Project & Task Balance**
6. **Communication**
7. **Technical Knowledge and Administrative Skills**

Activity 5 - Assessment - Virtual Team Member

Assessing Established Virtual Team Members

Some people are very well-suited to working on a virtual team. Generally, these people possess certain personal qualities that are highly desirable in virtual team members.

This assessment is provided to the virtual leader to help determine the virtual team member's **current strengths and areas of development**.

We will preview the tool now; however, to assess each team member, you will need to create **one copy of the assessment for each team member**.

For established teams, this tool will provide the opportunity to reflect on each established team member and provide development opportunities as appropriate. This tool can be also useful for potential virtual team members.

For each question on the following page, rate each team member on each of the techniques.

Rating as follows:

1 = Never   2 = Rarely   3 = Sometimes   4=Most of the time   5=Always

Team Member Names >>						
Personal Qualities						
Independent	Is comfortable working alone in a silo-like environment with little face-to-face interaction with others.					
Commun-icative	Is confident communicating via phone, Zoom (or other platforms), and email, depending on what is required. Is a people person and likes communicating with others.					
Proactive	Can work unsupervised, is organized, aware of the bigger picture and the part they play in it. Does not wait to be asked for information.					
Self-motivated	Focused, energized, words towards goals. Does not depend on others to motivate them.					
Articulate	Is a people person. Can adapt their language to suit any audience and has a knack of putting people they communicate with at ease. Is always positive and encouraging.					
Honest	Is ethical, can be trusted and does what they say they will do. Always speaks the truth even when it is bad news or negative. Does not mislead others.					

Team Member Names >>						
Personal Management						
Organization	Is super organized. Can streamline procedures and simplify the complex, creating easy to follow systems.					
Time Management	Projects and reports are always completed on time. Is aware of time zones with global virtual teams and considerate of time differences.					
Decision Making	Is confident making decisions. Methodically thinks through consequences and risk and adjust accordingly.					
Prioritization	Is confident at prioritizing jobs and aware of the bigger picture and overall vision for projects.					
Goal Setting	Is continually setting clear goals, reviewing their overall career and life plans. Can link their goals with their job and express results to team leaders.					
Tracking and Reporting Progress	Is financially literate and able to understand financial reports, explain budgets, costs and overheads to co-workers. Continually has their eye on the bottom line. Always stays within budget.					
Culturally aware	Understands, is interested and embraces the different cultures of team members who work in different countries, or regions.					
Embraces diversity	Supports a workplace that is inclusive of all team members such as race, spirituality, gender, sexual orientation or status as a disabled person.					
Working with Others						
Active Listening	Listens attentively, understands what is being said beyond the actual words. Is good at reading people. People they communicate with know they have been listened to.					
Coordination and Scheduling	Is well organized, and can manage and co-ordinate tasks, projects and schedules. Can clearly explain projects.					
Geographic-ally Sensitive	Schedules meetings that are appropriate for all groups, and if one geographic location is scheduled outside normal working hours that this is rotated amongst the team.					

	Team Member Names >>					
Conflict Resolution	Is very aware of diffusing situations before they explode into conflict. Is respectful of differences and can put a positive spin on most situations.					
Meeting Savvy						
Meeting Preparation and Attendance	Always arrives on time and is prepared for meetings. Skilled at preparing agendas and other meeting materials.					
Meeting Quality	Limits the duration of meetings, making the best use of time, making meetings focused work time, not general chit chat					
Meeting Quantity	Knows how many distance meetings can be dealt with personally in a day and doesn't overload calendar resulting in not having enough time for project work.					
Meeting Participation	Actively involved throughout the meeting. Ability to take notes and capture key points accurately.					
Post-Meeting Administrat-ion	Attention to detail to ensure notes are distributed in a timely manner.					
Presentations	Is a confident and clear presenter – both virtually and face to face. Clear communicator online, audio and video.					
Meeting Facilitation	Is a very experienced meeting chair and facilitator. Supplied agendas, keeps meet on track, starts on time, finishes on time. Takes control of online meetings					
Zoom (or other platforms), Functionality	Has a high skill level of the functionality of Zoom (or other platforms), and knows how to host, lead and participate in meetings, to share documents and to use meeting tools, etc.					
One-on-ones	Comfortable participating in one-on-one meetings with manager and other team members, colleagues and vendors via phone, Zoom (or other platforms), or other distance communication.					
Time Zones	Is time zone savvy and conscious of all virtual team members' availability, customs and differences. Regularly has full attendance at online meetings because of this.					

Team Member Names >>						
Project & Task Balance						
Project Quantity	Keeps the number of current projects to a manageable size					
Task delegation	Delegate tasks to colleagues where appropriate and follows up on the work that has been delegated					
Task prioritization	Prioritizes tasks according to what is important and can distinguish between 'urgent' and 'important' tasks					
Life Balance	Keeps work to a manageable number of hours everyday					
Communication						
Email	Communicates extremely well via email. Is clear, concise, creates no confusion with email correspondence. And is aware of netiquette to avoid conflict or confusion.					
Phone	Very confident using the phone with a clear speaking voice. Is an active listener and the speaker knows they are being heard.					
Instant Messaging	Uses instant messaging appropriately. Can condense a large message to an accurate short version without sounding rude.					
Email Management	Reads incoming emails on the day which they are received and responds in an appropriate amount of time, advising others if a response is unable to be given					
Maintaining Focus	Complete tasks without interruptions from other team members, maintain focus					
Technical knowledge and Administrative skills						
Computer Skills	Is adept in the technical ability for all virtual file sharing and storing, communication, project management, and other systems					
Administra- tive Attention	Has precision outlook when using systems to anticipate the needs of the team					
	TOTAL					

Reflecting on your answers

Reflect on the answers where you indicated 'Most of the time' and 'Always'. Where you answered 'Never', 'Rarely' or 'Sometimes' think about ways that you can develop this virtual team member to increase their skills and knowledge in these areas.

KEY POINTS SUMMARY

- If you are reporting to a virtual leader, you may like to analyze your virtual skillset and ensure that you are maximizing opportunities for development

- Analyze each team member's skills, attributes, and knowledge by continuing to use the Team Member Virtual Core Assessment provided within this chapter and create a program of continuous improvement for everyone on your team

- And finally, and most importantly, take action on your Skill Development Action Plan – the skills that you have identified need improving in your life. Change begins with you, so ensure that you commit to implementing your learning from this book.

How do you build virtual teams?

This chapter provides critical information for any virtual leaders establishing a virtual team and offers tips and traps for the everyday management of virtual teams. It provides ideas that can be implemented quickly and efficiently to maximize successful virtual leadership.

Virtual Team Interaction Types

There are several different types of virtual organizations. In large organizations, there may be all types present amongst various parts of the organization.

1.   Some remote team members

Managing a virtual team with some remote team members working away from the central location may sound straightforward. Managing some remote team members requires using virtual management tools and communication methods to reduce feelings of isolation. Local team members must be encouraged to use the tools and procedures to include remote workers.

2.   Split team members

Where an organization has two or more main offices, one team may be split among the offices. Each location may have its management hierarchy, with senior managers reporting to the headquarters. Virtual management skills and knowledge are the keys to project success. It's easy for an 'us' and 'them' mentality to develop. In the extreme, teams in different locations can become reluctant to work together, or help each other, and blame others for not achieving goals.

3.   Satellite team members

Where an organization has a central corporate office with numerous satellite team members around the globe or who work from home, the manager may be working onsite away from the rest of the team. It also occurs in a centralized network support system, such as onsite technical support and administrative resources. In a well run virtual organization having team members in different geographic locations, may be advantageous for conducting business, maintaining global or regional coverage, and reducing costs, such as salary costs and travel. The cost efficiencies lead to more competitively priced products and services.

4.   100% virtual team

The purest form of virtual management where an organization does not maintain a centralized office at all and has <u>100% of employees</u> working remotely from home or small offices.

Most large organizations prefer to keep centralized business functions such as accounting, legal, human resources, and IT in house.

5.   Outsourced team

A company that has a central corporate office and <u>outsource certain functions to other companies</u> may not seem like a virtual organizational structure.

However, if the outsourced services are vital functions or the outsourced team members are key players in the day-to-day projects, virtual management tools are usually put in place.

6.   Virtual work locations

Many organizations compete on a global scale, so it is a competitive advantage to have local and virtual employees forming a global team. Some organizations have strategic locations worldwide based close to their current clients and emerging markets. Employees in regional offices have the support of the infrastructure of the whole organization.

Virtual team members working from home offices need to be more independent and be comfortable with less support. Virtual team members are not limited by location and can work anywhere with an internet connection (home, hotel, airport).

Local versus Virtual Team Interaction

Local and Virtual team formal communication methods include:

- Phone calls and conference calls

- Audio calls and video calls

- Scheduled meetings

- Email

- Webinar and web conferencing platforms, such as Zoom (or other platforms)

- Peer-to-peer instant messaging

> Local team members have a considerable advantage through INFORMAL meetings and interactions throughout the day.

Local team members have a huge advantage through INFORMAL meetings and interactions throughout the day.

- These incidental interactions are great opportunities to share information, communicate project status, chat, and build rapport.

- These incidental interactions do not occur with remote employees.

- It's easy to forget virtual team members.

Local team member incidental interactions:

- In the kitchen, getting coffee

- At the water cooler

- In the elevator

- Before and after scheduled meetings

- In the restroom

- On the stairs

- In the cafeteria

- In the parking lot

Even when virtual team members call in via teleconference for meetings, they are often left out, and sometimes their input may be viewed as an INTERRUPTION to the local employees who are present at the meeting.

Virtual team members may be on an opposite time zone to the local team. Virtual team members can go days, weeks, or even months without actually speaking 'live' to the local team.

<u>Virtual management communication methods</u> have improved significantly over the past few years, making it possible to interact more informally across town, state, country, or the globe. These virtual management tools include communicating via many methods including:

- On the phone

- By email

- Over the internet using tools such as Zoom, Slack, Trello (or other platforms)

- Using a mobile or cell phone

VIRTUAL MANAGEMENT TIP: Virtual team members should have a daily presence with local team members.

Building Virtual Teams

Team Building & People Management

In Part 1 we introduced the model "Areas of Virtual Management Focus".

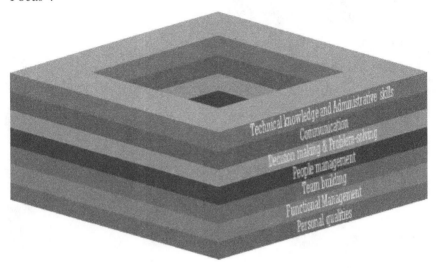

Figure 5 - Core Virtual Leadership Model

We discussed the first two areas of the model: Personal Qualities and Functional Management.

> A leader is someone who can create and communicate vision and inspire others to achieve the vision.

In this chapter we will deep-dive into Team Building & People Management skills.

Activity 6 - Team Building & People Virtual Management Assessment

People Management skills are required for virtual leaders whether or not they have direct reports. Virtual leaders manage by influence rather than authority, which requires a much higher level of people-management and communication skills. This assessment is for your personal use to help you determine your existing strengths and areas of development.

For each question[5], rate yourself on each of the techniques.

People Management Skills		1 Never	2 Rarely	3 Sometimes	4 Most of the Time	5 Always
Active Listening	High level of skill in active listening. Ability to listen and mirror back (paraphrase) what has been heard. Ability to "hear between the lines" and understand what is not being said as well as what is being said.					
Coordinating and scheduling resources	Coordinate and schedule resources. Ability to gain an understanding of remote team members' skills and interests to facilitate practical resource assignments and scheduling.					
Hiring and firing	Excellent distance interview skills. Understands when someone needs to be removed from the team. Understands how to undertake necessary steps leading up to termination. Be willing and able to take necessary action to terminate team members remotely or travel to do so in person. Know which course of action is most appropriate.					
Pay Decisions	Understand what pay decisions are appropriate for a virtual team.					
Goal Setting (individual)	Use team and management goals to set individual trickle-down goals for team members. Some goals might depend on geography or nationality.					

5 Adapted from: Managing without Walls, p 361. Managing Without Walls: Maximize Success with Virtual, Global, and Cross-cultural Teams, Colleen Garton, Kevin Wegryn (2006)

People Management Skills		1	2	3	4	5
		Never	Rarely	Sometimes	Most of the Time	Always
Setting Personal Objectives	Ability to communicate with and understand each remote team member. Set appropriate, measurable, and verifiable objectives for each team member. Work with each team member to define personal growth and development wants and needs.					
Performance Evaluation	Evaluate performance from a distance by accurately measuring and verifying individual accomplishments and results. Ability to successfully communicate performance feedback and ratings verbally.					
	Total					

Please total your scores and list them for Never, Rarely, Sometimes, Most of the time, and Always.

All of the skills above are necessary to lead virtual teams and will be discussed in this and later chapters.

Reflecting on your answers

Congratulations on all the statements that you answered, 'Most of the time' and 'Always.' Please don't worry, though, if you scored high on the 'Never,' 'Rarely' or 'Sometimes' columns. This book will guide you through the maze of virtual leadership and give you strategies to significantly improve the skills you have identified.

SETTING UP A VIRTUAL TEAM

- What is the purpose of the virtual team?

- A virtual team is a team that conducts business and operates virtually. However, many considerations for building a team are independent of how the team will function.

Successful virtual leaders understand the purpose of the virtual team and the project's goals and objectives. They also know the project's stakeholders and how the stakeholders are impacted. The virtual leader translates this information into meaningful content for their team. The virtual leader works to set the tone, style and direction for the team – the foundation for the rest of the team to work with. The virtual leader doesn't need to know how everything will be accomplished. The team will work together to be successful.

A virtual team does not have to be 100% virtual. Consider this: the occasional face-to-face meeting between virtual team members can build trust and teamwork. Interacting with virtual team members in person changes them from an email address or voice on the phone to a real person.

Hiring – Selecting Virtual Team Members From Within The Organization

There are two sets of skills successful virtual leaders consider when selecting team members for their virtual team. These skills are the **technical skillset** to achieve the project or team objective and **virtual team skills.**

Examples of technical skills could include therapeutic area knowledge, experience in clinical development, and phases of clinical research and understanding of Good Clinical Practice Guidelines.

The virtual team skills were covered earlier. As a refresher, successful virtual team members are self-motivated, demonstrate healthy decision-making and problem-solving skills, are strong communicators, mainly written, over the phone and teleconference, and independent but still view themselves as a team member and function as such. Successful experience in a previous virtual team and or as a virtual leader and familiarity with the tools your virtual team uses will allow new team members to integrate faster.

How can the virtual leader determine who will make the most successful team members?

Successful virtual leaders need to prioritize their hiring requirements, determine what skills/gaps can be overcome by training/mentoring and put in place a solid program for both on-board and new virtual team members and address the skill gap while taking into account team dynamics.

Some ideas for determining skill sets and possible gaps are asking open-ended and behavioral questions of the potential team member, obtaining samples of work (ideally that were created for a virtual team) and discussing with the applicants their previous experience with virtual leaders (local or virtual) and virtual teams.

Recruiting Virtual Team Members

Interviewing virtual team members may mean two different things.

Firstly, if there is an open position on the team, the virtual leader has the opportunity to recruit, post a job, interview, and choose an applicant to fill the vacancy.

The other situation is when virtual leaders are assigned team members for a project or inherit an existing virtual team.

Opportunity to recruit

With the chance to choose team members for a virtual team, the effective virtual leader will find the best fit for a virtual team and consider the virtual skillset in addition to the technical skills required for the role.

A virtual team is the hardest to manage as it will cross many departments and, indeed, probably many regions. The virtual leader needs to be concerned as to how a potential virtual team member will potentially manage competing priorities from within their departments and areas.

Assigned virtual team members

This situation arises when virtual leaders are assigned team members for a project by someone else. Selection under these circumstances is more likely to take into account technical expertise and regional or country representation rather than essential skills for working virtually. Decision-makers and key stakeholders who commission and assemble virtual teams may require your assistance in appreciating the personal qualities and key attributes required to work virtually.

Being assigned virtual team members is an excellent opportunity for virtual leaders to get to know the team members individually, to begin to build trust and identify areas of strength and expertise as well as potential training gaps.

While it may be tempting to simply integrate the assigned team member into the existing virtual team, we suggest carrying out a similar interview as if the new virtual team member was applying for the role via an advertised position.

This way, the virtual leader has an opportunity to ask broad-based interview questions, which will help to establish rapport and identify strengths and areas for development.

THE INTERVIEW SETTING

Conducting the Interviews

It has been well documented that interviewers form impressions and base evaluations on non-job-related factors such as a candidate's physical appearance.

Conducting interviews distantly, via telephone, videoconference, through online questionnaires, or email might offset common selection errors such as stereotyping and increase the accuracy of selection decisions.

One study demonstrated that interviews conducted over the telephone were **more** accurate than those done face-to-face[6].

Videoconferencing/Webcam Interview

A screening interview via teleconferencing is very similar to a face-to-face, or in-person interview, except a heads-up visual perspective.

Online virtual interview

When recruiting internally or externally for virtual team members establishing a virtual interview process may be beneficial for initial screening.

Candidates write their responses to a series of interview questions, attach their resume, and submit their application via their computers.

As a second-round interview, it may be appropriate to ask candidates to complete a lengthier questionnaire that, for all intents, is an 'online virtual interview.'

A final interview should be conducted via videoconference or telephone, or if possible, face-to-face.

The Online Virtual Interview method is useful for virtual team recruitment, especially if much of the communication methods of the virtual team will be via email and distance communication.

---

[6] Journal of Management June 2001: 363-381, Susan G. Straus, Jeffrey A Miles and Laurie L. Levesque

Nicola: Originally, when I was recruiting for my virtual team members, I set up face-to-face meetings with them.

On one occasion, I flew from Portugal, where I'm based, to Sweden, to conduct a series of interviews for a field position there.

I was there for a total of 3 days.

When I added up the cost of the flights, accommodation, meeting room hire at the hotel where I conducted the interviews and meals, it was several thousand Euros.

Then it struck me. The new team members need to work remotely, so why can't I interview remotely?

This may seem like a necessary thing, but I hadn't considered it because, in the past, I'd always interviewed face-to-face.

With the onset of COVID-19, we are recruiting many people, as we are in the industrial cleaning chemical industry. All of my interviews are via telephone, Skype or Zoom. We no longer have the choice to travel to conduct interviews.

Not only has it saved money, but it also saved me valuable time.

The biggest plus is that I get to see how potential candidates communicate with me from a distance – after all, that is how they will communicate in their day to day work, so it gives me a good idea of what to expect when they start in their role.

The Interview Process
Before the Virtual Team Member Interview

Conducting a virtual interview is similar to any other interview process. One key difference to focus on is to establish whether candidates have virtual team experience, or not.

When preparing the virtual team member interview:

- Read relevant information

- Prepare interview questions

- Decide on the interview format

- Decide on interview time. Ensure that the candidate is being interviewed at an appropriate time of day when they will be most effective.

- Invite all attendees to the interview 'location'.

Beginning the Virtual Team Member Interview

Starting a virtual interview via teleconference or videoconference is a critical time. It is essential to establish rapport quickly. Merely asking the weather at the candidate's location, or referring to a recent news item from their country will help to break the ice.

Then, provide an overview of what the candidate can expect during the interview.

Importantly, do not have 'silent attendees' during the interview. Ensure that you introduce *everyone* who is on the line and ask each person to tell the candidate why they are participating in the interview process.

Finally, explain what will happen if the call is disconnected and proceed with the background of the role.

When beginning the interview:

- Facilitate introductions and establish rapport

- Outline the length of the interview

- Introduce other people who may be joining the interview (even if their role is silent)

- Explain what will happen if the remote connection is lost (e.g., the interviewer will re-establish connection)

- Provide the background of the role

- Explain any additional information

CONDUCTING THE VIRTUAL TEAM MEMBER INTERVIEW

Based on the selection principle that the best predictor of further behavior is past behavior under similar circumstances, the selection of virtual team leaders and members might begin with an examination of **previous virtual team experience.**

We suggest using the STAR[7] process when interviewing. The STAR process is used for any behavioral questioning pattern and is useful not only for interviewing virtual teams but is also used for sales, project management, and conflict resolution.

	Definition	High Impact Interview Question
Situation	What was the situation the candidate was faced with, or what did he or she need to accomplish? What were the circumstances?	Describe a situation or problem that you have encountered.
Task	What tasks did the person need to accomplish to deal with the situation? You may need to ask probing questions on the Task and Action to ensure that you are finding out what the candidate did, especially if the candidate talks about what "we" did.	Describe the steps you took.
Action	What **specifically** did the candidate do to accomplish the task? (Note: Make sure you know what the *candidate's* actions were. Some people will use phrases such as "We did..." or "We discovered..." when they didn't do anything themselves. When you hear "we" statements make sure you follow-up and clarify.	Describe the steps you took. What were the obstacles that you overcame?
Results	What was the **result** or outcome? Were the tasks accomplished? Did the actions solve the situation with which the candidate was faced? What did the candidate learn from the experience?	What was the result or outcome? What were the outcomes achieved? What experience did you gain?

---

[7] Source: Victoria A. Hoevemeyer, High-impact interview questions

Situational Questions for Candidates with Virtual Team Experience:

For individuals with previous experience working virtually, interview questions **could probe how candidates coped with issues common to virtual teams**.

- Describe a virtual team project where team members might have underused available technology.

- Explain how he or she resolved the problem.

- Recall a situation where a virtual team member failed to post important documents to a teams' virtual workspace. Explain how they managed this unresponsive team member.

- Because of our global interests, we ask employees to often be at meetings at 7:00 am. Working until 9:00 pm is not unusual. Are you comfortable with this? What are your potential challenges with working outside of 'normal' working hours?

- Given that you will have virtual team members in a different time zone to you, how do you create a balance between work time and non-work time?

- Are there any other experiences that you think helped prepare you for virtual teams?

- Who was the person from whom you learned the most about working in a virtual setting? What did you learn from him/her?

- What do you consider are the unique challenges of having a boss who is from a different culture than yours? What about other virtual team members?

- What are the most important differences between being a part of an international team and a national team? What traps would you avoid?

- What kind of support did you get from your previous virtual leader that helped you succeed? In retrospect, what could your virtual leader have done that would have been helpful?

- Looking back at your experiences, is there anything you have learned that you would want to pass on to a talented younger team member that you think could help them work in a virtual environment?

Questions for Candidates WITHOUT Virtual Team Experience:

It is not uncommon for virtual team candidates to have never worked in a virtual team setting. The situational interview approach does not require candidates to have experience working with virtual teams. Two approaches include:

- Activities can be created that capture many of the challenges associated with virtual work. This activity could be given to candidates prior to the interview process, where they are asked to complete the activity and submit their responses. Then, successful candidates would advance to the 'next round' of the interview process.

- During a face-to-face or distance interview, questions around theoretical problems are posed, and candidates are asked to explain how they might respond.

Example Activity: Virtual Team Simulation

Candidates may be asked to plan, organize, and complete a short project with virtual teammates. They would be required to communicate using virtual team software to complete their virtual task.

The simulation created could build a variety of obstacles into the experience that must be overcome, such as cross-cultural misunderstandings, technological breakdowns, and mistrustful teammates.

Candidates for virtual team leadership positions might encounter situations requiring clarification of team goals, negotiation of tight deadlines, or the need to go off line to coach or counsel individual team members.

Example Hypothetical Interview Questions[8]

- Imagine you are on our virtual team, how would you maximize available technology?

- What is the difference between resolving problems in a local vs. virtual team?

---

[8] Some Questions adapted from: Developing global executives: the lessons of international experience By Morgan W. McCall, George P. Hollenbeck

- Imagine that your virtual team member failed to post important documents to the team's virtual workspace. Despite several attempts, the team member was unresponsive. How might you manage that?

- Ideas for candidates without virtual team experience continued...

- As a potential virtual team member, working with people in different zones, how will you create balance and manage this?

- What do you think are the special challenges that might be experienced by being a part of a virtual team?

Virtual Team Pressure Questions

Working on a virtual team can often be isolating and stressful. There is a big difference between *stress interviews* and *pressure interview questions*.

The old fashioned practices of **stress interviews** will most likely leave candidates defensive, which is multiplied when being interviewed at a distance. Questions such as:

- Why should I have you on the team?

- Why shouldn't I hire you?

- Why, with this resume, would you consider yourself remotely qualified for this role?

...only makes the candidate defensive, mistrustful, and unlikely to give you real answers. If you did appoint the candidate to the virtual team, a great deal of work would need to be done to repair trust and build rapport with you, their virtual leader.

> The aim is to balance your investigation so that candidates feel welcome to share insights with you freely while you gather factual data about their strengths, weaknesses, inclinations, and dislikes.

Following, are some of the more useful "pressure questions" that force candidates to volunteer self-critical insights. This approach can be helpful when handled appropriately. An entire interview based on this approach would cause ill will on the part of the candidate. So use "pressure questions" sparingly, and always with the best intentions.

Case Study B - Lois and Valmay

Let's look at an interview between Lois, a virtual leader and Valmay, the candidate:

Lois: Tell me about your last performance appraisal regarding the work you did on your current virtual team? In which area were you most disappointed?

Valmay: My greatest disappointment was that I didn't reach my goal of lowering the company's expenses for my department by 15%. I began an internal program that relied heavily on team members being engaged to self-manage their costs in five workplaces, UK, Sweden, South Africa, Australia, and the US. Because of market conditions and a less-than-ideal communication plan to co-workers, the program never really took off.

Pressure Question:

Candidates may refer to disagreements they have with their manager's perceptions. For example, they may speak of their frustration about receiving only a 'good' instead of an 'excellent' mark in one particular area. For issues of perception, make a note and enquire further with the candidate on specifics.

What to look for:

Look for areas of performance weakness that are really 'over strengths'. These so-called weaknesses hold a lot more future value than they do risk.

The ideal limitation of any employee's work history is time. High-performance virtual candidates do their jobs exceptionally well but continuously try to increase the impact of their results.

Alarm bells:

Beware of candidates who provide information regarding lackadaisical performance standards, low tolerance for adversity, inability to work independently, displays of negativity or reliability problems.

Examples of Other "Pressure Questions":

- How many balls in the air do you have at any given time, and how hectic a pace are you used to working at?

- Do you prefer to tie together all of the loose ends of a project, or do you typically jump from project to project? Tell me how a situation like that actually played itself out in the past."

- Can you tell me your understanding of the job you're applying for?

- What can you do for us if you were to join our virtual team, and when should we expect to see concrete results?

- What was an event in your career that stretched you?

Case Study C - Lois and Valmay (continued) - Getting Mileage from Pressure Questions[9]

Following is Lois's follow-up question and Valmay's response:

Lois: So tell me then, in hindsight, how could you have improved the results of that program?

Valmay: I still believe that the program could have been successful. When I first proposed my plan, I was told that it had been done before and failed miserably. I wanted to prove them wrong because it had worked well at my previous company. My boss, who was located on the other side of the world, had predicted failure from the outset.

After authorizing the project, he didn't actively participate in it or assist me when I hit barriers. My marketing colleagues, who were located in a different country, never seemed to get my story into the monthly newsletter, and I consequently let the program drift. Still, I can't blame anyone else; it was my responsibility.

If I had to do it all again, I wouldn't have given credence to all of the naysayers. I would have found ways to publicize the program myself via email, the lunchroom bulletin boards, our department web pages, and global training seminars.

I would have ensured that this project was listed on my weekly meetings with my boss – as a separate agenda item. That way, we would have talked about it regularly and potentially not let the project derail so much.

Most importantly, I learned that I shouldn't sit back and wait for others to abide by their commitments, especially when initially, they aren't enthusiastic about the project. I got the authorization to go ahead with the project, and I accept responsibility for not having reached the goals of the program."

Getting Mileage Lesson

Two key areas to look for in candidates responses are:

- What the candidate has learned
- How willing the candidate is to take responsibility.

---

[9] Adapted from: 96 Great Interview Questions to Ask Before You Hire, Paul Falcone, 2008

Ask the candidate if he/she would like to provide any other evidence.

Invite candidates to ask questions.

Explain the selection procedure with clarity on the timeline and next steps.

Thank the candidate.

> "That is what learning is. You suddenly understand something you've understood all your life, but in a new way."
>
> Doris Lessing

KEY POINTS SUMMARY

- Virtual leaders manage by influence rather than authority, which requires a much higher level of people-management and communication skills.

- There are two sets of skills successful virtual leaders consider when selecting team members for their virtual team. These skills are the **technical skillset** to achieve the project or team objective and **virtual team skills.**

- Working on a virtual team can often be isolating and stressful. There is a big difference between *stress interviews* and *pressure interview questions.*

What about virtual team dynamics?

Establishing Team Structure and Roles

It is critical to the success of your virtual team that each team member knows what their role is. Also they need to know who they are working with, and the roles and tasks that each person does, who they report to, and what their potential career path could be.

Without team structure, you will risk continual disarray and reduced productivity as no one will know where they fit in the bigger picture of your organization.

In a virtual team, some roles will default based on the person's professional area of expertise. For example, if there is a biostatistician on the virtual team, this person's team role will relate to biostatistics. If there is a sales manager on the virtual team, this person's team role will relate to sales.

Virtual teams also create several informal roles. An example of informal roles includes troubleshooter for a team specific software or document sharing site. Virtual team members often have multiple roles within a team and need to be flexible as roles evolve.

When a virtual team forms, best practice is for the entire team to be involved in the creation of both the structure of the team and the role or roles each team member will have in the team and the accompanying responsibilities. This maximizes the chance of success by decreasing confusion and ambiguity and helps ensure that all the roles and responsibilities are accurately captured. Providing a clear structure to a virtual team allows team members to understand what all the team members do and minimizes the chances of individual interpretation.

Virtual leaders will consider the best way to conduct these meetings. A meeting can be used to accelerate trust and team building as team members share a collective experience to build on and can maximize the non-verbal communication. However, in the constrained business environment, virtual leaders are creative with solutions to allow for team building and trust. A variety of technologies and tools can help allow for non-verbal communication such as videoconferences and online conferencing tools.

Regardless of the method of determining roles, the team members should be able to answer two questions at the end of the meeting:

- What is my role?
- What am I doing on the virtual team?

Considering Team Dynamics

Team dynamics occur in all teams, regardless of whether they are local teams or virtual teams. Team members are bringing their own unique experiences, cultures, values, backgrounds, and strengths. In successful organizations, virtual leaders will maximize the benefits of this diversity to create a strong team dynamic.

When teams are working in a virtual setting, some factors will be more of an influence on team dynamics. Virtual teams need to build trust, potentially without having met face-to-face. How does a virtual leader influence trust and team dynamics? Successful virtual managers exhibit the behavior they expect from their virtual team members – they show trust, openness, commitment, as well as both giving and receiving constructive feedback.

Strong virtual managers recognize potential dangers in virtual team dynamics. Trust needs to be created quickly to match the pace of the virtual team, but the lack of face-to-face time may impact building trust in some team members. Team members may not share anything in common, other than being on this team. Being separated by geography and time zones can isolate team members. Virtual communication techniques can increase the chance of miscommunication or a different interpretation of a message.

In addition to recognizing the dangers, good virtual managers will proactively plan and implement strategies to counter the risks.

Angelika: When I was appointed Regional Director, I was in an advantageous situation. The region was a new addition to our previously singular North American based organization. I recruited my entire team together, and we launched the region as an energetic, focused group.

When recruiting, I focused on hiring people who brought a variety of skills to the team. I remember being coached by a great manager, "hire giants around you, and you'll never go wrong." I've never forgotten that.

Our region EMEA (Europe, Middle East, and Africa), has offices in 40 countries. My team of 40 local Country Managers are diverse, spirited, share the company values.

I had the choice of relying on North American managers to transfer to the region under our expatriate program. However, I decided against it, favoring instead on the bedrock of indigenous managers, for without their local connections and knowledge, all of the sophistication that ex-pats acquire in foreign and home office postings means very little, especially in emerging markets.

Hiring locally was a pivotal decision and one that for our organization paid off in profitable growth and team diversity.

In February 2020, coronavirus hit our team hard. The manager's local connections and knowledge have now become our significant advantage of moving through this crisis. All of our US managers outside of the US returned home. My local managers are currently safe, and we are continuing with day-to-day business activities the best way we can.

Setting the Ground Rules

When teams are establishing the roles and responsibilities within the virtual organization, this is an excellent opportunity to develop the ground rules. These ground rules will govern how the virtual team functions, its expectations, and communication pathways. In a virtual team, ground rules help to eliminate confusion between team members and clarify expectations. Ground rules should be public and available to all virtual team members.

All the team members should be involved in the creation of the ground rules – their involvement creates a sense of ownership and begins the 'team-building' process. Shared experiences where all virtual team members contribute help to build a thriving virtual team.

The ground rules will shape the culture within the virtual team. They will also assist when a new team member joins an established group.

Ground Rules

- How virtual team functions, communicates, and its expectations
- Be public and accessible
- Involve virtual team members in the creation
- Creates a team-building experience
- Ground rules will influence culture

Establishing Virtual Team Ground Rules

Questions for discussion by the virtual team. How will we:

- Work together?
- Establish plans?
- Make work assignments and set schedules?
- Monitor and follow up on work assignments?
- Keep each other fully informed?
- Give feedback?
- Recognize accomplishments?
- Organize and conduct meetings?
- Ensure that everyone participates fully?

- Make decisions?
- Ensure that we achieve the desired results?
- Communicate regularly:
    - Timing
    - Type of communication
    - Meetings
    - Holidays (e.g. country based public holidays)
    - Vacation coverage
    - Back-up communication options
    - Informal communication between team members
    - Formal communication methods to other teams, customers, point of contact(s)
- Manage different time zones?
- Manage work hours vs. personal hours?

Case Study D - Creating Ground Rules For The Team

The Virtual Team works on creating the ground rules for the team. Examples of ground rules may include:

- Telephone or voicemail for time-sensitive messages
- Email for regular communication
    - Subject line options:
        - **FYI** – No Response Required
        - **Response Required** – Response required within 24 hours
        - **Approval Requested** – Receipt of request acknowledge with approval timeline given to the sender
- Team Meetings: Late afternoon Central European/early morning Pacific
- Progress reports through **electronic team space**
- Progress reports submitted weekly by the **end of the business day on Friday**
- Nathan appointed as European stakeholder communication
- Amanda appointed as North American stakeholder communication

All virtual team members must be clear on the ground rules and the importance of accountability. Clarity will prevent confusion, complaints, and misunderstandings.

KEY POINTS SUMMARY

- It is critical to the success of your team that each team member knows what their role is, who they are working with, and the roles and tasks that each person does, who they report to, and what their potential career path could be.

- When a team is created, best practice is for the entire team to be involved in the creation of both the structure of the team and the role or roles each team member will have in the team and the accompanying responsibilities.

- Team members are bringing their own unique experiences, cultures, values, backgrounds and strengths. In successful teams, the leader maximizes the benefits of this diversity to create a strong team dynamic.

PART 4
MANAGING YOUR VIRTUAL TEAM ON A DAILY BASIS

How do you create a virtual team culture?

Creating a virtual team from a group of geographically diverse team members requires an understanding of interaction styles, a desire to build rapport, respect and trust among team members, and the people skills needed to achieve this virtually. This chapter focuses on Team Building Skills.

Activity 7 - Team Building Skills for Virtual Management Assessment

This assessment is for your personal use to help you determine your current strengths and areas of development.

For each question on the following page, rate yourself on each of the techniques.

For each question[10], rate yourself on each of the techniques.

Team Building Skills		1 Never	2 Rarely	3 Sometimes	4 Most of the Time	5 Always
Understanding interaction and communication styles	At least a basic understanding of interaction styles. Virtual team members are missing the non-verbal 55% of communication that traditional teams generally enjoy. How team members interact determines how they will bond with each other.					
Discovering common ground	Ability to work with team members both individually and as a team to help them find out commonalities among themselves.					
Building rapport	Ability to encourage and facilitate the building of rapport among team members regardless of any geographical, cultural, or time-zone differences.					

---

10 Adapted from: Managing without Walls, p 361. Managing Without Walls: Maximize Success with Virtual, Global, and Cross-cultural Teams, Colleen Garton, Kevin Wegryn (2006)

Team Building Skills		1 Never	2 Rarely	3 Sometimes	4 Most of the Time	5 Always
Creating the "virtual water cooler."	Ability to develop a culture of openness and sociability on the team to facilitate team members keeping in touch daily. The Virtual Manager needs to set examples of collaboration for work and non-work related topics.					
Building "virtual bridges."	Ability to build bridges between team members, especially those with opposing interaction styles, where there is a high probability of conflict.					
Having fun	Ability to influence team members to have fun with each other and to enjoy virtual meetings with team members. More fun generally equals more participation and attention to the content of virtual meetings.					
Conducting virtual team building events	Ability to develop creative and practical ideas for participative and productive team events that span geography, culture, language, and time zones.					
	TOTAL					

Please total your scores and list them for Never, Rarely, Sometimes, Most of the time, and Always.

The skills above are necessary to lead virtual teams and will be discussed in this and later chapters.

Reflecting on your answers

Congratulations on all the statements that you answered, 'Most of the time' and 'Always.' Please don't worry, though, if you scored high on the 'Never,' 'Rarely', or 'Sometimes' columns. This book will guide you through the maze of virtual leadership and give you strategies to significantly improve the skills you have identified.

Building a Virtual Team Culture

Team culture develops among a group of people working together, and active virtual leaders will use their skills and abilities to make this culture as useful and team-based as possible. One of the most valuable tools a virtual leader can use is to model the behavior desired. We have mentioned examples of modeling, such as timeliness of feedback, honesty, authenticity, and information sharing.

> Create a culture of learning, productivity and team-based engagement

> As a virtual leader, model the appropriate behavior

There are two situations for a virtual manager in **creating a team culture**. The first situation is when a manager is involved in creating a new team from the beginning. An advantage of this situation is the whole team can be included in creating the vision of how the team functions. One way to accomplish this is by involving the team in the creation of ground rules and team structure. A potential disadvantage is the team members may not know each other and need to build trust amongst each other and contribute to the team culture. Virtual managers must be explicit about minimizing assumptions and being aware of personal cultures brought by individual team members that could influence the team culture.

Creating (a new team from scratch)

> Involve the team in the vision of what the team looks like and how it will function

> Be explicit: assumptions may differ between cultures

The second situation is when a virtual manager **inherits a pre-existing virtual team**. When assuming the lead of an existing team, take time to evaluate the current culture, how the team functions, and how effective their culture is. A new virtual manager provides a fresh perspective to the team culture. This activity can identify gaps created by the team culture. Contributing to a team culture of sharing, learning, and collaboration, involves the team in creating solutions to the identified gaps.

Inheriting (taking leadership of existing team)

Take time to evaluate the team's
current culture (how the team
functions and how well it functions)

Identify gaps

Involve the team in gap solutions

Team Building Activities

In a virtual team, there are opportunities to have team building activities. They just look different from traditional team-building opportunities. The objective is to have the group of remote-based individuals learn about each other to begin or continue to function as a team, with their focus on team goals and objectives.

When planning team face to face activities, good virtual leaders incorporate time in the schedule for non-work related activities – these activities contribute to building trust and creating a shared team experience.

Virtual team building activities are more challenging but typically less expensive than in-person ones. Such events can be synchronous or asynchronous, depending on what you want to accomplish. Establishing a culture of **trust and collaboration** are two critical outcomes of virtual team development activities.

Possible virtual team building activities might include:

Team Activity	Description
Virtual coffee break	Set aside time on team agenda before the start of an official team meeting for an informal conversation about non-work related topics. Encourage team members to bring a beverage of choice.
Virtual celebrations	Team members can celebrate life events of other team members such as birthdays, weddings, baby, or other personal accomplishments.
Team Member Photos	Distribute a team listing on photos and contact information for team members. Update as new team members join the group.
Celebrating milestones	As the project accomplishes milestones, celebrate with the whole team. With some advanced planning, the Virtual Manager can send appropriate 'party supplies' (either physically or ditigally) to the team members.
Culture trivia	For global virtual teams, create a trivia game to learn about the various cultures of team members. For example, holidays, customs, food.
Ground rules	When a virtual team is being formed, having the whole group create the team ground rules build the team culture and trust.

Team Activity	Description
Personal Page	Have each virtual team member build a personal page on the intranet or team site. This helps team members get to know each other and provides training on the apps that the team will be using for the project.
Ideas Page	Share information and ideas on an ideas page. Idea sharing fosters creative problem-solving and encourages team members to seek information actively.
Virtual Game Show	Using conferencing platforms such as Zoom, or similar, conduct a virtual game show for teaching company facts, history, terminology, and so on.
2 Truths and a Lie	An excellent activity for a video conference where everyone can see each other. In this 'get to know you' exercise, each team member tells two truths, and one lie about themselves and the other team members have to guess which are real and which is a lie.
Trivia Challenge	Great for familiarizing people with the company culture, history, and so on, as well as for training on specific tools.
Who am I?	Everyone is given a list of characteristics or hobbies and has to match the descriptions to the correct team member. This is an excellent activity for getting to know team members better.
One Positive Thing.	For groups that already know each other, each team member is given a list of all team members and has to name one thing that they like about each person. The facilitator collects them and assigns each team member with another person's list to read aloud.

Rona: I'm based in New York City with a global advertising agency.

My virtual team wasn't precisely cohesive at the news that we were being locked down due to coronavirus!

We had a 'them and us' attitude with those in New York City feeling more powerful because that's our headquarters site.

When I heard in one of my team meetings a team member say to someone in Auckland, New Zealand "Look, you people who are not here are just in the camping ground of New York," I knew I had to act! And fast!

Competition is what drives my team. So I set up a global competition. Over a series of a week, teams competed with each other for points.

Firstly, each team had to submit a team photo on our group intranet page. Hilarious photos of teams at iconic landmarks in their city came in. These were collages of photos of individual team members.

In all, we have held six events so far, including global scavenger hunts, best inspirational memes, a problem-solving activity for an imaginary team based on the Moon, best ideas to cope with COVID-19 isolation, an advertising campaign promoting the strengths of their local teams, and so on.

Employee engagement skyrocketed.

I was amazed at how 'into it' the teams were. Now, teams laugh, retell stories, and reminisce about our Global Team Challenge as we join our virtual global conference calls.

As everyone is saying now with coronavirus, "We're all in this together!"

Culture will also be created from shared experiences.

Take advantage of any opportunity to share everyday experiences, including situations at work, home or family. Use shared experiences to the virtual team's lead when creating a culture.

General Guidelines for Structured Activities that Build Positive Virtual Team Culture

Personally welcome everyone on the team

Make sure that you greet each person as he or she joins the virtual team call. For virtual meetings, introduce people joining calls for the first time and facilitate introductions to the rest of the group. Identify at least one personality trait, characteristic or ability that you admire about each individual or one strength that he or she brings to the virtual team, and make a point of telling him or her.

Involve the team in planning some of the activities

Ask team members what activities they think would help build team synergy. Then, implement them.

Pick the sides at random for activities

Creatively think of ways to randomly assign people to teams for activities, or just assign people to groups. Doing so avoids someone always getting chosen last, and keeps people who are already friendly from always being on the same side in an activity, which can cause clique formation.

Watch for social isolation

Many people are uncomfortable in group activities, especially if they do not know anyone. Others may lack business etiquette or social graces. Encourage participation from everyone, and if you see not participating in social interactions or group activities, make a point of talking to that person for a few minutes offline and introduce them to others who have similar interests or responsibilities on the virtual team.

Ensure that everyone has the opportunity to participate equally

Set up team building activities and business activities so that each member of the team has to contribute something to the effort. For example, in a brainstorming session, ensure that all participants contribute to the brainstorm. Especially noteworthy is not to favor participants from the same office or work location as the virtual manager.

Provide time to socialize casually after the meeting

Casual social time enables the team to relive and replay activities through discussion, stories, and laughter. Often, this social time provides more bonding than the activity itself.

Maintain a sense of humor

"Laughter shortens the distance
between two people."

Shared fun and laughter can provide strong bonds that enable teams to withstand difficult times later on. It is especially important to see the humor in the situation if the activities do not turn out exactly the way you planned or in other situations where something goes awry. Often, what happens is not as important as your response to what happens.

Managing a Team Split between Two Locations

Virtual managers often find themselves in a situation where their team is split between two or more locations. A risk when the team is divided into two areas or geographies is the creation of a 'Us versus Them' mentality. This is detrimental as it breaks the cohesiveness of the team, and the benefits of a virtual team are lost. Some examples could be North America and Europe, East and West Coast of the United States, or the UK and other European countries.

However, this is not an inevitable consequence of the team's split between two or more locations. Effective virtual leaders can overcome these location differences and create highly productive teams.

Strategies for creating highly productive teams at two locations are:

Not playing favorites with one location over another, especially if a virtual manager is co-located at one of the locations. If the other location perceives an advantage, real or otherwise, the virtual leader's integrity and objectiveness are questioned.

Team meetings should include all team members. Holding separate meetings for each location can exaggerate any perceived difference within the team. This influences transparency and information sharing among the group. Face-to-face team meetings should include the whole team to be considered a team meeting.

Also, virtual leaders should be aware of **time zones** and country based holidays. While this seems necessary, it's often overlooked. Successful virtual managers arrange meeting times so that they are equally convenient or inconvenient for all the team members.

For any **meeting requiring multiple time zones** ensure that all locations have equal opportunity and inconvenience.

The **virtual manager should also share their time with all locations** and makes efforts to be present.

Quick ways to boost team engagement

If you feel that your team engagement is lacking and culture needs a boost, the following ideas might be just what your team needs. Each of them are quick to deploy, especially if you are using a team sharing intranet, Slack, Trello or other platform.

1. Send an eBook or a physical book to each team member and have virtual team member's write their thoughts on the book and how it's helped them in their role.

2. Have your virtual team view download a motivational or education film, or documentary and write their thoughts about the film and lessons learned.

3. Have your virtual team watch a sporting grand final or a famous historical team sports event and write their thoughts about the winning team strategy and game plan.

4. Have your virtual team watch a Ted Talk from www.ted.com and write about the topic, key points, and action steps triggered by the talk.

5. Have your virtual team download a news article on something affecting your industry and write about their response to the article and the impact it might have on your organization.

6. Or, if you think fun is what they need, arrange a virtual cook-off, virtual yoga (with a professional instructor), virtual brain-teasers, virtual competitions, daily share or daily challenge.

Christine: Being a Chinese Manager with a team in Italy was, in the beginning, a big challenge. My position as manager began 2-years ago.

Our customs of our countries seem like worlds apart. To bridge the gap, we decided that our Italian colleagues should celebrate all of the Chinese holidays, and in China, we would celebrate theirs. This was a great idea, which we thought would be pretty straightforward. However, as each of the holidays came around, we realized that for many of our team, they didn't know anything about what happened on these special days. So, it became a cultural lesson.

My Chinese team had great fun on April 1st with Pesce d'Aprile (April Fool's Day) playing tricks on team mates, pinning paper fish to each other's shoulders. They cooked dishes from Florence on June 24 for San Giovanni Battista (patron saint of Firenze). In September, our Italian team celebrated the Chinese Mid-autumn Festival by eating moon cakes, and in February they surprised our Chinese team on a Zoom call with their Italian office decorated with Chinese Lanterns for the Lantern Festival.

They even went to their local Chinese restaurant and were eating yuan xiao, (rice dumplings). Both teams are now more culturally aware and share their customs, which bridges the geography of our teams.

What all seemed like fun and team bonding has now paid back in spades. With the COVID-19 early epicenters being China and Italy, my team has bonded to new heights. Today, we are no longer just work colleagues; we are like family.

Putting these grassroots techniques in place years ago has been an emerging miracle now. I would say to all virtual managers now: It's never too late to put in place the essentials. Do this, and you'll never regret it.

Evaluating Team Needs, Capabilities and Existing Tools

There is an almost limitless number of tools a virtual team can use, and this number continues to grow. The best virtual teams first determine what they are trying to accomplish, in terms of communication, reporting, or sharing of information, and then find the most appropriate tools. They are not trying to make their needs fit the technology.

A few points to remember when considering new technology:

- What's the available training, and how is the training provided?

- What support is available after the team begins to use the technology?

- What virtual team standards need to be developed to ensure the team members are using the tool in a consistent way?

- What restrictions may occur because of differing standards or technology? An example of this may be for calendar tools, do firewalls block the distribution of the information.

- How familiar is each virtual team member with each technology used by the team?

Considerations for Implementing New Technology

When considering implementing new technologies, there are some points to consider, which include:

- **Training** – be careful not to assume that everyone knows how to use the latest technology. Create a training plan for each individual or assign group leaders in various geographic locations to compile this information.

- **Support** – create a list of support, both locally and at a global level. Ensure that support is available 24 hours a day and doesn't rely on a help desk that is centrally located but closed at the times people in your team are working.

- **Standards** – ask your team to create standards for the new technology. For example, a new email system may prompt a standard signatory that everyone adopts for consistency.

- **Restrictions** – be clear about the limitations and boundaries of the new technology and offer other methods of working or workarounds for those impacted.

- **Individual team member skill level** – be very clear and open with team members about their skill level. Create a skill level map of competency with the new technology and offer support and training where needed, putting those with more experience in coach or buddy roles for others who are new or novices.

Case Study E - Virtual Team Communication Meeting – Training requirement

In this case study, a virtual team identified the areas that the team will use extensively in their communications. These areas may include:

- email for one to one communication,
- web-based meeting tool for conducting team and stakeholder meetings and
- a project collaboration tool for sharing best practices and reporting progress

The team members were asked to self-report their ability level with each of these technologies or tools, the results were as follows:

	Email writing style	Web-Meeting Tool	Project Collaboration Tool
Elizabeth	HIGH	MEDIUM	LOW
Michael	LOW	LOW	LOW
Amanda	HIGH	LOW	LOW
Nathan	HIGH	LOW	HIGH
Margret	HIGH	LOW	LOW

Based on the above results, their manager would potentially arrange training in the following areas:

Email Writing Style:

- Training for Michael only, with one of the other team members as a buddy for support

Web meeting Tool:

- Training for the whole group – using Elizabeth as potentially a future coach for the others

Project Collaboration Tool

- Training for the whole group – using Nathan as potentially a future coach for the others

Understanding Team Dynamics in a Virtual Environment

Team dynamics occur in the virtual environment and can provide Virtual Managers with additional challenges.

These challenges can result in the added difficulty between virtual team members to identify the emotions or values behind the behavior of a team member and the added difficulty in creating trust among team members who don't have a relationship formed.

This difficulty in building trust can be exhibited in the feedback behaviors of a team. Giving and receive feedback implies that the parties involved in the discussion trust each other.

It is more difficult to receive feedback from someone the team member has never met and may have a more limited trust basis.

Lifecycle of a Virtual Team[11]

Dr Bruce Tuckman published his Forming Storming Norming Performing model in 1965. He added a fifth stage, Adjourning, in the 1970s. The Forming Storming Norming Performing theory is an elegant and helpful explanation of team development and behavior. Similarities can be seen with other models, such as Tannenbaum and Schmidt Continuum, and especially with Hersey and Blanchard's Situational Leadership® model, developed about the same time.

Tuckman's model explains that as the team develops maturity and ability, relationships establish, and the leader changes leadership style. Beginning with a directing style, moving through coaching, then participating, finishing delegating, and almost detached. At this point, the team may produce a successor leader, and the previous leader can move on to develop a new group. This progression of team behavior and leadership style can be seen clearly in the Tannenbaum and Schmidt Continuum - the authority and freedom extended by the leader to the team increases. In contrast, the control of the leader reduces. In

---

[11] Tuckman's book Conducting Educational Research (first published in 1972) has gone through five editions and his Theories and Applications of Educational Psychology (first published in 1996) is now in its third edition.
Situational Leadership® is a trademark of the Center for Leadership Studies, which represents the interests and products of Dr Paul Hersey. Ken Blanchard (who incidentally wrote 'The One Minute Manager') went on to develop the Situational Leadership® system into what he called Situational Leadership II®, and which now covers a range of products marketed by his organization, The Ken Blanchard Companies.

Tuckman's Forming Storming Norming Performing model, Hersey's and Blanchard's Situational Leadership® model, and Tannenbaum and Schmidt's Continuum, we see the same effect, represented in three ways.

Bruce Tuckman's Team Development Stages Model - 1965

Lifecycle stage	As described in the original article[12]	Working Definition	Virtual team challenges
Forming:	Groups initially concern themselves with orientation accomplished primarily through testing. Such testing serves to identify the boundaries of both interpersonal and task behaviors. Coincident with testing in the interpersonal realm is the establishment of dependency relationships with leaders, other group members, or preexisting standards. It may be said that orientation, testing, and dependence constitute the group process of *forming*.	This earliest stage in team development is when the team begins to create their identity, understand the group goals, and build a trust relationship between group members.	Slower and more challenging to build trust virtually. Less informal opportunity to interact. Needing to build shared opportunities and experiences. Often distance plays an important role in slowing the forming process as virtual teams are not physically together and rely on virtual team meetings to communicate.
Storming	The second point in the sequence is characterized by conflict and polarization around interpersonal issues, with accompanying emotional responses in the task sphere. These behaviors serve as resistance to group influence and task requirements and may be labeled as *storming*.	Conflict and disagreement occur within the group as the team member's work on creating roles and responsibilities.	Virtual communication methods can allow for misunderstandings to escalate. Virtual team members can easily withdraw from team conflict and dynamics.
Norming	Resistance is overcome in the third stage in which in-group feeling and cohesiveness develop, new standards evolve, and new roles are adopted. In the task realm, intimate, personal opinions are expressed. Thus, we have the stage of *norming*.	Teams begin to work efficiently together as standards and methods of information sharing are established, and relationships develop.	Formalizing the standards regarding communication methods and response time.
Performing	Finally, the group attains the fourth and final stage in which interpersonal structure becomes the tool of task activities. Roles become flexible and functional, and group energy is channeled into the task. Structural issues have been resolved, and structure can now become supportive of task performance. This stage can be labeled as *performing*.	The team works effectively as a unit towards the group goals and objectives.	Communication among the team. Maintaining momentum of a virtual team.

---

[12] Tuckman 1965 - page 78 in the 2001 reprint

Tuckman's fifth stage - Adjourning

In 1977 Bruce W. Tuckman proposed an update of the model (in collaboration with Mary Ann Jensen). He has subsequently commented:

> We reviewed 22 studies that had appeared since the original publication of the model and which we located by means of the Social Sciences Citation Index. These articles, one of which dubbed the stages the 'Tuckman hypothesis' tended to support the existence of the four stages but also suggested a fifth stage for which a perfect rhyme could not be found. We called it 'adjourning'. (Tuckman 1984)

Adjourning involves dissolution. Adjourning is arguably more of an adjunct to the original four-stage model rather than an extension – it views the group from a perspective beyond the purpose of the first four stages.

The Adjourning phase is certainly very relevant to the people in the group and their well-being, but not to the main task of managing and developing a team, which is clearly central to the original four stages.

Lifecycle stage	Working Definition	Virtual team challenges
Adjourning:	The break-up of the group, hopefully when the task is completed successfully, its purpose fulfilled; everyone can move on to new things, feeling good about what's been achieved.	From an organizational perspective, recognition of and sensitivity to people's vulnerabilities in Tuckman's fifth stage is helpful, particularly if members of the group have been tightly bonded and feel a sense of insecurity or threat from this change. Feelings of insecurity would be natural for people with high 'steadiness' attributes (as regards the 'four temperaments' or DISC model) and with a strong routine and empathy style.

Mobilizing group potential to become a High Performing Virtual Team

Authors Jon Katzenbach and Douglas Smith have an interesting perspective on high-performance teams. The authors studied teamwork across several companies and base their findings on case studies spanning harsh business environments and work challenges. Their findings expose the factors that stimulate high performance in teams.

> 'High-performance teams typically
> reflect strong extensions of the basic
> characteristics of teams.'

According to their book The Wisdom of Teams, these durable extensions grow out of an intense commitment to the team's mutual purpose. The qualities that distinguish a high-performance team from other ordinary groups can be summed up as follows:

High-performance teams have:

- a more profound sense of purpose.
- relatively more ambitious performance goals compared to the average teams.
- better work approaches or complete approaches as the authors term it.
- mutual accountability including an acknowledgment of their joint responsibility towards a common purpose in addition to individual obligations to their specific roles.
- a complementary skill set, and at times interchangeable skills.

Mapping Team Effectiveness with Performance Impact
In the following diagram, we show a map of the Tuckman Model, together with the performance impact, to reveal the practical stages when a geographically dispersed group becomes a High Performing Virtual Team.

SOURCE: Katzenbach and Smith, 1993

Figure 6 - Mapping Team Effectiveness with Performance Impact

Reflective and Development Opportunity

The model provides an opportunity for reflection and the opportunity to develop a virtual team by reflecting on the state of the team development (the 5 Tuckman stages), and then aligning the state of the team to the current level of development.

Two simple questions can spark a strategic shift in direction and team development:

1. Where is your team today?

2. Where do you want them to be?

The answers provide the virtual leader the opportunity to create a new vision for her team and identify activities that will advance her team into a truly high performing virtual team.[13]

---

[13] The Wisdom of Teams: Creating the High-Performance Organization (Collins Business Essentials) by Jon R. Katzenbach, 2003

Challenges with Virtual Teams

Being a member of a virtual team has problems, and being a virtual leader has both the challenges of being part of a virtual team and leading a virtual team. Not every virtual team will have the same problems, but these are some of the most common ones:

- **Building Trust** – virtual team members are still human beings. It is easier to build trust between people that know each other, can work together, and can be together. Virtual team members may be communicating mainly through email, and it is harder to trust an email than a person who can look you in the eye. This is why video conferencing should be the first option for virtual leaders so that people are emulating face-to-face meetings as much as possible.

- **Time zones** – many virtual teams are global and working across several time zones. Scheduling a meeting may cross the boundaries of the 'typical work hours/day.'

- **Communication issues** – with the use of email and other virtual communication tools, it is difficult to interpret the emotion of a message. Team members can be overwhelmed by the different methods of electronic communication. Also important to remember is for some team members, English is their second language. This can affect team members' comfort in relaying messages and information in English as well as the impact on vocabulary.

- **Reliance on Technology** - Virtual teams are reliant on technology to get their work completed. Events such as a computer system upgrade, internet or phone outages, or poor teleconference connection impact the teams' interaction and ability to work together. Team members must quickly become comfortable using any virtual team required software or a virtual solution.

- **Informal Exchange between Team Members** – In co-located environments, the chance meeting between team members in the office kitchen sometimes results in a great new contact, lead, or collaboration opportunity. Virtual team members don't have the opportunities every day to have chance meetings – they need to reach out to team members and co-workers with purpose.

Tom: I was about six months into leading my team and COVID-19 hit. I knew other colleagues who were successfully leading global virtual teams hearing their stories of how united and exciting it was.

So what was wrong with me? My team isn't global, not even across time zones! My team is located in the Pacific Northwest in one city, ten clinics, each having two people reporting into me. So, how hard could it be? Twenty people, 10 locations, all within 30 minutes drive time from each other. It was a nightmare!!!!

When the virus hit, and we went into lockdown, everyone was fearful and panicked!

In one last attempt, I decided that it was my organization's goal to help people lead balanced lifestyles that incorporate physical activity. So that's how I based my decision to ask my virtual team members who would like to participate in a virtual walk from Seattle to Los Angeles. Every week, team members went for walks at lunchtime and recorded their steps. Some of my team walked around their living rooms because they were in apartment complexes and didn't want to go outside. Others had backyards or access to parks nearby.

The steps were tallied, and within a few weeks, together as a team, we'd walked the 1,140 miles.

In just under a month, we'd made our virtual walk to LA. We celebrated with a Hollywood themed lunch in our virtual Zoom office!

What a successful team building activity it was. It generated positive feedback and resulted from associates who worked together toward the same goal.

Last week, the team requested that we now walk to Miami, and then they want to walk to New York! So, we all have our walking shoes on, and we're on our way now to the Miami beaches! Virtual Beach Party…here were come!

Opportunities for Virtual Teams

There are also **great opportunities** with a virtual team and its' members. From a company perspective, the ability to form a team is **not limited by geography**. Virtual team members can be from around the globe and be the best-suited members for the team to meet the objective. This results in teams being **more representative of the global organization** and also of the worldwide economy.

From a virtual leader's perspective, the team will be **diverse** and bring different opinions, backgrounds, and experiences to the side. This heterogeneous group of team members should result in a variety of different solutions and approaches to achieve team goals. The chance of the group having only one method, resulting in **'group think'**, is low. Global virtual teams **can also work around the clock** as a result of their time zones. While one team member is finishing their workday, another is beginning and can build upon the work that happened while they slept.

Virtual team members have personal opportunities to be **part of a global team** that may not happen otherwise. For example, if the virtual manager is in London and had to have only co-located team members, this restricts the potential virtual teams outside of London have the opportunity to be on the team. However, employees located in any of the organization's offices have unlimited working opportunities to be part of the virtual teams.

Virtual Project Management

Managing projects in a virtual environment require excellent project management skills. The four phases of a project's lifecycle are shown.

The stages of project management will give virtual teams a clear definition of the team's goals and objectives, a roadmap in how to achieve these goals, a communication strategy to team members and stakeholders, and tools for tracking the progress of the project and managing any risks.

Successful project managers use existing reports that meet their needs and don't ask the team to recreate data. This allows the team to focus their energy on project-related tasks, rather than completing a task twice.

Successful project managers use existing tools that meet their needs and create tools when gaps are identified.

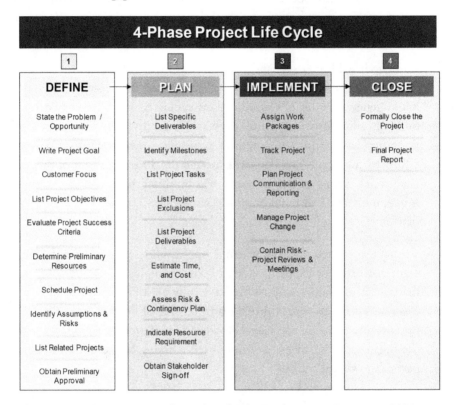

Figure 7 - 4-Phase Project Life Cycle - © The Performance Company, 2000

Conducting Virtual Project Reviews

Leading project reviews are a vital part of the implementation phase of the project management plan. The timelines or frequency of these meetings is determined in the planning cycle and is public information among virtual team members and stakeholders.

Information and tracking can be shared in the form of project dashboards, which allow for a quick overview of project progress.

By using tools to track progress and identify risks or issues, this allows the virtual team meeting time to be spent in problem-solving and resolving issues.

Conducting the review of the project at key milestones should be done with a meeting of the virtual team members and relevant stakeholders. This ensures everyone hears the same message or information and is involved in moving the project forward.

> Consider the benefits of having this
> meeting allow for non-verbal
> communication between participants,
> either through videoconference.

Using the Virtual Team Project Status Report

The Virtual Team Project Status Report is an example of a template approach for project status updates. The project leader or project administrator would complete this on a weekly or monthly basis, and it would form the basis of on-going communication to both key stakeholders and virtual project team members. As a communication tool, it forms the foundation of a meeting agenda and keeps visible the project challenges and timelines.

Virtual Team Project Status Report[14]

Virtual Team Project Status Report	
Project:	
Report #	Prepared by:
For the period from:	Report Date:
Accomplishments for this report period are:	
We are ☐ ahead ☐ behind ☐ on schedule	
List any changes to project objectives:	List any changes in our business climate that might affect your project:
What problems do we face that were initially unanticipated?	
What needs to be changed?	List anyone whose approval is needed for those changes:
List any additional *anticipated* problems:	Action steps which I plan to take:

---

[14] © The Performance Company Pty Limited, 2020

Conducting Virtual Team Members Reviews

Reviewing virtual team members' performance is another critical responsibility of the virtual manager. Developing team members and their skillset allows for a higher contribution to the virtual team and the organization.

Successful virtual managers provide **informal reviews** via regular feedback to their team members on an **ongoing basis. This feedback is timely**, relevant, and genuine. Team members can act on this feedback in a real-time way, rather than at preset review time points. For virtual team members, this feedback helps them know that they are on track and meeting the goals of the project.

With the **formal review process**, if the budget and COVID-19 restrictions allow, successful virtual managers have these **discussions face to face**. This helps minimize potential misinterpretation, allows for non-verbal communication for both the virtual manager and the virtual team member, and establishes trust and compassion.

> At the very least, a virtual manager
> should ensure that both themselves
> and their team member are using video
> conferencing with the video cameras
> switched on during the meeting.

Adding feedback on the **team member's virtual team performance and skillset develops the virtual skill set** and contributes to future success on virtual teams.

Miguel Ángel: I had a really successful performance review with Sharon, which I'd like to share. I'm located in Mexico, at our Engineering Plant; Sharon is in Glasgow in Scotland at our Head Office. The timing of conference calls between us is frequently a problem. In this case, I figured that if one person has to be inconvenienced, it should be me – so I scheduled the call at a time that I knew was in Sharon's typical business day. The challenge for me in a open office environment was to find a quiet area, so I took the call from home so that I would be in a private area where I would not be overheard or disturbed.

We discussed each of Sharon's goals: the degree to which they were completed, the quality with which they were finished, and any extenuating circumstances that made it difficult to achieve. As a native from Mexico who talks very fast, my accent is often hard for my Scottish team members to catch, so I was especially conscious in this call to speak more slowly and carefully than I usually might in a meeting and to check for understanding more frequently.

Together we set new goals for the upcoming year and discussed how Sharon's areas for development might be met by training. Last year, I suggested how Sharon should attend particular training courses, but not knowing the local Glasgow area messed this up!

So, this year, we identified Sharon's development needs, and Sharon will come back to me with her proposed professional development program for the year.

We spent about one hour on the call. It was the most productive performance review I had done. My pre-work and thinking around the call certainly was a benefit.

Key Points Summary

- Creating a virtual team from a group of geographically diverse team members requires an understanding of interaction styles; a desire to build rapport, respect and trust among team members; and the people skills needed to achieve this virtually

- Two simple questions can spark a strategic shift in direction and team development:

  - Where is your team today?

  - Where do you want them to be?

- Managing projects in a virtual environment require excellent project management skills. The four phases of a project's lifecycle include: Define, Plan, Implement, Close.

- Successful virtual managers provide informal reviews via regular feedback to their team members on an ongoing basis. This feedback is timely, relevant, and genuine.

Virtual Team Changes, Issues, Conflict and Challenges

Managing Team Member Changes and Issues

In an ideal world, the virtual team members would work together throughout the life cycle of the project from implementation to conclusion. Realistically, virtual team members will leave the team, and new team members will join throughout the project. Successful virtual managers work in reality and do their best to plan for these situations.

Ideally, the virtual team being managed is well-functioning.

To the newly joined team member, **because the team is functioning so well, it may feel like trying to join a clique.**

Virtual leaders assist in this situation by **facilitating the integration** of the new team member and ensuring appropriate introductions to both team members and key stakeholders, occur. Successful virtual managers manage this integration into the team to minimize the time between on-boarding and contribution.

Case Study F -   A New Virtual Team Member: Julio

In this activity, a new team member is joining the **Virtual Team**.

Julio is joining the team to address a gap identified in the project. He is responsible for sales development in emerging regions such as Singapore and Manila.

A list of activities is provided below to assist in integrating Julio onto the team.

Send a welcome note to Julio
Inform the team of the pending new member, Julio with relevant background
Meet with Julio and provide a background of team, objectives, ground rules
Assign a team mentor, if appropriate
Introduce Julio and have team introduce themselves at the next team meeting
Regularly check-in with Julio about integrating with the team

Consider your situation when
welcoming team members into the
virtual team setting.

What do you currently do?

What else might you do in the future
to welcome new virtual team members
and integrate them into the team?

Activity 8 -   Decision Making and Problem Solving Skills for Virtual management Assessment

Communicating decisions must be made clearly and assertively. Otherwise, virtual team members will be unclear about what to do with the information and how to action it. The first part of this assessment focuses on **Decision Making.**

Problems arise in many different areas, including technical, political, administrative, and managerial. No matter what type of problem, where it occurs, or who it affects, the Virtual Manager is responsible for ensuring it gets resolved appropriately and promptly. The second part of this assessment focuses on **Problem Solving.**

This assessment is for your personal use to help you determine your current strengths and areas of development.

For each question on the following page, rate yourself on each of the techniques.

Decision Making and Problem Solving Skills		1	2	3	4	5
		Never	Rarely	Sometimes	Most of the Time	Always
Making Decisions	Ability to take ownership and make decisions with authority and conviction.					
Communication Decisions	Ability to communicate decisions and reasons for decisions to virtual team members. Ability to ensure that decisions are accepted and adopted by all team members.					
Reviewing and Updating Tasks or Processes affected by Decisions	Ability to review and update processes, procedures, tasks, priorities, and assignments to align with new decisions.					
Detecting Problems	Ability to recognize that a problem exists whether or not it is reported to the manager. Ability to identify issues occurring remotely, or local issues negatively affecting remote team members.					
Evaluating Problems	Ability to assess the extent and criticality of a problem and to assess its impact on the team or project. Excellent virtual coordination and fact-finding skills to expeditiously complete the evaluation.					

Decision Making and Problem Solving Skills		1	2	3	4	5
		Never	Rarely	Sometimes	Most of the Time	Always
Identifying Root Cause	Ability to drill down into the details and identify the root cause of the problem. Ability to engage remote team members to assist with identifying the cause of the problem.					
Resolving Problems	Ability to define appropriate steps to resolve a problem and to roll out any required process or task changes to remove team members.					
TOTAL						

Please total your scores and list them for Never, Rarely, Sometimes, Most of the time, and Always. All of the skills above are necessary to lead virtual teams and will be discussed in this and later chapters.

Reflecting on your answers

Congratulations on all the statements that you answered, 'Most of the time' and 'Always.' Please don't worry, though, if you scored high on the 'Never,' 'Rarely', or 'Sometimes' columns. This book will guide you through the maze of virtual leadership and give you strategies to significantly improve the skills you have identified.

Managing Conflict

Conflict will occur within a local team and a virtual team; it is easier for conflict to inflate due to the virtual dynamics. However, virtual managers should remember that disagreement is not the same as conflict. It is healthy for team members to have differing opinions. The key is once a decision is made, the team members work with that decision.

> Conflict causes tension within the team
> and affects how well the team works
> together.

The virtual manager needs to manage this conflict to prevent further escalation or damage to the team. They don't need to resolve the dispute or solve the problem, but they manage it to ensure that it doesn't affect the team.

Philipa: She's driving me crazy! Cynthia that is. Cynthia's role is in marketing communications. I'm her manager in a Swiss micro-technology company.

I'm based in Switzerland, and Cynthia is located in Mississippi, USA. Cynthia has a diverse range of projects, and she is always saying how busy she is when what she produces, to me at least, is quite minimal.

Cynthia has gone into a frenzy over COVID-19. Understandably she has elderly parents and kids at home. However, she is almost unable to operate at this time due to her stress levels. It's very worrying for me to see her like this.

Before the virus, we had an important project to produce a prospectus and some other company information. Cynthia was responsible for the project and didn't deliver. When questioned, Cynthia blamed four other people in the team for not providing her with timely information. Each of these people sent me emails with proof that they had sent Cynthia their relevant parts before their deadlines.

Now, with coronavirus affecting us all, I don't know how we are going to get the prospectus out.

To add to the conflict that Cynthia is causing, she has become very close friends with the Head of Marketing, who in Mississippi based. Cynthia is continually complaining about our team and me to the Head of Marketing. So he hears all about our team dysfunctional behavior, which doesn't reflect well on me.

I tried to ignore it, but it is getting worse. I don't know where to start to resolve the conflict and internal team war I have going on right now. Coupled with the virus, I feel like everything is caving in around me.

Be proactive with managing conflict
Because of the virtual dynamics of a team and the nature of virtual communication, such as a difficultly building trust and the lack of non-verbal communication cues in communication methods, successful virtual managers are **proactive** and aware of situations where conflict may arise.

Identify triggers for conflict
They **identify potential triggers**, such as conflicting cultural values and norms, communication styles, or personalities.

Use the first opportunity to address conflict
When conflict is **first identified**, they address the parties involved at the first opportunity in a neutral manner.

Pick appropriate methods of initial communication
They recognize that the use of email to manage conflict often escalates the conflict situation and has minimal effectiveness, so the successful virtual manager **picks the most appropriate method for initial communication**.

Maintain neutral emotions
They **maintain neutral sentiment** and do not allow their own emotions to escalate or interfere.

Don't play favorites
They **do not play favorites** between the parties involved in the conflict.

Get the facts and keep to the facts
They get the **circumstances of the conflict** and keep to the facts.

The issue is the problem, not the person
They remember that the issue is the cause of the conflict, not the person.

> "Example is not the main thing in influencing others. It is the only thing."
>
> Albert Schweitzer[15]

---

[15] Albert Schweitzer (14 January 1875 – 4 September 1965) was a German (Alsatian) theologian, organist, philosopher, physician, and medical missionary

KEY POINTS SUMMARY

- To build and maintain relationships that allow virtual team members to work effectively with others in such circumstances, virtual managers have to figure out what the differences and similarities are between them and others with whom they work.

- Those differences affect expectations, approaches to work, views of authority, and other issues.

- A virtual manager's work is more complex and calls for a new kind of flexibility for handling differences and change.

How do you communicate for peak performance

Virtual Communication

Virtual Communication provides the essentials for communicating with team members across town, across the country, or the world. This chapter includes ideas and guidance on how to communicate with maximum efficiency and effectiveness to ensure business goals are accomplished.

Unlike local teams that operate in a shared physical space, virtual teams work in a collaborative workspace. This virtual workspace connects remote employees and allows them to learn from each other, to pool and leverage their knowledge and experience.

Understanding the communications required – both personal and technological – and effectively applying them is the goal of the virtual team manager.

Activity 9 - Virtual Communication Skills Assessment

This assessment introduces some key personal and technological communication skills and allows you to personally assess your current skills in this area.

It is designed for you to personally assess your current skills in this area. This assessment is for your personal use to help you determine your current strengths and areas of development.

For each question on the following page, rate yourself on each of the techniques.

Virtual Communication	1 Never	2 Rarely	3 Sometimes	4 Most of the Time	5 Always
I choose a method of communication that best fits the mutual needs of all virtual team members and the situation.					
I apply a communication technology that best fits the needs of the virtual team situation.					
I help all virtual team members apply available communication technology with skill and confidence.					
I help the virtual team to establish clear and inspiring shared goals, expectations and purpose.					
I lead by example with a focus on visible, measureable results					

Virtual Communication	1 Never	2 Rarely	3 Sometimes	4 Most of the Time	5 Always
I choose a method of communication that best fits the mutual needs of all virtual team members and the situation.					
I encourage all virtual team members in our conversations to participate fully.					
I guide communications to achieve a positive and constructive outcome.					
I conduct coaching and feedback in ways that convey respect and support.					
I model the behaviors expected of all virtual team members.					
I maintain the self-confidence and self-esteem of others.					
I honor commitments.					
I admit mistakes.					
TOTAL					

Please total your scores and list them for Never, Rarely, Sometimes, Most of the time, and Always. All of the skills above are necessary to lead virtual teams and will be discussed in this and later chapters.

Reflecting on your answers

Congratulations on all the statements that you answered, 'Most of the time' and 'Always.' Please don't worry, though, if you scored high on the 'Never,' 'Rarely,' or 'Sometimes' columns. This book will guide you through the maze of virtual leadership and give you strategies to significantly improve the skills you have identified.

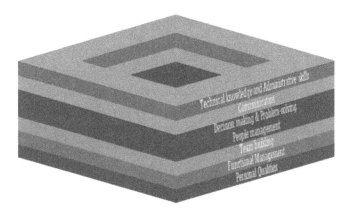

Figure 8 - Core Virtual Leadership Model

Review Model: Core Virtual Leadership Model

Earlier, we discussed the Areas for Virtual Management Focus. Before going on, let's review these now:

Virtual teams:

Virtual teams are groups of people, working interdependently across space, time, cultures, and organizational boundaries, with a shared purpose, while using technology. Many companies with a geographically dispersed workforce deploy several different virtual team types to achieve its goals and objectives.

Work or functional teams:

Work or technical teams are functioning specific - within a particular area e.g., finance, training or research.

These teams may operate virtually from different geographic locations, and exist to perform regular or ongoing tasks.

Project Teams

Project teams are mainly focused on specific tasks or initiatives – like executing a clinical study, designing a new information system, or solving a service problem for a significant customer.

These teams tend to exist only for a finite period. They may add or remove members of their team at any given time, depending on the expertise needed, and the stage of the project.

Project teams can include study management teams whose function may be to plan, execute, and deliver product development studies that are for a finite period of time.

Service Teams

Service teams are assigned to a particular service like customer support, data maintenance, or Help Desk support. Each team provides the service during their business hours, and at the end of the day, work is passed to the next group, in a different time zone, to deliver 24-hour coverage.

And regardless of the type of virtual team you're leading, how you communicate with your team members will be critical to its success.

Building a Unified Team Commitment via Setting Goals

Communicating with your team to inspire their best performance starts with **setting a dear and inspiring shared purpose and goals.**

Just as you do for the virtual team professional integrity code, involving all members in creating or understanding the group's purpose is a foundation stone for building unified team commitment.

Working with Different Needs and Goals

Each of your virtual team members has different needs and goals. Your role as their virtual team leader is to create an environment that works for individuals.

The following shows five ways to assist:

1. **Be dear on expectations upfront.** Let people know what is important to you and what you expect from them.

2. **Walk the talk and lead by example.** Step in to support your team at every opportunity. Maintain your sense of personal integrity at all times.

3. **Get to know your people and what makes them tick.** Be a student of understanding differences and adapt your style to meet their needs. Provide opportunities for people to operate from their strengths.

4. **Provide honest feedback and continuous coaching.** Encourage an environment where virtual team members can learn from one another, including from you and you from them. Tell the truth.

5. **Encourage and reward accountability.** Provide reinforcement when people take the initiative. Be a driver of personal responsibility. Admit mistakes and learn from them.

Personal and Virtual Team Motivation

Who motivates the motivator?

The ability to motivate virtual teams is the essential ingredient of all good virtual leaders. In order to get individuals to achieve personal and group targets, motivation is particularly important. Consequently, a virtual leader who cannot motivate her team to perform is likely to not achieve personal or organizational goals.

Motivation comes through good leadership.

All great leaders in business, politics, and history have been superb motivators because they were great leaders, not the other way around. If you can capture your virtual team's imagination and excitement, they will be motivated. If you lose their respect, you will lose their motivation.

There is no single theory of human motivation.

There are many ethical theories of motivation. This doesn't mean that these theories cannot give us profound insights into human nature, but we shouldn't be afraid of drawing our conclusions and acting on them. The best place to learn about the motivation of your virtual team is by listening to them and understanding them as people.

Motivation is ultimately to do with the self.

Motivation is never concerned with telling people to do what you want. It involves instead getting people to want the same thing as you do, so they see your task as their task. This is vital in a business where most things depend not on what you do, but on how you do it.

Motivation comes from your own belief and enthusiasm.

Your virtual team will expect you to set the tone of their work. If you believe in your goals, your company and your products, so will they. If you do not, you will never be able to motivate them.

Herzberg's Hygiene Theory[16]

The two-factor theory (also known as Herzberg's motivation-hygiene theory and Dual-Factor Theory) states that certain factors in the workplace cause job satisfaction. In contrast, a separate set of factors cause dissatisfaction. It was developed by Frederick Herzberg, a psychologist who theorized that job satisfaction and job dissatisfaction act independently of each other.

Herzberg's theory is well respected as it recognizes two factors that affect motivation – motivators and hygiene factors. He found that when people felt dissatisfied with their jobs, they were concerned about the environment in which they were working. One the other hand, when people felt good about their jobs, this feeling had to do with the work itself.

Herzberg called the first category of needs **hygiene** (or maintenance) factors. Hygiene because they describe people's environment and service the primary function of preventing job dissatisfaction; maintenance because they are never delighted – they have to continue to be maintained. He called the second category of needs **motivators** because they seemed to be effective in motivating people to superior performance.

Herzberg's theory helps us make sense of how to motivate people and keep them motivated. It also shows us how such intangible things as sparse office decorations can gradually demotivate people.

---

[16] Herzberg, F., Mausner, B. & Snyderman, B.B. 1959, The Motivation to Work. John Wiley. New York.
Frederick Herzberg, Work and the Nature of Man (Cleveland: World Publishing, 1966); F. Herzberg et al., The Motivation to Work, 2nd ed. (New York: John Wiley & Sons, 1959). Herzberg, "The Motivation-Hygiene Concept and Problems of Manpower", Personnel Administration (January–February 1964), pp. 3–7.
Herzberg, F. (1968). "One more time: how do you motivate employees?". Harvard Business Review 46 (1): 53–62.

Virtual Team Motivators:

Provide virtual teams with positive motivation to do something. They include achievement, praise, and opportunity for growth, job satisfaction, and interest. If you do not offer your virtual teams these motivators, they will not be motivated.

Virtual Team Hygiene Factors:

Do not, in themselves, motivate. They provide the **right environment** for virtual teams to be motivated. They include adequate pay, working environment, administrative backup, company policy, atmosphere. If hygiene factors are non-existent, it will be challenging to motivate your team no matter what motivators you use.

MOTIVATOR	HYGIENE FACTOR
The job itself	Environment
Achievement	Policies and Administration
Recognition for Accomplishment	Supervision
Challenging Work	Working Conditions
Increased Responsibility	Interpersonal Relations
Growth and Development	Money, Status, Security

Motivators found in the workplace

Pride

- Most people want to take pride in the work they do. If nothing else you must:
- Encourage them to take pride in their work
- Make your virtual team feel their effort are important
- Let them know you value their skills

Use phrases such as 'set the right example,' 'I can count on you,' 'the others will take their lead from you.' However, don't over-flatter: feel free to use such criticisms as 'I was surprised by your action,' 'I want to talk to you before your behavior becomes a problem,' and so on. Don't belittle the pride motivated person – it can lead to resentment or even a resignation.

Peer Group Pressure

- The person motivated by peer group pressure does not want:
- To let the side down
- Be the odd one out

- The lowest performer

Use phrases like 'the virtual team are counting on you,' 'we can all do this together'. They are unlikely to be the one to initiate action.

Interest

- Involve this person in problem-solving. Ask for their ideas. Leave tasks open-ended. Offer opportunities to gain product knowledge or training.

Security

- Show that by doing what you are asking:
- They will become more secure.
- Their lives will be more comfortable.
- Their work is more predictable.

Someone with a great need for security will particularly dislike any system that exposes him or her to failure or managerial scrutiny. Provide routines and structure. Regularly reassure your virtual team that they are doing well.

Loyalty

- Encourage and reward with praise and recognition.
- Never take people for granted.
- Be loyal to your virtual team.
- People often leave jobs because they don't feel their manager repaid their loyalty.

Habit

Most of us do most things for no better reason than habit. Habit also makes us reluctant to change. Overcome habit by managing change sensitively. Encourage good habits by establishing routines for your virtual teams.

Greed

Show how your advice, encouragement, and so on will help your virtual team earn more money. Praise high earners and never make them feel 'guilty.' Only beware: don't let any of your virtual team members cut corners for quick results or give up if results are slow in coming. Never insult someone by assuming that his or her only interest is money.

Power

Offer people some power over their environment, or show how they can achieve potential if they are successful. Power means:

- Control over their work (e.g., sales territory)
- A position of team leading
- The personal freedom that comes with higher earnings
- The power comes from getting a customer to say, "YES!"

Competitive Spirit

Encourage completion with praise and prizes.

Focus and channel competitive natures by showing them where they can compete successfully.

For instance: 'you could be our best regional manager,' you could have the best-kept records in the team,' 'it's between you and Pedro for the best figures this afternoon.'

Don't make work too competitive; people can resent having to compete against each other pointlessly; others can shy away from competitions. People only want to fight for things that they might win that are worth winning.

Desire to be liked

Wanting to be liked is a prevalent emotion. Sometimes it can be counterproductive in sales, as it can make your virtual team reluctant to "upset" their customers by pushing for business. It does have its positive side; people will want to please you and want to be good virtual team members.

Desire to be helpful

If someone is keen to help harness this energy; can the person spend time inducting the new virtual team member, or collecting data for you? Present comments in such language as 'Could you help me with this?' 'I don't find your current attitude very helpful,' 'What ideas do you have?'

The desire for praise or recognition

- Be keen to bestow praise – whenever it is deserved.
- Never praise indiscriminately – always explain why you are praising.

- Reinforce the excellent performance, show sincerity.

Whenever you praise, pause for a second to let them enjoy your praise. Establish eye contact; smile warmly. Even over a teleconference call or Skype or Zoom (or similar platform) your warmth and friendliness will show through. Never praise grudgingly. Praise your virtual team in front of managers.

Excitement

Be fun and dynamic yourself. Don't always do the predictable. Encourage spontaneity.

Ease

Most people prefer the easy option. Harness this as best you can; make it easy for virtual team members to do things "by the book"; introduce changes smoothly. Beware of short cuts.

Fear

Managers often use fear needlessly or because they are afraid to confront the real problem; sometimes, it is easier to threaten to dismiss a poor performer than, to be honest and tell them the reasons for their poor performance.

Rather than fear for fear's sake, give fear a purpose – set the virtual team member clear, precise, achievable goals, and when they have achieved, give praise.

Activity 10 - Personal Motivation Questionnaire – What motivates me?

YOUR MOTIVATORS

Break down what each of these needs means to you. Analyze your own needs by completing the following table. Then invite your virtual team members to complete the table.

On a scale of 1-5, X in each box which of the following motivates you the most. (1 being the highest motivator and 5 being the lowest motivator.)

YOUR MOTIVATORS	Score 1-5 for each motivator
Pride	
Peer group pressure	
Interest	
Loved Ones	
Security	
Loyalty	
Habit	
Greed	
Power	
Competitive spirit	
To be liked	
To be helpful	
Praise	
Ease	
Fear	

Remember, do not add hygiene factors, such as money. What you do **with the money** is the motivator.

Activity 11 - Virtual Team Motivation

Reflect on your perception of what motivates each of your team members. If you don't know, leave it blank. For each of your team members rate each of the Motivators 1-5 (1 representing the Highest Motivator, 5 representing the lowest).

Virtual Team Motivation Questionnaire – What motivates my team?

TEAM MOTIVATORS	Score 1-5 for each motivator							
Team Member Name >>								
Pride								
Peer group pressure								
Interest								
Loved Ones								
Security								
Loyalty								
Habit								
Greed								
Power								
Competitive spirit								
To be liked								
To be helpful								
Praise								
Ease								
Fear								

Remember, do not add hygiene factors, such as money. What you do your team members do **with the money** – that is the motivator.

MOTIVATION AND MONEY

Why might people want to earn more money?

Pride:	The employee equates what they earn with their worth as a person.
Peer Group:	The employee wants more money because their friends just had a pay rise.
Greed:	The employee just loves money!
Power:	The employee feels more powerful and has more control over their living conditions.
Comfort:	They love to eat out and buy luxuries.
Care for loved ones	They want to treat the children to a holiday.
Peace of Mind:	They don't want to worry about cash flow.

Ways to Motivate in other ways than money

The point to be learned here is that instead of relying on money to keep our virtual team enthusiastic and committed, we should be motivating our virtual team members in other ways. For instance:

Pride:	Might be better motivated if they are offered a new job title or given public recognition.
Peer Group:	Tell them how essential they are to the virtual team, or they may be motivated by a company party.
Greed:	Bonus, new commission incentive will produce more than a simple pay rise.
Power:	A promotion or some sort of responsibility or administrative function may satisfy this need.
Comfort:	A dining or clothes allowance – it will be less than a pay rise.
Care:	More interest in families, medical insurance or long-term products.
Peace:	Give virtual team members other sources of security; offer praise, say what they need to make them feel their position is secure.

Planning for motivation

- What steps can you take to reduce the risk of lack of motivation within your virtual team?

- What practical steps can you take to increase the motivation of the individuals on your team?

Goal Setting in the Virtual World

The more comfortable you make goal setting for your virtual team, the quicker you will see the results. A simple seven-step goal setting model is:

1. Decide on the goal

2. Write the goal down in an activity book or folder.

3. Use positive language, present tense and a time frame.
    - For example – This year in December I am holidaying with my family in the country.
    - This year I am saving $200 every week towards a new car.
    - This month I will go to the gym three times per week.

4. Read the goal twice a day, preferably morning and night.

5. Write victory across the goal as you achieve it.

6. Write goals in at least seven areas of your life – health, finance, career, relationships, spirituality, travel, special interest.

7. Aim to have a total of at least 100 goals.

Set Goals with your Virtual Teams

One of the most powerful things you can do with your virtual team is to set goals around productivity and targets jointly. The more input the virtual team has in setting these targets, the more committed they will be to achieve them.

It is best to give your virtual team notice that you will be conducting this goal-setting session and set up the parameters of this activity. Make sure you allow sufficient time to hear from the whole team.

Don't be surprised if your virtual team exceeds its target.

Goal Buddy

It can also be very productive to allocate a goal buddy to each of your virtual team members. Two or three of your virtual team will link up and be accountable to each other and connect every week for an update on each other's goals. Confidentiality is part of the goal buddy process, and each team member agrees to not discuss each other's goals outside of their goal group.

> THE ME THAT YOU SEE,
> IS THE ME THAT YOU WILL BE

Set Ground Rules

Your virtual team also needs **ground rules** for expectations on how to work together. How quickly are people expected to return an email or phone call? What is the protocol when people are out of the office or on vacation? If you require regular updates – what exactly does that look like, and how frequent is 'regular'?

Working with your virtual team to negotiate and decide these rules (rather than you mandating them) gives them ownership and increases the chance of them being followed.

Professional Team Integrity Code

Once agreed, your Professional Team Integrity Code, Virtual Team Purpose, and Ground Rules should be freely available for virtual team members. Publish your code, purpose and goals, and ground rules.

Foster Positive Connections

You can also help to **drive peak performance by fostering positive connections** between team members. Virtual team members who respect and trust one another are more likely to feel motivated to support their colleagues and to deliver their best. Look for ways to build connections of trust between virtual team members.

Previously, we saw lots of ways to build a positive team culture. Here are two more ideas on ways to foster positive connections based on trust and respect.

BE AWARE OF FIRST IMPRESSIONS

The first way to foster positive connections based on trust and respect is to be aware of **the initial impressions of trust among virtual team members**. So, in situations where you are introducing virtual team members to one another, or a new member to the group, steer the conversation towards experience, skills, and abilities that can be related to the virtual team's purpose and goals.

Case Study G - Fostering and building connections – First Impressions

As an example, read these two introductions. Which one do you think is more effective in building positive connections and trust between virtual team members?

EXAMPLE 1:

'Say hi to Michelle, who's just joined our virtual team. She's been around the company for a long time, and knows just about everybody! I also hear she's a pretty mean pool player! She's going to be designing all the customer specifications for us ... er, is that right, Michelle?'

EXAMPLE 2:

'Say hi to Michelle, who's just joined our virtual team. Michelle has more than eight years' experience with our company designing customer specifications as well as a post-graduate degree in software design. She won a company award last year for her designs. I've given Michelle the authority to design all the customer specifications for us. I'm pleased that Michelle is joining us and during the next week I'll ask her to reach out to each of you for a personal introduction so that you can get to know her.'

Encouraging your virtual team members to share their professional qualifications and experience helps to set a positive expectation about what each person will bring to the virtual team.

Be Aware of Perceptions of Unfairness

The second way to foster positive connections based on trust and respect **is to be aware of how motivation to contribute can be influenced**, and performance impacted when there is a perception of unfairness, or that not all virtual team members are contributing evenly to the group work.

An action or situation that prompts virtual team members to perceive unfairness can directly affect their contribution and support to the virtual team and its goals. If there is a sensed hint of bias, cultural insensitivity, or unfair or unbalanced treatment of others, the typical reaction is to withhold or reserve full effort and creativity.

On the Job Coaching is Essential

Effective job coaching is challenging when you don't have the opportunity to observe virtual team members carrying out tasks and interacting regularly. But leaders of virtual teams need to monitor team and individual progress and give feedback, just as they would if everyone was sharing the same location.

Regular Feedback

Plan regular feedback for the virtual team in a group environment, such as a virtual meeting or conference call. Schedule regular catch-ups with individuals via phone or conference call and use face-to-face meetings wherever you can.

Counsel Non-Performance

Counsel non-performance promptly – offering constructive support to help the virtual team member to get back on track.

Maintain your Virtual Presence

As the virtual team leader, you have an individual responsibility to have a constant virtual presence to keep the team on track and to be available for all virtual team members.

Communicating to Build Skills

At its best, work can be a highly educative process for employees. Meaningful and challenging work promotes growth, connectedness, expression, and a continuous context for learning and self-knowledge.

Participating in a well-managed virtual team provides unique opportunities for employees to learn and grow, by managing their learning, and cooperating with others in their knowledge, through processes of negotiation and discussion.

And the nature of collaboration (from the words co-labor) means working together, which implies shared goals, to create something new or different through the collaboration, rather than merely exchanging information or passing on instructions.

> The successful virtual manager plays a
> crucial role in all of these outcomes.

A good starting point is to help your virtual team members build their skills in using the relevant distance technology tools – like task manager, team sites, Zoom and other web conferencing platforms, and Discussion Boards.

Model the skills yourself and help them to build their skills and confidence, so they become active participants, not silent observers.

You may need to:

- Direct them to an online learning tutorial or guide
- Spend time with them yourself or assign another virtual team member to buddy up with them

To encourage learning and further advance skills, virtual team members need to feel comfortable talking about and sharing mistakes. Virtual teams have the added concern that everything they say, write, draw, or do recorded for posterity in an online archive. Raise this issue with the team at the outset. Look for non-threatening and positive ways to encourage the frank discussion of mistakes and learnings.

And think about rewarding those willing to share their learnings with others. Read how a team member explains how this works in her virtual team.

Patty: "We wanted to get a culture where we all learned from our experiences. So we introduced the 'Mistake of the Month' award.

It's an award that goes to the person who made the biggest mistake …we submit our entries, …and the rest of the team judges them at our monthly video conference.

The digital-trophy gets shipped to the winner via email. We also post on our team intranet board each month's winner.

You might think 'this will never work,' or its 'naming and shaming,' but its opposite.

The idea of sharing the biggest mistakes is so that we can concentrate on what we learned from the situation.

It was slow to start, but three months down the track, there's stiff competition for that trophy!

And I think the best thing is we pick up a lot of knowledge along the way that we're all using."

Helping virtual team members to grow and develop is the responsibility of every virtual manager. You should include a discussion about skills as part of your regular review conversation and help them to develop an action plan to build their skills over time.

When to Communicate Face-To-Face

Most people will agree that there are lots of benefits to communicating with colleagues face to face – whether in a formal meeting setting or informally between two or more people. While this is difficult and infrequent when working with a virtual team, technology through webcams helps bridge the gap between the distances.

Face to face meetings, even via Zoom (or similar platforms):

- Provide human contact between team members.

- Allows members to judge and evaluate competencies and skills not easily evaluated via other mediums.

- Allows members to develop strong relationships among themselves.

- Allow 'sideline' conversations that are often valuable in achieving various tasks.

> 'When give-and-take is required, there
> is no form of communication that
> works better than getting out of one's
> chair and speaking to the person face
> to face.'
>
> Business leader

People rely on multiple modes of communication when conversing face-to-face, such as voice tone, inflection, volume, eye movement, facial expression, hand gestures and body language.

As we previously discussed, most of these aspects can be achieved by ensuring every one of the team has their video camera on during meetings.

These cues provide for a methodical conversation process. They serve to facilitate turn-taking, convey subtle meanings, provide feedback, and thus regulate the conversation flow.

Because of the practical challenges for virtual teams to come together, your problem as a virtual leader is to pick and choose those times when a face-to-face meeting is likely to have maximum effect.

For instance, calling a face-to-face meeting will be most appropriate:

- For critical tasks that can make or break a virtual team's outcome

- For complex issues that require everyone's commitment and input

- For delivering bad news that affects the virtual team's direction or future

- For making decisions that affect the whole virtual team or that need a whole virtual team consensus

- For confronting poor, unsatisfactory performance or dealing with major conflict

- For situations where lots of ambiguity or confusion needs to be clarified with immediate feedback

- For celebrating a major virtual team milestone or achievement

If occasional face-to-face meetings are within your budget and practicality, hold them. If not, ensure that your virtual meetings are 'camera on' meetings. You can also leverage the opportunity of bringing your virtual team together to cover other agendas, like team updates, training, and coaching and skill development.

Communicating Bad News

Giving bad news is never easy for virtual leaders, but there are right ways and wrong ways of going about it. For the virtual team leader, as well as planning the encounter itself, it's essential to think about what communication type to use in delivering the message.

The best option for communicating bad news is face-to-face.

However, where this is not practical, the next best option is a telephone or conference call.

Virtual team members receiving lousy news are likely to feel anxious and vulnerable. They are likely to have many questions.

So you must choose a channel that allows them the best chance of receiving and processing the information to vent their anxiety and concerns and raise their questions with you.

For small groups, contact each member individually and ask each to keep the news in confidence to give you time to reach the rest of the virtual members directly.

On no account should you use email or other electronic written channels.

It might seem tempting to avoid a challenging conversation, but as virtual leaders, we have a responsibility to treat our employees with respect and integrity. So, a personal discussion is essential.

Celebrating from a Distance

Celebrating contributions and accomplishments is a vital part of virtual team leadership.

You should celebrate at the end of a project or project phase, and it can also be done periodically at critical milestones, and to recognize individual contributions and behaviors.

Recognizing and celebrating achievements provides a sense of accomplishment for your virtual team members and motivates them to continue.

It also provides recognition and reinforcement to virtual team members for doing things right and increases the chance of them repeating the proper behavior.

While celebrating is best-done face-to-face, it is still possible to celebrate adequately in a virtual meeting environment.

Telephone and video conference calls are an excellent medium for publicly acknowledging success and achievements.

And thoughtful email messages or posts on the team site can also convey your messages.

> The celebration is most effective when
> it's specific, targeted, and meaningful.

Mention the specific behaviors or outcomes being applauded and why they are worthy of recognition. The more specific you can make the feedback, the more meaningful the recognition.

For major team celebrations, involve your virtual team in planning. Ask for their input and how to make the celebration meaningful and fun, regardless of where they are located.

KEY POINT SUMMARY:

- A celebration is most effective when it's specific, targeted, and meaningful.

- Mention the specific behaviors or outcomes being applauded and why they are worthy of recognition. The more specific the feedback, the more meaningful the recognition

- You *can* celebrate in a virtual environment.

    - Try: Telephone and video conferences or email messages or posts on team sites

- Get your virtual team involved

- Virtual teams are groups of people, working interdependently across space, time, cultures, and organizational boundaries with a shared purpose, while using technology.

- Communicating with your virtual team to inspire their best performance starts with **setting a clear and inspiring shared purpose and goals** then building on those goals through every interaction you have with each virtual team member

How do you communicate in a collaborative world?

Communicating in the collaborative workspace

This chapter outlines the different communication tools available for the collaborative workspace, what to use when, and how to use them effectively.

- Which communication method to use in which situation?
- Types of virtual communication
- Effective use of the email
- Effective use of meetings
- Effective use of audio and video conference
- Effective use of Live Meetings
- Effective use of online collaboration tools

The collaborative workspace provides a myriad of communication tools for connecting virtual team members, storing and tracking work, and sharing ideas.

When leading a virtual team, it's important to consciously think about the types of communications you use and when to use them.

For each of the following communication scenarios, select the communication type that you think would be *most* appropriate.

Communication type options include:

A telephone call, audio conference call, video conference call, email, instant messaging, webinar and conferencing platforms (such as Zoom, etc), electronic discussion board, Face to face meeting (if available), and electronic team site.

Activity 12 - Match the Communication Type – Speedy 10

From the communication type options – please select the one most appropriate for the following situations:

1. Telephone call

2. Audio conference call

3. Video conference call

4. Email

5. Instant messaging

6. Webinar and web conferencing platforms (such as Zoom etc)

7. Electronic discussion board

8. Wiki

9. Face to face meeting

10. Electronic team site.

Using the numbers 1-10 above, which communication method would be the most suitable for the following situations?

- Reschedule the starting time for a video conference call._____

- Provide constructive feedback and suggestions to a team member on a quarterly report._____

- Weekly team 'check-in' meeting on progress against project milestones. _____

- Quarterly update to team on strategic priorities. _____

- Alert team members that you'll be 10 minutes late for weekly meeting. _____

- Advise virtual team members of new budgetary constraints that have significant impacts for some team members and activities._____

- Coach a new virtual team member on navigating around the team site. ____

- Run a virtual team brainstorm on solutions to a particular team or project problem._____

- Counsel a virtual team member on poor performance over the past six months._____

- Celebrate the virtual team's achievements over the last three months

Special Communication Situations

1 – Managing employees who work from home

Some **virtual** or **hybrid teams** will include one or more employees who work from home.

These employees are technically no different from other virtual team members, and the same behaviors for managing these employees will apply.

In cases where the employee is the only virtual member of the team, be aware of the challenges they face as isolated members – as the lone member dialing into a lively face-to-face meeting, or logging on to the network long after others have gone home.

Make sure other virtual team members are sensitive to their situation.

You should also check that the employee's home office area is appropriate to the nature of the work and that he/she has access to the same technology and tools as on-site employees have to ensure they can participate fully as virtual team members.

2 - Leading people who don't report to you

In virtual teams, it is quite often that you will have team members who don't directly report to you. For example, you might be leading a project team, and the project virtual team members may be from various parts of the organization, only coming together for that particular project.

The guidelines for leading non-direct reports are very similar to leading those who report to you because while they are members of the virtual team, they are accountable for deliverables associated with the team or project.

It is a good idea to make it clear to those people how you will be evaluating their performance.

You should also pass your feedback on their performance on to their manager.

Types of Virtual Communication

Communicating clearly and effectively with colleagues when you can't see them is a challenge.

Fortunately, virtual team managers and members have a range of communication tools at your disposal.

Communication	Virtual Communication Options
▪ Some of the most common types of communication for **interacting with virtual team** members	▪ Phone calls ▪ Conference calls – audio and video ▪ Email ▪ Online chat/instant messaging – such as Slack, etc
▪ There are **collaborative meeting tools** that allow teams to interact and share documents and information	▪ Zoom, Microsoft Teams, Skype etc.
▪ There are other communication types for **generating and sharing ideas and solutions**	▪ Blogs, discussion boards, Online collaboration ▪ Trello, Slack, etc ▪ Team sites ▪ Microsoft Project
▪ There are also a range of other online communication types for **storing and sharing team files**,	▪ Dropbox, Google Drive, Microsoft OneDrive etc.
▪ **And, for scheduling and tracking progress,**	▪ Team sites ▪ Trello, etc ▪ Microsoft Project, etc ▪ Other online project management software

When leading or working in a virtual team it's important to consciously think about the types of communication you use and when to use them.

The right choice will help you to leverage the collective skills, experience and learning of virtual team members to find better solutions, resolve problems creatively and react swiftly.

The wrong choice of communication tool or technology can be detrimental for virtual teams.

So make careful choices that help you to consider the best common denominator for all virtual team members and avoid excluding anyone.

Effective Use of Email

One of the most commonly used tools for most virtual teams is email. Used judiciously, email is a highly effective and efficient communication tool.

Used poorly, it can waste time, distract employees, and at its worst, damage the very personal connections that you are trying to build.

Activity 13 - Email Effects

Read these examples of virtual team members talking about recent email experiences.

As you read, ask yourself:

- What is the problem?

- What is the effect?

- What should the sender have done to avoid the problem?

Read the following comments and see how many email mistakes you can spot.

- "She writes the longest emails I've ever seen! They go on forever; it's hard to work out what their point is!"

- "I'm always getting copied on these emails from Ted with the word 'update' in the subject. Update on what?"

- "Well, Janice might be the manager, but she's a horrible speller. I can hardly make sense of some of her emails. I don't think she's discovered Microsoft Outlook spell-check!"

- "So I get to work yesterday and find out that I'm being dropped from the project. And you know how I found out? On an email!"

Maria: I had a contract virtual team member, Sharon, located in the mid-west USA. For approximately <u>four months</u>, Sharon told me, her manager, and other virtual team members that her computer video camera was broken.

Then, Sharon didn't show up for a meeting. Then, she wasn't responding to emails.

About a week later, in an email with the subject line 'update' Sharon said "I'm sorry to have to tell you via email, but last weekend I had a baby.

My husband and I are thrilled, and honestly, I just forgot to mention it to you!"

In shock, I continued to read on about how she had meant to tell me, but simply 'forgot.'

Sharon went on, "The baby won't really impact my work in any way. If I can just take a couple of weeks off, that would be appreciated."

This is, without a doubt, the oddest email I've ever received.

Yes, this is a lesson both ways in management and also the appropriateness of message delivery via email.

To this day, I think I must have been dreaming it – but it was absolutely true.

Once you've decided to send an email, keep these email etiquette tips in mind.

- Keep your message brief and to the point.

- Break longer messages up with subheadings and paragraphs.

- Include a meaningful subject heading to indicate content and purpose.

- Include a date and time by which you need a response.

- Remember that email isn't private.

- Don't put anything in an email that you wouldn't put on an open postcard.

- Don't use email for complex or emotional messages, or as an excuse to avoid a personal conversation.

- Remember that your tone can't be heard in an email. What might be sarcasm or irony to you could be offensive to someone else.

- Be sparing with CC and 'reply all' emails.

Effective Meetings

Meetings are often the 'glue' for virtual teams because they create the opportunity to bridge the geographical and other divides and bring team members together in some format.

However, most of us have been to enough bad meetings in our careers to knowing that a poorly run meeting, or a 'no point' meeting, can be worse than no meeting at all. And virtual meetings present particular challenges for the virtual team manager.

Let's start with reviewing some universal meeting guidelines:

- Starting and finishing on time

- Having an agenda and sticking to it

- Circulating any items to be read or printed well in advance of the meeting (not five minutes before)

- Setting the context for the meeting

- Establishing any ground rules

- Introducing participants who don't know each other

- Involving all participants in the discussion, including quiet or shy ones
- Summarize key points, actions, and next steps

It's most likely that your meeting will be via an audio or video conference call. The mode you select will depend on the number of participants and the nature of the meeting.

Regular team, project, and status update meetings can usually be handled via an audio conference.

You may want to augment your regular audio conferences with occasional video conferences, at critical project points, or to review quarterly progress.

As a general guide, follow these virtual meeting tips:

- Try not to squeeze too many things into a meeting. Keep the focus on one or two topics.
- If you must cover more items, then give people time to stretch, take a bathroom break, or replenish their coffee.
- Keep each segment of the meeting short – no longer than 30 minutes.

Effective Use of Audio and Video Conference

Virtual Meetings are Still Meetings

Audio and video conference tools are both excellent for connecting you virtually with small and large groups, and both require preparation and understanding to be used effectively.

To start with, if you're hosting an audio or video conference, all the same rules of standard meeting etiquette apply. But there are new things to think about when you are hosting a virtual meeting.

Let's look first at some principles that apply to both audio and video conferences.

1. The first thing to remember is that you are in a *meeting*. That means giving your full attention and courtesy to participants precisely as you would if you were in the same room.

2. Introductions are especially important. You and others can't see who's on an audio conference, and it's often hard to recognize people's faces on a large group video conference call.

3. So broker the introductions precisely as you would in a regular meeting. That includes announcing late arrivals to the conference, who miss the first round of introductions

4. **Meetings should move at a slightly slower pace than a regular meeting because of a few second delays for most systems to communicate.**

5. Allow for sufficient pauses after asking a question or making a comment to give participants time to hear and digest it.

6. Ask a specific person a specific question. Asking open-ended questions to a broad remote audience will often result in 'dead air' and then multiple people talking at once. When requesting a general question precede it with language like: "I'm going to ask some general questions, please make sure that you are ready to answer, or type your answers into the chatbox," then pause and ask your first question.

7. For video conference calls there are some extra things to think about:

   - Movement can be quite stilted on camera so keep body movements to a minimum, and move and gesture slowly and naturally.

   - If you want to say something, bring attention to yourself before addressing the group by signaling with your hand or saying 'question' or 'comment' and waiting a couple of seconds before continuing. Some products, like Zoom, have a 'raise hand' feature. Encourage your team to use this so that as the meeting facilitator, you know who has a question, comment, or is ready to answer a question.

   - Try to avoid loud shirts or clothes, large, shiny, or noisy jewelry as these can be distracting.

   - Have attendees sit as close as practical to the camera. If you are using a board room or similar ample space, move to the front of the room.

Effective Use of Webinar and Conferencing Platforms

Webinar and conferencing platforms (such as Zoom, Web Ex, Skype, GoToMeeting and similar products) allow you to hold a live meeting with one or more participants, computer to computer. You can also share documents, share screens, and edit each other's documents, all live and online.

Many of the principles for using these types of products are similar to an audio or video conference call, but with some important additions.

Even though you are the only person at your desk, and you might be making the call from home, or on a weekend or evening, you *are* in a meeting.

How you present yourself to your audience can improve the effectiveness of your meeting, as well as your credibility as the virtual manager.

When hosting or being part of a webinar meeting or similar, follow these simple tips:

1. Make sure there is sufficient natural light
2. Ensure there is light in front of you, to illuminate you as the participant. Having the light behind you will create a dark silhouette. The most flattering light is from directly in front and lower than eye level
3. Be aware of where your camera is, and look directly at the camera as often as possible
4. Avoid bright lipstick or large shiny jewelry
5. Dress appropriately for your audience
6. Sit straight, and avoid slumping or moving unnecessarily
7. Avoid eating or drinking during the meeting
8. Select a quiet and discreet area to avoid interruptions

Activity 14 - Webconfercing Quandary

Look at these images of Zoom conference participants. For each one, ask yourself:

What's wrong with the picture?

What is the effect on the audience?

What could the person do differently?

Person sitting in their pyjamas

Laptop monitor at angle and camera not at face level

Person with partner kissing them – distracting to the audience

Laptop monitor at angle and camera not at face level

Eating a sandwich – poor presentation to the audience

Laptop monitor at angle and camera not at face level

Laptop monitor at angle and camera not at face level

Potential noise from outside

Light source from side – better light if it was front on

Sitting slumped – poor presentation to the audience

Laptop monitor at angle and camera not at face level

Sitting slumped – poor presentation to the audience

Laptop monitor at angle and camera not at face level

Light source from back – better light if it was front on

Person staring down– not aware of where the camera is

Eating – poor presentation to the audience

Laptop monitor at angle and camera not at face level

Person very hard to see – not enough light in the room

Potential distraction by child

Laptop monitor at angle and camera not at face level

Light source from side – better light if it was front on

Laptop monitor at angle and camera not at face level

During this coronavirus outbreak, just because you **can** wear your track pants on the couch for a meeting, doesn't mean you **should**!

Your co-workers will empathize if you are home-schooling your children, but do the very best you can to minimize distractions and maintain your professionalism.

Try to set up your home working environment as a dedicated space, or at least a space that you can quickly arrange each day. During the COVID-19 crisis it will help you to feel like you are in a business mindset.

Effective Online Collaboration

As we've already learned, the collaborative workspace provides a myriad of communication tools for connecting virtual team members, storing and tracking work, and in particular, sharing ideas and information.

The concept of a virtual team of experts seated at their respective desks in New York, London, Paris, Sydney, Vancouver, Sao Paulo, and Berlin – all being able to pool their knowledge and experience towards a particular end collectively, is an exciting prospect.

> The concept of a virtual team who was only a few weeks ago seated together in their offices and now, due to coronavirus, are working from home, struggling to continue to work amongst the chaos, might be a frightening prospect.

Online discussion boards are a good tool, but come with some challenges, in particular, because computer-mediated environments make coherent conversations difficult.

> These issues have the potential to influence the interactions negatively, and virtual leaders have a role to play here.

Case Study H - Alison's Considered Response

Read the situation as these issues can unfold in a real-life scenario. Consider this real-life scenario, which describes what commonly happens in the flow of an electronic discussion or message board (Slack, etc).

What virtual team members are reading and thinking	What virtual team members actually see on the Electronic Discussion Board
	BOBBY: The new SOP came out. Training due by the end of the month
Team member ALISON reads a message from team member BOBBY, and then signs off the computer to ponder over the news and carefully craft and edit her response. In the meantime team member KATE reads the same message, and then decides to make an immediate comment and move the point of discussion beyond the issue to which ALISON is preparing a response.	
	KATE: No problem, does the SOP include the updated form for reporting?
Team member CHARLES may decide to change the conversation and discuss something else.	CHARLES did anyone get the agenda for tomorrow's meeting?
No one responds to team member CHARLES, but team member DAN decides to change the conversation.	DAN: Anyone know which grocery stores are open early – I'll go before the meeting?
	SALLY not sure, check with Sandy
	JOE I think Ralph's Supermarket is open at 7 am ERIC I hope so – Dan, get there early as milk was in short supply yesterday
However, member ALISON decides to post her message anyway and notes the response is in response to an earlier comment offered by member BOBBY.	ALISON Hi Bobby, just responding to your earlier message, I've already completed the training, just needed to check the date
During the same time frame, various members (SALLY AND ERIC) post responses to member KATES's discussion.	SALLY Yes, I think so Kate ERIC I believe it's attached as part of the training, Kate
Other team members (FRED, JOHN) join in responding to KATE, CHARLES, BOBBY, ALISON, and DAN.	FRED Yes, it's attached, Kate JOHN It's attached Kate, I got the agenda Charles, and Ralph's is open Dan!
Even though they note that they are responding to the respective team member's comments, when member PENNY signs onto the conversation, she is bewildered and not quite sure how to participate.	
	PENNY Can someone please tell me what we're talking about? I'm lost.

A few practical solutions:

- **Apply dialogue structuring** – questions or rules that guide the conversation and are inserted into the communication interface. Virtual team members are required to abide by the rules and respond to the questions if they want to participate in the conversation.

- **Assign a moderator to each discussion**, to observe the discussion, and shepherd it back on track via comments to contributors.

- **Run discussions over defined periods** – with a start and end time – to capture all conversation in a short period.

- **Have the virtual team establish clear ground rules around discussions** – and let the team self-censor those who 'break the rules'.

> The ultimate measure of a man is not where he stands in moments of comfort, but where he stands at times of challenge and controversy."
> **Martin Luther King, Jr.**

KEY POINTS SUMMARY

- As the virtual leader, you have a special responsibility to have a **constant virtual presence** to keep the team on track and to be available for team members.

- **Celebrating contributions** and accomplishments is a vital part of virtual team management.

- When leading a virtual team, it's important to consciously think about the **types of communications** you use and when to use them.

PART 5
TAPPING INTO VIRTUAL TEAM POTENTIAL: CREATING HIGH PERFORMING VIRTUAL TEAMS

TRUST – the most fragile of all leadership skills

TRUST DEFINED

> "If you don't trust people, people will
> not trust you."
>
> ~ Lao Tzu

Mutual trust is a shared belief that you can depend on each other to achieve a common purpose.

Regardless of whether a team is local or virtual, the business of the team is conducted through personal relationships. And trust is the foundation of personal relationships.

When team members feel trusted by their manager and trust one another, it creates a strong bond that unites the team, encourages creativity, collaboration, and productivity.

By contrast, when trust erodes, relationships are compromised, and people shut down, pull back, and hesitate to engage. Without trust, employees have little interest in being creative, taking risks, and collaborating.

More comprehensively, trust defined as "the willingness of a party (trustor) to be vulnerable to the actions of another party (trustee) based on the expectation that the trustee will act important to the trustor, regardless of the trustor's ability to monitor or control the trustee."

People sense how you feel about them. If you want to change their attitudes toward you, change the negative beliefs you have toward them.

Building relationships requires the building of trust. Trust is the expectancy of people that they can rely on your word. It is built through integrity and consistency in relationships.

What is trust in a virtual team world?

Trust - an understanding the other
person's standpoint

- **Part of the 'empathy process' is establishing trust and rapport.**
  Creating trust and rapport helps us to have sensible 'adult' discussions

- Building trust is about listening and understanding – not necessarily agreeing (which is different) – to the other person. Listening without judging.

- A useful focus when listening to another person is to try to understand how the other person feels, and to discover what they want to achieve.

- Dr. Stephen Covey ('The Seven Habits of Highly Effective People') was one of many modern advocates who urge us to **strive deeply to understand the other person's point of view**.

- **We must work with people collaboratively**, to enable them to see what they want, and then help them to see the ways to achieve it.

- The act of doing all this establishes trust.

Activity 15 - Defining Trust

The following table lists words that define what trust is and isn't. From the following list determine 'what trust is' and 'what trust isn't'

Definition / Prompting Words	What trust is ☑	What trust isn't ☑
• keep your word		
• tell the truth		
• keep their promises		
• honest, decent, respectable, loyal and fair with others build trust		
• build integrity		
• reputation and credibility is given by others		
• surveillance		
• auditing		
• reputation		
• authorization		
• closed-loop control		
• insurability		
• belief		
• accountability		
• hope		
• intuition		
• faith		
• unqualified		
• the inverse of risk		
• the absence of risk		

Suggested Answers:

What trust is	What trust isn't
<ul><li>keep your word</li><li>tell the truth</li><li>keep their promises</li><li>honest, decent, respectable, loyal and fair with others build trust</li><li>build integrity</li><li>reputation and credibility is given by others</li></ul>	<ul><li>surveillance</li><li>auditing</li><li>reputation</li><li>authorization</li><li>closed–loop control</li><li>insurability</li><li>belief</li><li>accountability</li><li>hope</li><li>intuition</li><li>faith</li><li>unqualified</li><li>the inverse of risk</li><li>the absence of risk</li></ul>

How You Create Trust

Trust is a choice.

While there is no ironclad guarantee
that you will never be betrayed, you
have the power to create trusting
relationships.

Case Study I -   Three Virtual Team Encounters

As you read the following statements from virtual team members relating their recent team experiences, ask yourself:

What is the problem?

What is the effect?

What could the team manager do to avoid or solve the problem?

Situation 1

We're supposed to have a 30-minute team audio conference every week to check in on project status and identify roadblocks. Last week, Lois, my manager, dialed in 10 minutes late and then left before the end. And this week, Lois didn't dial in at all! I didn't get to raise my issue, and I'm worried that I won't meet my deadline."

Situation 2

'I've joined this global Customer Solutions team, and we're all supposed to be combining our input on this common team site. I've asked the manager twice to get me access, and I still don't have it. It's hard to be on the team when I can't contribute. Since COVID-19 hit we haven't seen or heard from him.'

Situation 3

'At the beginning of our project, we agreed what our outputs should be, and when to deliver them. But since then, I keep getting these little 'how's it going' instant messages from Roger, hinting that he'd 'like to know how I'm tracking with my project tasks outside of the formal communication process that we agreed to. It's like he's checking up on me. I've asked the others on the team, and they say it's the same for them. No one likes it. Why can't Roger just keep to the process and stop pestering me?'

Situation 4

'I have two children, aged 2 and 6. We are all in lockdown due to the coronavirus. I have no way of keeping regular hours and am struggling to meet my usual project deadlines. I'm working at odd times when my husband returns from work – he's a doctor at the hospital, caring for patients. He comes home exhausted, but I have to hand over the care of the kids to him, so I can get my work done. Yesterday, they were having lunch I took a photo and posted it on Facebook. I thought it was a good way for family and friends to see them happy and playing. In today's team virtual huddle, my manager said, "oh Ashley's having fun with the kids, we can't ask her to do that." My heart sank. I'm doing my best.'

Each of the above examples shared examples of broken trust – by being let down by the manager in some way.

Building Trust

Trust is integral to the success of a
virtual team.

Building trust from a distance is a unique challenge for Virtual leaders. We're more practiced in starting and building our working relationships in-person – relying on the non-verbal cues and signals we get from face-to-face contact.

But, while the mechanisms for delivery might be different, the behaviors required for building and maintaining trust are precisely the same for all teams.

Increasing internal networking and partnering capability through trust is vital to all virtual relationships. In every interaction, your team should feel satisfied with the outcome, regardless if they agree or disagree with your direction. This is underpinned by ensuring that within each of your relationships with your team members, there is a high degree of trust involved. Building trust is based on the willingness to partner.

PARTNERING DEFINED

"A long-term professional relationship
of mutual support between you, the
global/virtual leader and the team
member, both of whom are focused on
improving business results."

To be successful, a partnership requires a mutually beneficial focus on expectations, trust, results, and opportunities to seek win/win outcomes. The successful leader in a global virtual leadership role builds a relationship of trust and open communication by learning the fundamentals of the business, and particularly each of her team's internal clients, external vendors, and other key stakeholder's business issues and goals.

Through understanding their perspective, the successful person in a virtual leadership role becomes a valuable partner in delivering value-added solutions to the organization.

Three Types of Trust

"To be trusted is a greater compliment
than to be loved."

~ George MacDonald

Capacity for Trust

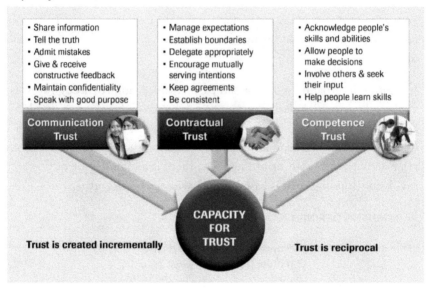

Figure 9 - Capacity for Trust Model[17]

Communication Trust

Communication trust is built by sharing information, being truthful, and giving constructive feedback. This establishes information flow and how people talk with one another.

In a virtual team, when Communication Trust is present, virtual team members feel comfortable, to be honest, share their experiences, and speak openly in meetings. Most importantly, when Communication

---

[17] Capacity of Trust Model (Adapted from 'Building Sustainable Trust, By Dennis S Reina and Michelle L Reina, 2007)

Trust is present, less gossip takes place in a team because team members know that this can destroy trust and damage relationships.

Contractural Trust

Contractual trust is built by setting and managing clear expectations, delegating, and keeping agreements. This sets the tone for engagement and shapes roles and responsibilities.

In a virtual team, when Contractual Trust is present, virtual team members strive to do what they say they will do. They work together to manage expectations, projects, and keep agreements with each other and the rest of their organization. They know their roles and responsibilities and openly ask questions if they are unsure of precisely what their deliverables are. They understand that breaching this trust means a failure to deliver on expectations and that in doing so, they would let their virtual colleagues down.

Competence Trust

Competence trust is built by acknowledging people's skills and capabilities, letting people make decisions, and helping people to learn new skills. This allows your team members to use and further develop their skills, abilities, and knowledge.

In a virtual team setting, Competence Trust is vital. Trusting those team members who are geographically spread are competent to deliver expectations. Virtual leaders often compromise Competence Trust by micro-managing and not delegating. This common mistake by virtual leaders causes virtual team members to become disengaged and disheartened. In the extreme, they may feel isolated, and due to their geography may feel unable to progress to other positions within the organization. Competence Trust in a virtual team allows virtual team members to leverage their existing skills and be rewarded for their professional growth.

> Knowing what behaviors are required
> to build and sustain trust, and applying
> those behaviors as a leader, are critical
> to the performance of your virtual
> team.

When Trust is Broken

Betrayal

> "A breach of trust or the perception of
> a breach, from major to minor,
> intentionally or unintentionally"

Reina & Reina

HOW TRUST CAN BE BROKEN

Trust is the most fragile of all the skills you will share with your team. Unknowingly, virtual leaders can break trust with their virtual teams by:

- Not doing what they commit to doing, without explanation.

- They are selective with the email responses that are sent. Sometimes leaders are just too busy to address all the queries their virtual teams send over days or weeks. However, rather than ignoring messages, it is far better to send one short email that explains you will not be available for x number of days or weeks, giving a reason for that situation. The virtual team may still be disappointed in you, but they will appreciate your honesty.

- An empowered virtual team will be happy to make decisions for them without continually consulting you if they have noticed that you will be unavailable.

- Asking "what do you think?" in a situation when you have already made up your mind. Within a short time, the virtual team member realizes this and is annoyed they had wasted their time when you ignored their recommendations.

- They are not setting up systems ahead of time when they are going to be unavailable for an extended time.

- They are allowing critical time frames to be ignored during your unavailability.

Trust can be broken through a series of stages:

1. **The confusion stage.** Your virtual team is confused by your behavior, as questions go unanswered due to your unavailability or unexplained reduction in communication.

2. **The disappointment stage.** Your virtual team has moved to the disappointment stage as they still have no answers for your behavior or lack of response to their queries.

3. **The broken trust stage.** Sometimes it takes weeks or months to get to the broken trust point. Basically, your virtual team wants to trust you, you are their leader, and they have faith in you. Your virtual team will continue to make excuses for you and your behavior until they get to the point where they run out of excuses for your unexplained behavior. At that point, trust is broken. When trust is broken with one team member, electronically, this broken trust can spread throughout your team very quickly. And when messages are continually ignored, the 'virtual grapevine' may go into overdrive, and your reputation will be damaged.

Activity 16 - Build or Betray Trust

Listed below you will find a list of management behaviors that are commonly demonstrated by virtual team managers.

For each behavior, evaluate whether it would be likely to build trust with team members, or betray trust. In the column, choose between Betray trust or Build trust by placing a ✓ depending on your opinion.

Behavior	Betray Trust with team members	Build trust with team members
Admitting on a virtual team conference call that you have made an error that impacts the project timeline.		
Insisting that all virtual team members use project software that only some have been trained to use.		
Posting internal management reports on the team site for all virtual team members to access.		
Criticizing the report of a virtual team member on a whole team video conference call.		
Working with the team to agree on virtual team purpose, ground rules, milestones, and deliverables and publishing these on the team site.		
Asking all virtual team members for their opinion on a reasonable project deadline.		
Requesting that all decisions be directed via you for approval before action.		
Taking a call on your cell phone during a live Zoom meeting.		
Using instant messenger to send a light-hearted joke about a virtual team member to another member during a team audio conference.		
Sending out an advance agenda for each videoconference meeting		

As we've just learned, high levels of trust across the team are critical to encouraging creativity, collaboration, and productivity – all critical ingredients in the recipe for peak performance.

And as you learned previously in this book, communication style for the virtual manager is LESS about being directive and more about guiding, coaching, and advising team members.

Another critical factor will be the effective handling of conflict. One strategy is to address perceived discontent as early as noticed. In essence, emotions left unchecked in the virtual environment might erupt into sequences of negative comments, which will be challenging to resolve asynchronously.

Another strategy in handling conflict will be to address, as much as possible, only the concerned individual and to avoid copying the entire team to messages that might be best to address to a single individual where a potentially conflicting problem has arisen.

How to heal trust in a virtual setting

When leading virtual teams, it can often be emotionally draining when trust is broken. However, as successful leaders know, it's up to them to begin the healing process to allow the virtual team member or members to move on.

The first recommendation in healing trust is that if possible, the process should begin face-to-face. Having an in-person meeting will speak volumes regarding your commitment to rebuilding trust. If this is not possible, then a series of conversations with a web camera is the second-best option. It's tough to have such sensitive discussions over the phone because, as the lead communicator, all body language is invisible, and you are reliant solely on the words that you and the other person are using and the tone of voice.

Case Study J -   Greta and Liz

Greta is a high potential corporate manager working in Europe. Her manager, Liz, is located in North America. Due to one project mishap where Greta didn't inform Liz of a project delay, Liz lost all trust in Greta and became a complete micro-manager requesting daily reports on all projects.

Greta felt that all communication and competence trust had been destroyed. Liz had no time for Greta, was blunt, officious, and abrupt. Greta dreaded taking phone calls when she knew Liz was working in the different time zone, in case it was Liz calling.

Liz had to conduct Greta's performance review and had 'save up' some feedback so that it could become part of the evaluation. Greta was already nervous and was sleepless the night before the review. Frustrated, Liz phoned at the allotted meeting time. Greta was pleased that Liz wasn't on a Zoom as she knew that Liz *wouldn't* be able to see her during the call.

Liz gave Greta her performance review praising her on a project that Greta had completed earlier in the year. Then, with a swift blow, Liz provided a massive list of negative feedback and said: "you don't get on with your colleagues – in fact, I wonder if you are even a human being because you don't seem to feel anything!" With tears running down her cheeks, Greta was crushed.

Liz ended the meeting with a plan that she had created without Greta's input. Greta put down the phone, picked up her handbag, and walked out of her European office. Liz was unaware that Greta was upset and crying.

A few months later Greta transferred to another position in the company.

Steps for Healing Trust

> People say that 'time heals wounds.'
> While this may be true for some, we
> think that 'taking action' heals wounds
> and rebuilds trust.

Case Study K -   Greta and Liz - continued

In the previous story, Liz did nothing to acknowledge during Greta's performance review what had happened to cause the mistrust that had developed between them. Firstly, the forum of a performance review is entirely inappropriate for this type of conversation. Liz might have chosen a coaching meeting where the specific issue could have been focused on, and trust has begun to heal and rebuild.

The flow of the coaching meeting might have been something like:

- To begin the coaching meeting, Liz might start by openly acknowledge exactly what happened and seek a mutual agreement to resolve and build trust between them.

- Then, Liz might have asked Greta **how she was feeling,** which would have been an excellent way to open up the conversation and to give Liz the opportunity to listen carefully with a view to also sharing how she felt. This approach would have begun to bridge a level of communication trust between them.

- Liz might have also suggested that Greta **reach out to others** on the virtual team to assist her in areas that she either wasn't confident or feeling skilled in. This way, Greta could have been the person to come to her own admission of areas for development, rather than Liz *telling* Greta where she was incompetent!

- As a competent leader, we would have expected Liz to create a 'lessons learned' coaching opportunity for Greta, asking her to reflect on what happened. This would have allowed Greta to **reposition the incident as a problem to an opportunity for professional development**.

- Taking **shared responsibility** to work together to avoid future situations would have built not only communication trust, but contractual trust.

- Finally, stating clearly that the situation is in the past and agreeing to move on again builds trust and the potential for a positive future professional relationship.

If only Liz had done any of these things, Greta might not have got a job in another department. Liz remains blind to what happened. By contrast, Greta, who now leads her new virtual team, is vitally aware of how the breakdown of trust can cascade into the demise of all parts of a working relationship.

KEY POINTS SUMMARY

- Regardless of whether a team is local or virtual, the business of the group is conducted through personal relationships. And trust is the foundation of personal relationships.

- Trust can be broken through a series of stages

- Confusion stage

- Disappointment stage

- Broken trust

- The behaviors required for building and maintaining trust fall into three categories

    - Contractual trust

    - Communication trust

    - Competence trust

Managing Global and Cultural Adaptability

This chapter provides virtual leaders with valuable information about the complexities of globally dispersed virtual teams by focusing on two areas:

1. everyday communication with a cross-cultural team
2. managing and adapting to cultural differences

The earlier chapters in this book mainly focused on the physical and technical challenges of leading and communicating with teams spread across more than one geographic location.

Cross-cultural teams add an extra dimension of complexity to the mix, especially when you combine it with distance. This chapter focuses on strengthening your cultural adaptability when managing your global virtual team.

The first part of this chapter will concentrate on some of the more fundamental day-to-day aspects of managing a cross-functional team – and incorporating elements like time zones, and communicating with people where English is not the native language.

- Fundamental aspects of managing cross-cultural teams
- Managing Globally

The second part of the chapter focuses more on the deeper cultural challenges presented by cross-cultural teams.

- Cultural Challenges
- Developing Cultural Capability

Review Model: Core Virtual Leadership Model

Let's begin by reviewing the Virtual Management model that's been presented so far:

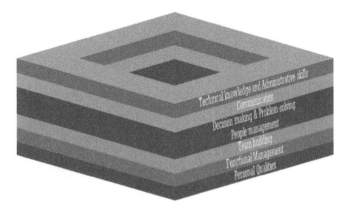

Figure 10 - Core Virtual Leadership Model

Previously we introduced the model "Core Virtual Leadership Model". We discussed the first two areas of the model: Personal Qualities and Functional Management.

> Leader – someone who can create and
> communicate vision and inspire others
> to achieve the vision.

Then, we concentrated on the next focus areas:

- Team Building

- People Management

- Decision Making and Problem Solving

- Communication

- Technical knowledge and administrative skills

Managing Globally and Cultural Adaptability

Figure 11 - Core Virtual Leadership Model grounded in Cultural Adaptability

The underlying foundation of successful global virtual leadership is **cultural adaptability**. Being able to manage globally, know and understand cultural differences, and adapt to different cultures are essential skills of the successful virtual leader.

If you are leading or participating in a virtual team, there's an excellent chance that you are dealing with people of nationalities and cultures different from your own.

Activity 17 - People Management Skills for Virtual Management Assessment

This assessment looks at some of the personal qualities and skills needed to lead cross-cultural teams.

This assessment is for your personal use to help to determine your current strengths and areas of development.

For each question, rate yourself on each of the techniques.

People Management Skills	1 Never	2 Rarely	3 Sometimes	4 Most of the Time	5 Always
I can adapt my behavior according to different situations					
I am comfortable with uncertainty					
I can trust when dealing with the unfamiliar					
I am willing to have my views and beliefs challenged					
I am tactful in my dealings with others					
I am invigorated and excited by differences (rather than threatened or intimidated by them)					
I am patient when I am not in control					
I am able to see a familiar situation from unfamiliar vantage points					
I am sensitive to nuances of differences					
I have genuine respect for others who have different backgrounds, cultures and experiences to me					
I am willing to change myself as I learn and grow (vs. changing others to fit me)					
I am able to laugh at my own mistakes					
I can empathize with others by putting myself in the shoes of another person					
I take a win-win attitude (rather than 'I need to win' attitude)					
TOTAL					

Assessing your Cultural Adaptability

Activity 18 - Global People Management Assessment

Now, we ask you to complete a second assessment. This one focuses on the attributes of cultural adaptability. Again use the same 5 part rating scale to answer each question.

Global People Management	1 Never	2 Rarely	3 Sometimes	4 Most of the Time	5 Always
I am clear, direct and open when communicating with virtual team members					
I am confident to take risks when dealing with global virtual team members					
To get to know the people on my global virtual team, I am friendly and talk about non-work related things with my global team members					
I am patient and take time to understand exactly what is being communicated by team members whose native language is different to mine					
I am sensitive to the different cultural needs of team members who are from a different country to me					
I express my expectations around my global team member's requirement for physical travel and the exact needs of attending virtual meetings					
I respect people's personal beliefs, even if they are different to my own					
I take the initiative to learn about the cultural differences between myself and my global team members					
I am adept at changing my language to more simplified versions for those whose native language is not the same as mine.					
I am patient with people whose native language is not the same as mine.					
I tolerate change even if I disagree with the action or content of the change					
I understand how people feel when they travel long distances for work and the adjustment to different time zones.					
TOTAL					

Please total your scores and list them for Never, Rarely, Sometimes, Most of the time, and Always. All of the skills above are necessary to lead virtual teams and will be discussed in this and later chapters.

Reflecting on your answers

Congratulations on all the statements that you answered, 'Most of the time' and 'Always.' Please don't worry, though, if you scored high on the 'Never,' 'Rarely', or 'Sometimes' columns. This book will guide you through the maze of virtual leadership and give you strategies to significantly improve the skills you have identified.

Managing Globally

Regardless of your skills and experience in leading virtual teams, a team which is geographically spread, and which comprises people from different cultural groups, presents many global challenges, starting with some major ones.

Two of the most apparent challenges include:

- Coordinating your communications across **different time zones**
- Communicating with people where **English is not the native language.**

Case Study L - Global Sales Virtual Project Team

Even the deceptively simple task of pronouncing unfamiliar names correctly can be a challenge. Let's explore those challenges now as we look at some case studies.

First, let's meet a virtual project team, comprising representatives from different countries. The team's brief is to develop topics and content for a range of online and printed materials that will be given to customers for a new product.

The sales representatives are all subject matter experts who have experience developing marketing and support materials for customers in their local geographies. Part of their brief is to identify standard information that can be shared across all geographies, as well as to clarify those aspects that will need to be more tailored, depending on the audience.

The materials will all be drafted in English, and then final versions will be translated into local languages.

- John is based in Dallas, USA and leads the team.

Other representatives include:

- Neen – Philadelphia USA
- Tom – San Francisco USA
- Margaret – London UK
- Alfonso – Frankfurt Germany
- Sanjit – Mumbai India
- Amina – Shanghai, China
- Juanita – Sao Paulo Brazil

We will be working with this virtual team throughout this chapter.

Their objectives:

- The cross-cultural virtual project team
- Representatives from different countries
- Develop topics and content for a range of materials for upcoming global project
- All subject matter experts
- Experienced in their local geographies

Time Differences

One of the simplest and most profound challenges for a geographically spread virtual team is time differences.

Let's think about our case study team members and the impact of time differences.

Starting with Neen on the East Coast of USA, imagine Neen decides to schedule a two-hour team meeting for 10 am Friday her time, and daylight saving isn't effecting any time zone.

- For Tom, on the West Coast, it's 7 am (3 hours behind Neen).

- For Juanita in Sao Paulo, it's 11 am on Friday (*one hour ahead*).

- For Alfonso in Frankfurt, it's 4 pm *(6 hours ahead)*.

- For Margaret in London, it's 6 pm on Friday evening *(8 hours ahead)*

- For Sanjit in Mumbai, it's already 8.30 pm on Friday night. *(10.5 hours ahead)*

- For Amina in Shanghai, it's 10 pm on Friday night. (*12 hours ahead*).

- While the meeting time seems perfect for Neen, Juanita, and Alfonso, it's less than ideal for Tom and Margaret and probably unreasonable for Sanjit and Amina.

For a global team, no single time slot is always possible and convenient for all members.

Useful tips for scheduling cross-time zone meetings

There is probably no easy solution for managing time differences, but here are five useful tips.

1. Only invite people to a meeting when they need to be there.
2. Think about splitting your meeting into two groups, according to the different time zones.
3. Plan your meetings well in advance, so everyone has time to get organized, regardless of the time
4. Ensure that minutes of each meeting are recorded and distributed to all team members

And – perhaps most importantly:

5. Rotate the meeting times, to share the inconvenience equally between team members.

> As one seasoned virtual team leader
> says, "We rotate the meeting hours, so
> everybody gets to work at crazy
> o'clock at times.'

A simple solution to a 10 to 13 hour time difference is to have someone work a little later. In contrast, others get up a little earlier than usual (for example, 6:00 AM in San Francisco is 9:00 AM in Philadelphia and 7:30 PM in Mumbai).

Let's check back in on Neen, and our case study team.

To manage meeting times, and to streamline communication, Neen did several things with her team.

- She asked each virtual team member to identify what their preferred meeting time would be, and then set a rotating schedule, based on those times.
- The team's charter included an agreement to respect the schedules of team members.
- Virtual team members also agreed to be explicit in their communication regarding intent, relevance, situation, and purpose.
- They agreed to set a response time of 24 hours from the time of receipt for urgent communications.
- And they agreed to take responsibility for prioritizing communications as urgent, important, routine, or information-only.

Pronouncing Names – What's In A Name?

Pronouncing names right is extremely important in cross-cultural relationships because it communicates respect for the other person.

Often it's difficult because the sound and spelling of names outside your cultural boundaries may be unfamiliar and hard to remember.

Customs around Names

The custom of countries like the United States of jumping to a first-name basis immediately is not widely duplicated in other cultures. It can be perceived as an unwelcome presumption of intimacy, or at best, a sign of ignorance and arrogance.

Here are five guidelines on how to use names:

- If necessary, ask the person to say their name more than once, until you can pronounce it correctly. Make it clear that it's important to you to get it right.

- Ask the person if they prefer to be called something different – like a shortened version or nickname.

- Don't translate a name into a similar name in your language, just because it's easier for you to pronounce.

- Write down a phonetic spelling of the person's name to help you remember.

- Think of something that rhymes with the person's name – when you come to say it aloud; it's easy to recall the pronunciation by remembering the rhyming word.

- Make sure you understand the order of names. For instance, in some Asian countries, the surname comes first. In Latin American cultures, the mother's maiden name is part of the surname.

Activity 19 - Cultural - did you know?

In Switzerland only children immediately address each other by their first names. Always address Swiss adults by their title, plus surname.

In German language the most important word in a sentence is usually the final one, so Germans are in the habit of listening for the end of the sentence. Half sentences and unfinished sentences can be very annoying and confusing for German people!

There is no equivalent to 'get' in many languages. But English speakers use **get** in many different ways, like:

- become lost ('get lost')
- understand ('get the main point')
- leave ('get out of here')
- start ('get going')
- continue ('get on with it')
- purchase ('get some supplies from the store')
- explaining ('what I'm getting at')

No wonder non-native English speakers get confused!

- In the Middle East: the thumbs-up sign is considered vulgar.
- In **Lebanon**: raising a closed fist in the air is considered a rude gesture.
- In **England**: the victory sign with your palm facing in is considered vulgar.
- In **Mexico and Argentina**: Hands-on hips is a sign of hostility.
- In **Saudi Arabia**: shaking the head from side to side means yes.
- In **Colombia**: women hold forearms instead of shaking hands.
- In **Egypt**: it's rude to show the sole of your shoe.
- In **Zimbabwe**: it's rude to maintain eye contact.
- In **France**: the OK sign means zero.
- In **India**: people grasp their earlobes to express remorse or honesty

Most Americans are comfortable with only about four seconds of silence during a meeting or conversation. But other cultures, like the Japanese, like to take much longer to consider questions and formulate their answers. They might wait 40 seconds or even longer before offering a response

English is just one of five significant languages of world trade and the mother tongue of only 5 percent of the world's population.

Jokes and things we find funny often depend on assumed understanding and history. It's deeply rooted in cultural assumptions. For example, a British trainer who works in China used to open her session with a joke or humorous anecdote. Then she learned from a Chinese-American colleague that instead of translating her joke or story, the translator usually says to the audience

'Our presenter is telling a joke right
now. The polite thing to do will be to
laugh when she stops.'[18]

Poles will do just about anything for a visitor who demonstrates a love of Poland. Poles are more enthusiastic about Hungarians than about other Slavs.

When dealing with people from Finland, be faithful and dependable. Remember that according to Finnish tradition statement is often regarded as a promise. If you commit to something it is a promise

When dealing with Swedes, remember that they believe strongly in group consensus, so don't ask them for quick individual decisions. They are not as profit-minded as you may be, so don't focus too much on the bottom line.

When working with Russians, avoid talking down to them, discussing past failures, causing loss of face, bad manners, and being too casual or flippant.

Arabs expect regular praise when they have done good work, and are more hurt by criticism than Westerners, who are content to keep their job. Westerners want to be fair, but just; Arabs want to be just, but flexible.

Bahrain is the smallest Arab state in terms of both population and area (only 1,000 square kilometers/300 square miles). It is an archipelago of 33 islands, all tiny, sandy, and low lying, with Manama, the capital, located on the largest island, Bahrain Island.

Indonesians rarely say anything that might be offensive; consequently, it is often difficult to judge the relative success of your presentation. Although they show great humility, Indonesians are well aware that they are the fourth largest country in the world. Show respect for the size of their market.

Singaporeans are courteous, careful listeners in the Asian manner. They do not interrupt but give good feedback at the end. They often reply with, "My modest opinion is....."

In Thailand, confrontations must be avoided at all costs; everyone's face must be maintained. Socializing includes meals, theatre, and music, kickboxing, going to the beach, and badminton. Care should be taken to observe the pecking order in social and business situations. Superiors are not to be challenged, but they generally strive to get on well with subordinates.

---

[18] Adapted from – When culture collide – leading across cultures by Richard D. Lewis, third edition isbn 978 – 1-904838-02-9

In the Philippines, public criticism of any person must be avoided. Gift giving is relatively common, but do not accept a gift (or any other service) without first refusing it twice.

In Vietnam remember women play an essential role in the workplace. Avoid talking down to them or humiliating them in any way. Avoid assuming they have a natural alignment with China (they don't). Avoid expecting things to be done quickly.

In China don't hesitate to do business through go-betweens. It often speeds up progress strikingly. Avoid rejecting a Chinese proposal out of hand. When you negate someone's idea, you deny the person.

In Japan remember that anything you say they take literally. Flippant remarks such as "this is killing me" or "you must be kidding" will be misconstrued. You must never hurt their feelings.

Mexicans are courteous and polite listeners, always ready to learn from people of other nationalities. They are, however, very suspicious of Americans. Mexicans do not follow agendas rigidly and feel they can discuss any point when it seems timely.

Brazilians often find it difficult to compete with their peers for a promotion, and even talented individuals need frequent encouragement and ongoing training to further their careers. They are hesitant to accept responsibility; you may find that you always need to build up their confidence.

Chileans are somewhat nervous listeners since they wish to break in, but are often too polite to do so. Because they often believe they know best, they can barely tolerate long monologues from others.

In Japan, avoid saying "No" or "It's impossible" or "We can't." If you disagree, just be silent. Avoid cornering them or making them lose face.

When dealing with the Irish, avoid confusing them with Scots and trying to delude them and talking down to them.

When working with New Zealanders, affectionately known as Kiwis, avoid too much flattery – some males react against it. Avoid any form of hard sell or making statements you cannot back up.

South Africans are courteous listeners, though some repetition is advisable. They do not like being rushed verbally – their elders have innate patience.

When working with Germans, say what you mean – irony, subtle undertones, and sarcasm usually fall on deaf ears. Avoid falling into the trap of oversimplifying. Germans like facts, figures, and reliable information.

In a working relationship, the French are not initially generous, but they will respond quickly to generosity from your side. Avoid sarcasm and irony.

Italians like to share details of families, vacations, hopes, aspirations, disappointments and preferences. No matter how hard you try, the Italian will always consider you reserved (and talk ten times as much as you).

When English is the Second Language

If you are leading or participating in a virtual team, it's likely that for at least some of your team members, English will be their second language.

Hi there

Good morning

Buongiorno!

Guten Morgen

Zao shang hao

Suprabhaat

Bom dia

Case Study M -   Global Sales Virtual Project Team (continued) – What's their native language?

Think about our case study of the project team.

- Neen, Tom and Margaret are native English speakers, (though there are some subtle speaking and spelling differences between American and British English).

- Germany based Alfonso's native languages are Italian and German.

- Amina speaks Chinese, Sanjit speaks Hindi, and Juanita speaks Portuguese.

- While the meetings and interactions might be conducted in English, Neen - and indeed, each team member - must take these backgrounds into account when meeting and communicating.

Helping those whose native language is not yours

Adapting your speaking style will help you to communicate effectively with all team members. Let's take a look at these ten tips.

Tip 1 Speak slowly and clearly – but not loudly

Be sure not to speak insultingly slowly, and be sure not to shout. Your team members may not be native English speakers, but they are not deaf! So be careful not to portray arrogance and avoid condescension – just speak slowly and clearly.

Tip 2 Keep it simple

Sometimes when we're trying to speak properly or clearly, we choose lengthier, formal words, like 'utilize' instead of 'use' or 'verbalize' instead of 'say.' This can be more confusing and more difficult for non-native speakers.

Most importantly, try to avoid long run-on sentences. Use shorter sentences, and give the others adequate time to absorb what you say, instead of rambling on into more complex ideas.

Tip 3 Avoid idiomatic expressions

Idiomatic or slang expressions are an excellent way to introduce informality into meetings, but they can be confusing for non-native English speakers.

For instance, instead of saying 'Let me run this one past you', it's safer to say 'There's another idea I'd like to talk to you about.'

Graphic: slang expressions may include:

Knocked it out of the park (US)	From soup to nuts (US)
Don't throw the baby out with the bathwater (Australia)	Gone pear-shaped (Australia)
I think you're pulling my arm (German)	I slept like a woodchuck (German)
All talk but no trousers (UK)	Flogging a dead horse (UK, Australia)
First-class outcome (INDIAN)	On the anvil (INDIAN)

Tip 4 Give and seek feedback

Even if you speak clearly in simple English, you can't be confident there has been communication until the receiver acknowledges it with feedback. So ask for feedback often to make sure the listeners heard what you intended to say.

Close-ended questions like 'Is this making sense?' will not always work because sometimes people will say yes even if they don't understand. This might be true for Amina and Sanjit, for example, where saving face for the speaker is essential, and who may have a less direct communication style. **Open-ended questions** are better. 'How does this plan sound so far?' or 'How do you think we should approach this problem?' This will help to clarify how much of your message has been understood.

Tip 5 Offer examples

Examples help to support an idea. For instance, a question like, 'How long do you think we need for this stage?' might elicit silence. Clarifying this question with examples – 'Two weeks? A month? Two months?' helps your listener to answer your question.

Tip 6 Write it down

Non-native English speakers are often more used to reading English than speaking it so written material that can be read at a leisurely pace without pressure is helpful.

Words on a screen during webinar and conferencing platforms (such as Zoom, Skype etc.) are not only VISUAL aids, they are also HEARING aids. They help people HEAR the words better. Of course, this needs to be balanced without creating a script on the screen that you simply read.

Think about sending out your key discussion points in advance or using virtual tools like discussion boards, Zoom to share documents to support the discussion.

Tip 7 Summarize

Summarizing what has been discussed is helpful to recap on key points, and gives everyone an extra chance to clarify their understanding.

You can also ask team members to summarize. For example, 'May I suggest that we stop for a moment and summarize what you understand the options to be? I'd like to make sure we all have the same understanding before we go any further. Alfonso, would you please do this for us?"

When stopping the meeting to summarize, be sure to do it in a way that is not offensive or confronting.

Tip 8 Use clear and common gestures

If you are in a face to face or video conference meeting, support your words with precise, impromptu gestures.

For example, point to your watch as you ask, 'What time should we come back?' Hold up your hand as you say, 'Could we just pause on that point for a minute, and come back to it?'

Remember, though, that certain gestures have different meanings, depending on the culture. The western sign for okay – thumb and forefinger together making a circle – is an offensive gesture in Brazil.

Tip 9 Repeat if necessary

Listening to a foreign language can be exhausting, and it's easy for listeners to get behind. If you sense this is happening to your audience, offer to repeat the last point.

Tip 10 Relax...Take it easy

Don't take offense if you are asked to slow down, if you have to repeat yourself, or if you can't get your point across. It's not a personal criticism.

And remember, by speaking your language, your international colleagues are already going more than halfway to communicating effectively with you.

Case Study N - Global Sales Virtual Project Team (continued) – Idea: Meeting Warm-up: The Virtual Water Cooler

Neen quickly realized that some of her team members found it easier to communicate in a meeting than others, especially during a teleconference. In response, Neen instituted a 'warm-up' at the beginning of every meeting.

Neen likes to call this the 'virtual water cooler' discussion!

She would ask each participant to 'check in' with the team by relating a one minute story in English about some event in their personal or business life. The topic, Neen explained, isn't important. '

At one meeting we discussed the World Cup. It got everyone going. Or sometimes we'll take turns in choosing a topic – like a quick weather report, or what we each did on our weekend.'

As a result, team members get to practice speaking, and just as important, listening in English. 'They also learn more about each other – which builds trust – and get a sense of what skills other members bring to the team.'

Avoiding Idioms in Speech

Below we have listed some idiomatic expressions commonly used during business conversations by different cultural groups, and a matching list of the same expression, using more neutral universal language.

Activity 20 -   Translate the idioms

As you read each expression in the first list, see if you can "translate" that expression into the real meaning it has for you. Then look at the number in brackets at the end of the expression and read the equivalent expression with its more universal equivalent listed on the next page.

Idiomatic expression

- We need a more level playing field. (9)

- The original proposal has been watered down. (13)

- She's like a cat pacing around a bowl of hot porridge. (1)

- Even monkeys fall from trees. (18)

- Let me run this idea past you. (15)

- This project is a basket case. (10)

- That option has been sidelined. (4)

- Am I in the ballpark? (17)

- Are we all breathing from the same nostril? (19)

- Joe really shoots from the hip. (20)

- Fire off an email to Christine. (8)

- There is no magic bullet. (12)

- Blah blah blah (14)

- We need to go for the low hanging fruit. (6)

- Who wants to pick this one up? (11)

- We want to make each other's breathing be in harmony (5)

- We have two possibilities on the anvil. (16)

- There are a few roles up for grabs. (2)

- We'd better wrap this up soon. (7)

- I think his ears are lined with ham. (3)

Universal expression

1. She's avoiding the issue.
2. There are a few roles available.
3. I don't think he can hear what is being said.
4. That option has been postponed.
5. We want all of our thinking to be aligned.
6. We need to investigate the easy options first.
7. We'd better finish this meeting soon.
8. Quickly send an email to Christine.
9. We need conditions to be fair.
10. This project is hopelessly broken down.
11. Who would like to work on a solution for this problem?
12. There is no universal solution.
13. The original proposal has been weakened.
14. And so on, and so forth.
15. Let me tell you my idea.
16. We have two possible solutions that could potentially happen.
17. Am I right/accurate/close?
18. Even skilled/experienced people can make mistakes.
19. Are we all thinking the same way?
20. Joe doesn't plan carefully.

KEY POINTS SUMMARY

- The underlying foundation to successful global virtual leadership is cultural adaptability.

- Adapting your speaking style will help you to communicate effectively with all team members.

- Remember, by speaking your language, and your international colleagues are already going more than halfway to communicating effectively with you.

How do you tap into potential cultural intelligence?

Developing Cultural Capability

It's simply not possible to understand all the cultural nuances from all the world's cultures.

In a global business environment, if you want to work effectively across all cultural boundaries, you must be able to communicate respect for the customs, habits, and rituals of others, especially for the people who work for you.

As you become more aware of these differences and more skilled at communicating across those cultures, you will become a more effective virtual leader.

The goal is not to become an expert on the perfect word, delivery, and non-verbal behavior for every situation.

Instead, the key is to develop the ability to expect and anticipate differences, observe the behavior of others, reflect on it, and learn where and when to modify your own actions in response.

- Communicate respect for the customs, habits, and rituals of others
- Especially for people who work for you
- Cultural awareness = more effective leader
- Expect and anticipate differences
- Observe the behavior of others
- Reflect on it
- Learn from it
- Modify your actions

The notion of culture and cultural differences is familiar to all of us.

But what does it mean? And what does the cultural difference look like?

We can define culture as the relatively stable set of inner values and beliefs generally held by groups of people in countries or regions and the noticeable impact those values and beliefs have on the people's outward behaviors and environment.

Defining culture and its potential influence

"Inner values and beliefs held by
groups of people in countries or
regions and the impact those values
and beliefs have on the people's
behaviors and environment."

Brooks Peterson[19]

We can think about the many aspects of culture a bit like an iceberg.

There's the part you see straight away – which we can call 'tip of the iceberg' or 'above the waterline' culture. Then there's the part you only see as you get closer - the 'bottom of the iceberg', or 'under the water' culture.

Tip of the Iceberg

Above the waterline culture

Bottom of the Iceberg

Under the water culture

---

[19] Cultural Intelligence, A Guide to Working with People from Other Cultures, Brooks Peterson, Intercultural Press, 2004

Tip of the iceberg culture is anything you can perceive with your five senses – like:

- Language
- Architecture
- Food
- Music
- Clothing
- Art
- Literature
- Emotional display
- Gestures
- Eye contact
- Pace of life.

Compare these two pictures of colleagues meeting in a business setting.

The different greeting behaviors you see are different examples of 'above the waterline' culture.

The under-the-water part of the iceberg represents what we *can't* perceive with our senses, and the deeper we go, the more critical the items are.

Remember also, that just like an iceberg, these under-the-water aspects make up to 80% of the most critical aspects of culture.

They include:

- Opinions
- Viewpoints
- Attitudes
- Philosophies
- Values
- Convictions

Let's take a closer look, using the 'values' as an example. Beneath the water surface line of the iceberg, values can determine a person's:

- Notions of time
- How the individual fits into society
- Rules about relationships
- Importance of work
- Tolerance for change
- Comfort with risk
- Expectation for macho behavior
- Preference for leadership systems
- Communication styles
- Attitudes about men's/women's roles
- Preference for thinking style

And many more things besides.

Case Study O - Virtual Managers Reactions

Let's look at some examples of virtual managers describing their reactions to different situations, and think about the role that culture plays in influencing their responses.

'Why doesn't she just say yes or no?' In one culture, an indirect answer may signal indecisiveness, while in another, it signals deference and respect.	Indecisiveness? Or deference and respect?
'Why is he always staring at me like that?' In one culture, staring can signal aggressiveness or intimidation, while in another culture, direct eye contact shows attention and esteem.	Intimidation and aggression? Or Attention and esteem?
'Why does he have to be right in my face when he talks to me?' In one culture, the halo of personal space and privacy can be much smaller than it is in another culture.	Too close? Or just close?
'Why doesn't she tell me if she doesn't understand something?' In one culture, asking questions is accepted as a useful tool for communications, while in other cultures questioning superiors may signal insolence.	Good communication? Or insolence?
'Why does he sit there smiling when I'm talking about his performance problems?' In one culture smiling during a severe discussion may signal contempt and disinterest, while in another culture, a smile may reflect sincerity and attention.	Contempt and disinterest? Or sincerity and attention?
'Why does she make a joke out of everything?' In one culture, a glib nature can signal a lack of confidence or seriousness, while in another, it's a sign of deference.	Lack of confidence? Or deference?

As those examples highlight, as virtual leaders, it's crucial to look for cultural traits both at the tip of the iceberg and below the waterline.

Cultural Confusion

Case Study P -   Virtual Leader: Della

In the following case study, we'll hear from a UK manager Della based in London who is leading a virtual cross-functional development team, with four of the six members located in Mumbai India.

Here she expresses her frustration to a local colleague who asked her about her interactions with the team.

'It's actually rather frustrating. I'm finding I need to give much more detailed, specific instructions to the team in India, just to get the simplest things done. And unless minute detail is provided, things seem to go wrong. They don't seem to take the initiative to do anything other than what is clearly agreed in advance.

I know they're brilliant... I've seen lots of innovative work from them... they have a lot of creative ideas. But they seem very reluctant to share them with me! I feel like they just want me to tell them what to do and then leave them alone to do it. What am I doing wrong? What can I do to get them more comfortable with me? And get some progress?!'

Cultures of countries such as India, Pakistan, and China tend more towards a hierarchical style. Countries such as the UK, the US, and Switzerland, are based more on equality.

Here are seven possibilities that might explain Della's frustration.

Read each one and select all of the options you think are likely.

1. The people from India Della deals with respect to her position as a virtual manager and expect her to tell them what to do.

2. Della is experiencing cultural adjustment issues, and because of this, she is easily irritated by even small things that seem to go wrong.

3. Indian employees are not very detail-oriented, so the details must be provided to them.

4. The Indian employees in Della's team are accustomed to a definite style of top-down leadership and do not usually presume to participate in decisions with their superiors.

5. Della must have pushed the Indian employees too far already, and they are not interested in working for her.

6. Indian employees are lazy, and unless given detailed instructions, they won't perform.

7. Indian males don't like reporting to British women as they think males should be managers, not females. Women are not respected in India, so Della has no hope of success with any of the Indian men on this team.

Let's look at these options in the light of what we've just heard about culture.

Options 3, 6, and 7 are absurd racial stereotypes, and not at all helpful in explaining what's going on.

Options 2 and 5 use behaviors to explain what's gone wrong – Della becoming easily irritated because of cultural adjustment issues, and Della having pushed the Indian employees too far.

However, while we don't know from the small example of what happened, they don't offer us a general principle to follow, because people's behaviors change in every situation.

The remaining options, 1 and 4, give us insights into some general principles that could apply to a variety of situations that Della might encounter when dealing with people from India (and likely, other Easterners).

They address the more profound level leadership phenomenon of focusing on either *equality* (where employees are granted the power to take the initiative even if they don't have a position or title after their name) or hierarchy (where the manager is expected to take control and make decisions).

The point of this example is **not** to suggest one leadership style as being better than another. Both models are highly effective business models.

Instead, it is to emphasize the importance of looking below the waterline, at the values and beliefs that shape a culture, to understand a colleague's behavior.

Once Della understands this, she can adjust her expectations and her style of working with her Indian colleagues.

Equality:

Where employees are granted the power to take the initiative even if they don't have a position or title after their name

Hierarchy:

Where the manager is expected to take control and make the decisions

Case Study Q - Anne, An Australian Trainer on presenting in Japan

Just to emphasize how different people's perceptions of a situation can be, note the contrast between what Anne, an Australian trainer said, compared with what Yoko, one of the Japanese who sat through her training, said.

Anne, Australian trainer, describing her presentation in Japan:

- 'They were so engaged. They sat and listened, and they didn't get up and go for a toilet break every five minutes or constantly ask for breaks. The room was sweltering and humid, but that didn't seem to faze them. They were so respectful,'

Yoko, Japanese employee, was a participant in the training class:

- 'I'm glad she felt respected. But she needs to realize we would never think about talking or getting up in the middle of a lecturer's presentation. It would be unheard of for us to do that to a teacher, much less for a foreign guest. It doesn't necessarily mean the content was engaging.'

Cultural Intellligence

The most effective way for a virtual manager to deal with the challenges of culture (both above and below the water of our culture iceberg) is by developing and applying **cultural intelligence.**

> Put simply; cultural intelligence is your capability to function effectively across national, ethnic, and organizational cultures.

> More specifically, we can think of cultural intelligence as your ability to engage in a set of behaviors that use skills and qualities that are tuned appropriately to the culture-based values of the people with whom you are interacting.

> And to go one step further, it's the ability to read the intentions and desires of others, even when they've been hidden.

It's impossible to understand all the cultural nuances from all the world's cultures, and cultural intelligence does not mean having an exhaustive and in-depth knowledge about every culture.

We can break cultural intelligence into three steps:

- Step 1 is being sensitive to different cultural styles.

- Step 2 is recognizing signals of culture clash.

- Step 3 is modifying your own communications accordingly.

Case Study R - Global Sales Virtual Project Team (continued) - Being Sensitive To Different Cultural Styles

Let's explore these steps in more detail, by revisiting our case study of Neen and her virtual project team:

Being sensitive to different cultural styles starts with awareness. That means starting from the premise that if your team member is from a different culture, there are likely to be some aspects of their culture that will influence your interactions, and that you should therefore be aware of.	Look for different cultural styles
With Neen and her project team, one of the first things Neen did was to raise the issue with her team. She included it on the agenda at an early team meeting and invited everyone to air their concerns and issues.	Put it on the agenda
She also makes time to speak to each team member individually, recognizing that team members like Amina, from Shanghai, and Sanjit from Mumbai, are less likely to volunteer their views as easily than say, Tom from San Francisco. Neen understands the importance of listening. So she actively tries to spend around 50% of her time in these meetings listening to the views of each team member.	Talk with team members individually Spend 50% of your time listening
Neen makes a point of finding out a bit about what's going on in the countries of her team members. She subscribes to, and consumes a range of alternative news sources – not just American ones – and notes the different ways that news stories are reported, depending on the source. She even uses those news sources to follow popular culture - so she can reference what she reads when she talks to team members – like popular local books, films, and theater.	Learn about the countries of your team members
Most importantly, Neen starts from the assumption that there *are* different cultural styles to be aware of, which will require sensitivity. Therefore her chances of a successful outcome for her team, are already much greater.	Assume there will be differences

Recognizing Signals of Culture Clash

The differences that can arise between cultures working together are almost infinite. But let's explore just three of these differences.

CONVERSATION FLOW

Different countries have different 'rules' for who talks when and how they communicate.

The **Taking Turns** style operates in places like the US, Australia, and the UK – with the conversational partners taking turns to speak.

Interrupting is the style of the South American, European, Middle Eastern, North African people. With this style, several people might talk at once.

Then there is the **Halting** style. Asian people, in particular, are usually comfortable with silence, so they converse in what can be perceived as a halting manner – where person 'a' talks, both pause to reflect, then person 'b' makes a comment, then another pause, person 'b' adds another comment, both pause … and so on.

These pauses for reflection can be off-putting for those who crack under the pressure of short silences and need to say something.

Conversation flow can be:

- Taking turns style
- Interrupting style
- Halting style

Comfort with Silence

Related to this conversational style are the varying levels of satisfaction with silence between different cultures.

Most Americans and Australians are comfortable with only about four seconds of silence during a meeting or conversation.

However, cultures like Japanese like to take much longer to answer the questions, issues, and formulate their answers. They might wait 40 seconds, or even longer, before offering a response.

$$10 - 9 - 8 - 7 - 6 - 5 - 4 - 3 - 2 - 1-$$

As you see, even 10 seconds is quite a pause!

Cognitive Style

Our third example relates to cognitive style – or how people from different cultures think.

Thinking for many Westerners, for example, tends to follow a fairly predictable sequence – from point A to point F, with a predictable passage through points B, C, D and E. These thinkers like to organize their thoughts in this **linear** fashion so they can accomplish their objectives in short order.

By contrast, thinking for many other cultures tends to be more **circular or systemic,** more 'meandering'.

Japanese speakers, for example, sometimes prefer to circle the point when getting straight to it might appear blunt.

Speakers who have relaxed views on time, notably Arabs, Africans, and Indians, might seem to meander to the point, inserting stories and tangents.

They may then circle it with an anecdote or three. Their path may zigzag and become sidetracked; however, they eventually reach the same point.

When the two styles mix, there can be clashes. The meanderers may be put off by the Americans, who appear to them to be pushy and incapable of appreciating subtlety. The Americans meanwhile may be frustrated by all the tangents and what they perceive to be 'wasted time'.

For the virtual team manager, each of these cultural differences presents challenges that need to be managed.

Case Study S - Global Sales Virtual Project Team (continued) - Culture Clash

And as we move through each example, think about the impact of each on our project team, with its representatives from the USA, England, Germany, India, China, and Brazil.

Think about Neen, and our case study team.

Because she's aware of these issues, Neen can manage their impacts during her meetings with the team more effectively.

She includes a discussion of these different styles as an agenda item on an early team meeting. As a result:

- The team agrees to some ground rules, that includes being sensitive to taking turns during discussions, and accepting silence as an essential part of meeting flow

- Neen calls on each team member at an appropriate point during each conversation - particularly helpful for quieter contributors

- Neen provides a summary at the end of each discussion segment, to ensure everyone is at the same point

    o   Make it an agenda item

    o   Set ground rules

    o   Call on all team members

    o   Summarize key points

Straight to the point cognitive style

Brain   The point

Meander to the point cognitive style

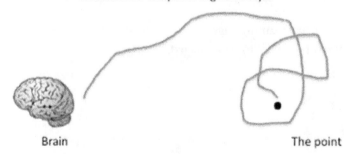

Brain   The point

Cultural Comparison

From this section, you can learn more about some of the cultural characteristics that typically apply to these different nationalities.

It's imperative to note that these characteristics are **generalizations** only – and we can't say that every attribute applies to every individual.

Instead, think of them as **descriptive stereotypes** and a helpful starting point for differentiating between cultural groups.

The following countries are included in this section:

- United Kingdom
- Switzerland
- Germany
- United States
- India
- China
- Australia
- Japan
- Brazil

This is followed by a Cultural Style Audit for you to assess your cultural approach.

UNITED KINGDOM

Hello, I'm Thomas, and I live in London and lead a virtual global team. Let me introduce you to a few of the cultural nuances of the United Kingdom. The United Kingdom is culturally very vast with people from England, Wales, Scotland, and Ireland, all having their own unique cultures. However, we all share some commonalities in business, which may be worthwhile for you to know when managing a team with people from the United Kingdom as team members.

At business meetings, the British are rather formal at first, sometimes using first names only after 2 or 3 encounters. Our company policy for team members is they will call each other by their first name immediately, however, when working with suppliers, customers, or clients, don't be surprised to hear a very formal greeting.

British people like to show themselves as family-oriented, and it is normal for us to discuss children, vacations, and reminiscences during and between meetings.

The British are very time-oriented; we are somewhat anxious about deadlines and results. We do not like to be rushed towards a decision. Humor is vital in business sessions.

You'll find that the British will often use humor against themselves or colleagues. It could be for:

- self-deprecation,
- to break up the tension in a situation
- to speed up a discussion, when excessive formality is slowing it down
- to direct criticism towards a superior
- to introduce a new or wild idea
- So it's always a good policy to use self-disparagement with British people and laugh at yourself

The British **rarely disagree openly** with proposals from the other side. We agree wherever possible but may qualify our agreement (Hmm, that's a fascinating idea).

English people, in particular, like instructions to be given in the form of suggestions or hints. 'Perhaps we might try ...' is better than 'I want you to do this.'

- Statements and actions should be low key.
- We British like everything to be – and appear to be – under control.
- You'll find that virtual managers usually want to be considered as part of the team but may maintain a slight distance from it.
- In discussions, British people are good at accepting occasional ambiguities and are prepared to read between the lines.
- When you do wish to criticize, disagree or even praise, do it obliquely

I do hope you've found these suggestions useful.

Summary - United Kingdom

▪ Formal at first	▪ Time oriented
▪ Family-oriented	▪ Don't like to be rushed

SWITZERLAND

Bon Giorno, I'm Flavio, and I live in Lugano, in southern Switzerland's Italian-speaking Ticino region. Let me introduce you to some of the cultural nuances of my beautiful country.

There are three official languages in Switzerland – French, German, and Italian, so most of us are multilingual.

We're very patriotic, interested in our country's politics, and very concerned about the environment.

We look forward to July and August when we take our summer holidays. Swiss people work hard and play hard.

If you have a Swiss person on your virtual team, these tips might help.

- Punctuality is essential to us. – The Swiss are famous for it! So we expect our meetings to start and end on time.
- Business is quite a serious affair for us. We like to get straight down to business, and we don't have much time for small talk or jokes.
- If we do make a joke, you'll find our humor tends towards understated wit, more likely to elicit smiles than laughter.
- Swiss people don't like to display strong emotions in public. And most Swiss never reveal what they're thinking – at least not initially. French and Italian speaking Swiss are more emotional than the Germans.
- We're entirely private people, and we usually take a long time to establish personal relationships.
- In terms of decision-making, the individual makes the decision, so we take it very seriously. And making decisions can take time – we don't like to hurry it.
- Age and seniority are quite crucial to the Swiss.

Summary - Switzerland

- Very punctual
- Like to pause and reflect, rather than rush into decisions
- Very patriotic
- Business is serious and unemotional

GERMANY

Guten Tag, I'm Brigitte, and I live in Munich in Germany.

Let me tell you a little bit about our culture. When we're not working, many Germans enjoy outdoor activities, like hiking, camping, and skiing. We take advantage of our six week vacation time each year.

If you have a German person on your virtual team, congratulations, you are fortunate. These tips might help to work with your German colleague.

- Punctuality is essential. We're second only to the Swiss in our desire for timeliness.
- We like to deal in facts. We're quite analytic and conceptual in our processing of information.
- Our reputation for quality is based on slow, methodical planning. We believe it takes time to do a job properly.
- For this reason, our pace of decision making is much slower than that of the US or Great Britain.
- Once we decide on a position, Germans will rarely budge from that position.
- Germans like directness, and we dislike hype and exaggeration. Case studies and examples are beneficial for Germans.
- We expect a job to be well done, so we don't expect or give compliments. Why compliment people who are merely doing their duty?
- We like to work through tasks one at a time, rather than doing many at once. We wish to be thorough rather than speedy.
- You'll find our communication style is frank, open, direct, and often loud. For Germans, the truth comes before diplomacy. If we disagree, we will say so. And our arguments are logical, weighty and well thought out.
- You'll find we don't like changes. Sudden changes – even if they may improve the outcome – are not welcomed.

We don't like to discuss personal matters during business meetings, and we don't appreciate the humor in a business context.

SUMMARY - Germany

- Punctuality is important
- Reputation for quality
- The slow pace of decision making
- Direct, case studies, examples
- Thorough rather than speedy

- Deal in facts
- Take time to do a job properly
- Hold firm to our decisions
- Keep business and personal separate
- Frank, truth before diplomacy

UNITED STATES

Hi, how are you doing? I'm Cheryl from Woodland Hills, California, USA.

Let me tell you a little bit about our culture. We're incredibly patriotic and proud of our country and love our country more than any other on earth.

If you have a North American on your virtual team, it's your lucky day! These tips might help to work with your American colleague.

- We like to start our meetings on time – punctuality is highly emphasized.
- We love to introduce informality right off the bat. That means first names, sharing personal details, swapping family stories – the whole deal.
- Our pace of business is lightning fast compared to many cultures.
- We love to use humor in our meetings. We'll use it wherever we can.
- We like to lay our cards on the table from the start.
- Americans are very individualistic. We're very self-oriented, and we put a lot of emphasis on individual initiative and achievement.
- Our work ethic is very strong.
- We value innovation over tradition. And we're persistent – we believe there is always a solution and we'll explore all options until we find one.
- Americans are pretty blunt – we'll make it clear when we disagree.
- We like to get the big picture sorted out first, and then go back and sort out the details.
- And we do love our technology – it's common to take a call on our cell phone or blackberry during a business meeting.

SUMMARY - UNITED STATES

- Punctuality is important
- Very informal meeting style
- Fast pace of business
- Love to use humor
- Cards on the table

- Strong work ethic
- Value innovation over tradition
- Persistent
- Blunt and direct
- Big picture first

INDIA

Namaste. I'm Chakori, from Mumbai, India.

Let me tell you a little bit about our culture. Religion plays a significant role in the daily lives of most Indians. The majority of Indians are Hindu, and others are Muslim or Sikh.

If you have an Indian colleague on your virtual team, these tips might help to get the best out of that relationship.

- We appreciate punctuality but are relaxed about it ourselves. We have a less hurried attitude about time than most westerners.
- As well, we have a strong sense of what westerners call 'fatalism', so time is not a significant source of anxiety for Indians.
- Business is not conducted during religious holidays, and these are numerous.
- Our personal feelings form the basis for the truth for Indians, but a strong faith in religious ideologies is always present. The use of objective facts is less persuasive than a combination of feelings and faith.
- India is a moderately collectivist culture, so the decisions of the individual must be in harmony with the family group and social structure.
- The word 'no' has harsh implications in India. We are more likely to use an evasive refusal because it's considered more polite.
- We have a communication style that is quite loquacious and talkative compared to other Asian cultures.
- We like to show and share our emotions – joy, disappointment, and grief are expressed without inhibition.

SUMMARY - INDIA

- Relaxed about punctuality
- Less hurried attitude about time
- Strong sense of 'fatalism'
- Frequent religious holidays
- Strong faith in religious ideologies

- Collectivist culture
- 'No' has harsh implications
- Loquacious communication style
- Show and share emotions
- time is not a significant source of anxiety

CHINA

Ni hao. I am Amina, from Shanghai, China.

Our culture is shaped very much by our history. China sees herself as the Chung-Kuo – the middle kingdom, the center of the universe, and the world's oldest culture and society. So, it's hardly surprising that we have a sense of cultural superiority, which does affect our view of foreigners.

We are also influenced by the teaching of Confucius, who taught us:

- We should observe and respect unequal relationships. Parents, teachers and bosses must all be obeyed.
- We must behave in a virtuous way towards others. Everybody's 'face' must be maintained.
- Education and hard work must be prized.
- We should be moderate in all things. Save, stay calm, avoid extremes and shun indulgence.

Collectivism is very strong in China. A Chinese person belongs to four basic groups; the work unit, family, school and community. Obligations to each group mean that Chinese people have limited social or geographic mobility. For this reason, the issue of 'face' is very important.

If you have a Chinese colleague on your virtual team, it is important for you to understand these things about Chinese people and culture.

- Chinese people are extremely punctual; we abhor wasting anyone's time.
- We are courteous and considerate communicators, and regarded as more direct than our Japanese neighbors.
- Politeness is observed at all times. Confrontation and loss of face (for all parties) must be avoided.
- When dealing with Chinese colleagues you are advised not to reject a Chinese proposal out of hand. When you negate the idea, you negate the person.
- Chinese people rarely say no directly. We prefer to hint at difficulties and obstacles rather than confront them directly.
- Power distance is large, so inequalities are expected and desired.
- We believe that age brings seniority.
- We also believe that the ideal boss is a benevolent autocrat, that subordinates expect to be told what to do and Individualism is taboo.
- Relationships are more important than tasks.
- Confrontation is to be avoided – harmony and consensus are the ultimate goals.

SUMMARY – China

- Sense of cultural superiority, shaped by history
- Confucian influence:
  - Observe and respect unequal relationships
  - Everyone's 'face' must be maintained
  - Education and hard work highly prized
  - Moderation in all things

- Punctuality is important
- Courteous and considerate communicators
- Politeness observed at all times

- Rarely say no directly
- Inequalities expected and desired

- Believe age brings seniority
- Benevolent autocrat
- Relationships over tasks

AUSTRALIA

Hi, I'm Sarah, from Sydney, Australia. We think we live in the luckiest country on earth, with our great weather, beaches, and laid back lifestyle.

Because of our isolation from so much of the rest of the world, we're pretty comfortable doing business with people we've never met.

We're curious, creative, and not averse to risk – we'll usually adopt new technologies as soon as they're available.

We respect people with opinions, even if they conflict with our own, and arguments are considered entertaining, so don't be shy about sharing your beliefs with an Aussie.

'Fair go' is essential to the Australian outlook, based on common sense, equality, and a healthy disregard for authority and ideology.

If you have an Australian colleague on your virtual team, these tips might help to get the best out of that relationship.

- You'll find us friendly and easy to know. We're quick to move to a first-name basis.
- We value punctuality, though we're not obsessive about starting on time.
- Individualism is fundamental in our decision making. We don't find it difficult to say no. You'll find us very direct and to the point, and we value directness in others.
- Sport is a favorite topic of conversation, and we love a good sporting analogy.
- We like to make jokes, often at the expense of a colleague and like to laugh at ourselves.
- Our business style is closer to American than European, and we make decisions quickly.

SUMMARY – AUSTRALIA

- Comfortable doing business remotely
- Not adverse to risk
- Respect people with opinions
- 'Fair go' ideology
- First name basis

- Value punctuality, but not obsessive
- Individuals make the decisions
- Direct communication style
- Sport
- Humor – at ourselves or others

JAPAN

Konnicihiwa. I am Hiroto, from Tokyo, Japan.

It's been said that we are culturally different from anyone else. This is because of our history of isolation, the crowded conditions of our geography, and our complex language.

Japan was almost completely isolated from the rest of the world for more than 250 years until the mid-1800s, and during that time developed a very distinct culture, society, and language.

Communication in Japan is often marked by great subtlety; information is left unspoken yet is entirely understood.

If you have a Japanese colleague on your virtual team, that is excellent news. These tips might help to work with your Japanese colleague.

- We are incredibly punctual. We will prefer to be 20 minutes early for a meeting than to be late. Tardiness is considered rude by the Japanese.
- We are willing to go over the same information many times to avoid later misunderstandings and achieve clarity.
- We are cautious, skilled, and do not like to be rushed.
- Work is a serious issue for us. We don't try to 'lighten things up' with humor.
- For Japanese, silence shows respect for the speaker.
- We don't like to offend by showing open disagreement or refusal. Maintaining face for all parties is extremely important to us.
- Japanese people are often quite shy to speak another language, which makes it difficult for us to initiate conversation. We are also reluctant to show when we have not understood something in another language.
- We generally prefer teamwork and group decisions to individualism.
- One important aspect of Japanese behavior is an apology. Individuals will apologize, almost as a matter of course. It is considered a sign of politeness.
- We dislike strong displays of emotion. Displays of anger or frustration during meetings are poorly regarded by Japanese people.
- Japanese do not expect to be complimented for good work, because the group and not the individual are rewarded. It is considered a bad idea to single out Japanese workers.

SUMMARY – JAPAN

- Culturally different from everyone else
- Subtle communication
- Very punctual – tardiness considered rude
- Focus on avoiding later misunderstandings and achieving clarity
- Cautious and skilled
- Reluctant to show when we have not understood something
- Prefer teamwork and group decisions

- Don't like to be rushed
- Work is serious
- Silence shows respect
- Maintaining face vital
- Shy to speak another language
- An apology is central to Japanese behavior
- Dislike strong displays of emotion

BRAZIL

Bom dia! I am Juanita, originally from Taquaraçu De Minas, Brazil. Unlike the rest of South America, we speak Portuguese in Brazil, so don't try to speak Spanish with us!

People describe Brazilians as typically talkative, exuberant, compassionate, imaginative, and patriotic. We're very proud of our beautiful country!

Concepts of class and status are strong, and will often determine what job a person has in Brazil.

Let me give you a few tips about working with Brazilians, which might be useful if you have one of us in your virtual team.

- You'll find we're very relaxed about punctuality. 15 to 30 minutes late is not considered late in Brazil.
- Brazilian conversations are highly animated, with lots of interruptions, to the agenda, and to each other. We use gestures and facial expressions to emphasize our point of view. Understand that what we are saying comes 'from the heart.'
- In a face to face meeting, we use a lot of eye contact and physical contact by touching arms, hands, or shoulders.
- The sign for 'ok' (a circle of first finger and thumb) is considered vulgar in Brazil, so we never use this.
- We're very open to discussion on most subjects, but home and family are private topics that we don't tend to talk about until we know you better.
- We tend to approach problems indirectly, and we allow our feelings to dictate the solution, as well as facts.
- The individual is responsible for decisions (as opposed to collective decision making).We conduct business through personal connections and expect long-term relationships.
- Like Americans, we tend to be very futuristic in our outlook, dispensing with the old and continue building the new.

SUMMARY - BRAZIL

- Relaxed about punctuality
- Highly animated
- Lots of interruptions
- Gestures and facial expressions, physical contact
- Home and family are private
- Feelings dictate the solution
- Individuals make the decision
- Long term relationships important

Activity 21 - Auditing your Cultural Style

The scale below will give you a snapshot view of your cultural style.

Each dimension represents a different aspect of culture, evidence of which is likely to show itself in a meeting situation.

For each dimension, rank yourself on the number that most closely represents where you rank.

Auditing your Cultural Style

		1	2	3	4	5	6	7	8	9	10	
Role of Managers	The boss											Team player
Decision making style	Consensus											Command
Conflict style	Direct											Indirect
Work priorities	Live to work											Work to live
Views on change	Positive											Negative
Courtesy, protocols, formality	Informal											Formal
Planning style	Ready, aim, fire											Ready, fire, aim
Workstyle	Multi-task											Mono-task
Level of control over life and business	In control											Not in control
Rational or emotional communication	Rational											Emotional
Physical space	Near											Far
Reasoning styles	Start with conclusion											Finish with the conclusion
Comfort with silence	Embrace silence											Avoid silence
Flow of conversation	Interrupting (fast)											Halting (slow)
Freedom vs. collective identity	Freedom											Identity

Reflecting on your answers

The previous assessment is impossible to say 'correct' or 'incorrect'. This assessment is purely based on your personal perception which is drawn from your values, beliefs and previous experiences. Reflect on how you think your personal choices might align with those in your virtual team. Then, consider how you may have to flex some of your choices in order to successfully lead your virtual team.

Advantages of Cultural Differences

Finally, while this chapter has been primarily focused on the *challenges* of cultural differences in virtual teams, it's important to remember the many very significant advantages – both for your organization and for the individual.

For a global business, meeting global needs, it's vital that we harness and utilize the collective resources, perspectives and experiences from across our business – and cross functional teams allow us to do that.

Diversity can reduce the occurrence of 'group think' and allow a team to make better and more creative decisions. Effective ideas from one country or market can be adapted successfully for others.

Learning to work internationally fosters a sense of creativity that can't be gained any other way.

Reaching a successful outcome when dealing with multiple cultural backgrounds grows an overall sense of innovation and creativity that can be applied across other facets of life and work.

It's one thing to understand the cultural differences between Germany and China; it's quite another thing to have creatively found a way to develop a working relationship that achieves the respective performance objectives while demonstrating respect and dignity for one another.

We all live with the objective of being
happy; our lives are all different and
yet the same."

Anne Frank

KEY POINTS SUMMARY

- To work effectively across all cultural boundaries, you must be able to communicate respect for the customs, habits and rituals of others, especially for the people who work for you.

- The most effective way for you to deal with the challenges of culture is by developing and applying cultural intelligence.

- Self-awareness is critical part of cultural intelligence, and to improving your cultural capability.

- Develop your ability to expect and anticipate differences between cultures. Take the time to observe the behaviors of others.

- Reflect on what you observe, and use those reflections to choose where and when to modify your own actions.

- Analyze your own cultural style and recognize that your team members will almost certainly have a different style.

PART 6
BE HEARD AND GET AGREEMENT IN A VIRTUAL WORLD

Be Noticed, Be Heard: Virtual Presentation skills

Preparation = confidence =
more relaxed

Types of Presentations

The further you progress up the corporate ladder, the more opportunities you will be given to present to audiences. These may range from a staff meeting in a workplace through to a board meeting with shareholders, not to mention media releases, product launches, and speaking engagements.

The more confident you are as a presenter, the more confident you will come across as a leader. Remember, leaders have followers, and every audience you speak to has the opportunity to become your followers.

The power and opportunity we are given every time we present is enormous, yet many presenters have no idea of their potential to influence. A dynamic presentation gives you a platform to communicate your message effectively, influence your audience, and spark the desired action.

There are many different types of presentations, including:

- Informative presentations
- Instructional presentations
- Attention-grabbing presentations
- Persuasive presentations
- Decision-making presentations
- Communicating bad news

Planning Your Presentation

- know your audience
- set clear objectives
- create content overview and gather content

- create content detail and visual aids
- adding impact – telling stories
- handling question and answer sessions
- rehearse
- consider co/multi-presenters
- review

Effective presenters use the energy of their audience to deliver lively and memorable presentations. They also spend a considerable amount of time preparing for their presentation, ensuring that the structure, content, and communication style is appropriate for their listeners. It is what happens before the presenter enters the room that dictates the success of the presentation.

Today's business environment calls for a variety of presentation types, including convention speeches, keynote addresses, reports to the board of directors, communication at a team meeting, delivery of good and bad news, or communicating organizational change. The goal of the presentation may differ with each of these occasions. However, whether you aim to motivate, enthrall, entice, deliver facts, provide data, or influence behavior change, solid presentation skills are essential for communication success.

The ability to present professionally is a beneficial skill in business, sales, training, public speaking, and self-development. In addition to solid presentation techniques, confidence and experience are critical skills in determining the success or failure of a presentation. However, you are not alone if the thought of speaking in public terrifies you. Presenting and public speaking regularly tops the list in surveys of our greatest fears – more than heights, flying, or dying.

Preparation = confidence = more relaxed
Good preparation is the key to confidence, which is the key to being relaxed. Good preparation and rehearsal reduce your nerves, decrease the likelihood of errors, and communicates to your audience that they are important. Preparation and knowledge are the pre-requisites for a successful presentation, and confidence and control will flow from good

preparation. Remember and apply Eleanor Roosevelt's maxim that "no-one can intimidate me without my permission."

A great presentation does not just happen. It is planned, rehearsed then delivered with flair. A good presenter is one who learns the skills of presenting – not one who hopes for talent to carry them through. Public speaking is a skill, not a talent. You can be an excellent presenter if you learn the skills for presentation success. You will be a great speaker if you learn from every presentation you deliver.

We can all learn from the great speakers of the world.

- Who are the public speakers you admire? Ask yourself why you admire them.
- What techniques do they use in their speeches that you can use?
- What principles can you adapt to your presentations?

Activity 22 - Presentation Skills Assessment

Creating and delivering a dynamic and meaningful presentation that provides your objective is a core skill for a virtual leader. The following assessment looks at some of the individual abilities and presentation components for success.

It is designed for you to assess your current skills in this area personally. This assessment is for your personal use to help you determine your existing strengths and areas of development.

For each question, rate yourself on each of the techniques.

Presentation Skills Assessment I......	1 Never	2 Rarely	3 Sometimes	4 Most of the Time	5 Always
Include as many relevant facts and research data as I can to persuade my audience and let the facts speak for themselves					
Begin my presentations with a greeting such as "Thank you for having me," "Good morning," "It's nice to be here", or "Ladies and gentlemen."					
Almost always use PowerPoint in my formal presentations					
Use different words and a different mannerism when I am at a relaxed dinner party with friends than I do when I am giving a formal business presentation					
Focus on delivering intelligent and thoughtful presentations rather than presentations which are humorous and entertaining					
Structure my presentations in parts and within each part I delve into specifics.					
Avoid gimmicks and concentrate on the matter at hand – conveying the concepts as clearly as possible.					
Believe that people should remember the information I present, rather than the way I present.					
Present visuals that combine text, numbers and suitable business graphics.					
Tend to be more factual than speculative in my presentations.					
Rely on experience, research and case studies to drive my point home.					
Use relevant personal and business stories, analogies and metaphors to help explain difficult data or new concepts					
TOTAL					

Please total your scores and list them for Never, Rarely, Sometimes, Most of the time, and Always. All of the skills above are necessary to lead virtual teams and will be explored in this and later chapters.

Reflecting on your answers

Congratulations on all the statements that you answered, 'Most of the time' and 'Always.' Please don't worry, though, if you scored high on the 'Never,' 'Rarely', or 'Sometimes' columns. This book will guide you through the maze of virtual leadership and give you strategies to significantly improve the skills you have identified.

Types of Presentations

The following is an overview of several common types of presentations and their purpose.

Informative Presentations

The purpose of an informative presentation is to **communicate information, facts, and data.** Keep an informative presentation brief and to the point. Stick to the circumstances and avoid complicated details. Use one or a combination of the following structures to communicate this information.

Chronological Structure

- Explains when things should happen.
- Works best with visual people or people who can see the overall organization or sequence of events.
- Use words like "first," "second," "third," to list order.

Location Structure

- Explains where things should happen.
- Works best with people who understand the group or area you are talking about.
- Use words like "Region 1, 2, 3, or 4" to explain order.

Cause and Effect Structure

- Explains how things should happen.
- Works best with people who understand the relationship between events.
- Use phrases like "Because of_____, we now have to _____"
- Simply list items in their order of importance.

Instructional Presentations

The purpose of an instructional presentation is to give specific directions or orders. Your presentation will probably be slightly longer, given that it has to cover your topic in detail, in an instructional presentation, your listeners should come away with new knowledge or a new skill.

- Explain why the information or skill is valuable to the audience.

- Explain the learning objectives of the instructional program.

- Demonstrate the process.

- Provide the participants the opportunity to ask questions, give, and receive feedback from you and their peers.

- Connect the learning to actual use.

- Have participants state how they will use it.

Attention-Grabbing Presentations

The purpose of an attention-grabbing presentation is to make people think about a specific problem or situation. You want to arouse the audience's emotions and intellect so that they will be receptive to your point of view. Use vivid language in an attention-grabbing presentation to project sincerity and enthusiasm.

- Gain attention with a story that illustrates (and sometimes exaggerates) the problem.

- Show the need to solve the problem and illustrate it with an example that is general or commonplace.

- Describe your solution for a satisfactory resolution to the problem.

- Compare/contrast the two worlds with the problem solved and unsolved.

- Call the audience to action to help solve the problem.

- Give the audience a directive that is clear, easy, and immediate.

Persuasive Presentations

The purpose of persuasive presentations is to **convince your listeners to accept your proposal.** A convincing persuasive presentation offers a solution to a controversy, dispute, or problem. To succeed with a persuasive presentation, you must present sufficient logic, evidence, and emotion to sway the audience to your viewpoint.

- Create a great introduction. A persuasive presentation introduction must accomplish the following:

  - Seize the audience's attention
  - Disclose the problem or needs that your product or service will satisfy.
  - Entice the audience by describing the advantages of solving the problem or need.
  - Create a desire for the audience to agree with you by describing exactly how your product or service will satisfy their needs.
  - Close your persuasive presentation with a call to action.
  - Ask for the decision that you want to be made.
  - Ask for the course of action that you want to be followed.

Decision-making Presentations

The purpose of a decision-making presentation is to **move your audience to take your suggested action.** A decision-making presentation presents ideas, suggestions, and arguments strong enough to persuade an audience to carry out your requests.

In a decision-making presentation, you must tell the audience what to do and how to do it. You should also let them know what will happen if they don't do what you ask.

- Gain attention with a story that illustrates the problem

- Show the need to solve the problem and illustrate it with an example that is general or commonplace.

- Describe your solution to bringing a satisfactory resolution to the problem.

- Compare/contrast the two worlds with the problem solved and unsolved.

- Call the audience to action to help solve the problem and give them a way to be part of the solution.

Communicating Bad News

No one wants to be the bearer of bad news. However, there are things you can do to soften the blow. The next time you have to present less-than-favorable information, keep the following tips in mind.

Tailor your presentation appropriately

Don't use bright colors, cartoons, sound-effects, or zany fonts if your PowerPoint presentation contains a series of grim statistics. Stick to the simple background color (or use a standard corporate template) and san-serif font. Save the transitions and animation effects for a more upbeat presentation.

Don't invite extra spectators

When you schedule a bad-news meeting, it's particularly important to invite only those people necessary to the discussion.

Include a positive spin

The bad news is always easier to take if it's delivered with a positive spin. For example, if you must report that the results of your company's latest advertising strategy are less than favorable, you'll also want to include some positive news. After you've reviewed the key findings of your research, conclude with a recommendations section. If consumers hated the look of the ad, but thought the copy was well written, recommend that future advertising use the same copy direction but a different layout.

Don't 'sugar-coat' it

On the other hand, be careful not to 'sugar-coat' the information. You have an obligation to share the facts, even if they're alarming or upsetting to others within the organization. After all, it's business. Numbers fall, campaigns fail, employees don't work out, and the economy slumps. People cope with bad news every day. Be forthright, objective, and optimistic. It's the best way to deliver bad news.

SUMMARY OF PRESENTATIONS:

Terms	Definitions
Informative presentations	The purpose of this presentation is to communicate information, facts, and data. Stick to the facts and avoid complicated information.
Instructional presentations	The purpose of this presentation is to give specific directions or orders. Listeners should come away with new knowledge or a new skill.
Attention-grabbing presentations	The purpose of the presentation is to make people think about a certain problem or situation. You want to arouse the audience's emotions and intellect so that they will be receptive to your point of view.
Persuasive presentations	The purpose of this presentation is to convince your listeners to accept your proposal. You must present sufficient logic, evidence, and emotion to swap the audience to your viewpoint.
Decision-making presentations	The purpose of this presentation is to move your audience to take your suggested action. You must tell the audience what to do and how to do it. You should also let them know what will happen if they don't do what you ask.
Bad news presentations	The purpose of this presentation is to deliver unfavorable information.

"Ask yourself, if I had only sixty
seconds on the stage, what would I
absolutely have to say to get my
message across."

Jeff Dewar

From Presentation Start to End – Overview for Success

Creating Impact – The Presentation Start

- Generally, you have 4 – 7 seconds in which to make a positive impact and good opening impression, so make sure you have a good, robust, and reliable introduction and rehearse it multiple times. Try to build your credibility and create a safe, comfortable environment for your audience. Smiling helps.

- Don't start with a joke unless you are supremely confident that you can 'pull it off.' Jokes are a high-risk strategy at the best of times, let alone at the start of the presentation.

- Don't apologize for anything up-front unless you have made a severe error. This will be perceived as a lack of confidence and a sign of weakness by your audience.

- Try to start on time, even if some of the audience is late.

- The average attention span of an average adult listener is only 6-8 minutes, so present your material using a variety of stimuli, media, and movement to maintain maximum interest.

Adding interest throughout the presentation

- Memorize a couple of good quotes and always credit the source. Having quotes and other devices is vital to give your presentation depth and texture, as well as keeping your audience interested.

"If the only tool in your toolbox is a hammer, you'll treat everything as a nail."

Abraham Maslow

- Be daring and bold and include the level of entertainment in your presentation that is appropriate for your audience.

- Create opportunities to take notes via handouts and other items that you distribute. Create analogies and themes and use props to illustrate and reinforce them. The more senses you can stimulate, the more fun your audience will have, and the more they'll remember.

Examples of interest that you can use to bring your presentation to life, and keep your audience attentive and enjoying themselves:

- Stories

- Questions

- Pictures, cartoons, and video-clips

- Sound-clips

- Straw polls

- Audience participation exercises

- Quotations

- Props

- Examples

- Analogies

- Statistics (which dramatically improve audience 'buy-in' if you're trying to persuade)

- And your body language, and changing the tone and pitch of your voice

Managing longer presentations

- For longer presentations, if you're not an experienced speaker, you must schedule a break every 45 minutes or so for people to get up and stretch their legs. Otherwise, you'll be losing them regardless of the amount of interest you include.

- Take the pressure off yourself by not speaking all the time. Get the audience doing things, and make use of all the communication senses available.

Creating Impact – the presentation close

- Prepare a great close. Quotes, a personal or professional story, a concise summary are all examples of ways of ending your performance with impact.

- To ensure the audience knows it's "the end," by simply saying "thank you" or "I'd like to conclude with...."

- If the audience applauds, stop, and silently acknowledge their applause before leaving the podium. Remembering to smile will leave your audience with the memory of a great presenter.

> "If you wouldn't write it and sign it,
> don't say it."
>
> Earl Wilson

Seven Deadly Presentation Mistakes

1. Apologizing in advance.

2. Failing to explain the reasons why the subject has any relevance or value to the audience.

3. Using a presentation designed for one audience – for a different audience.

4. Telling the audience more than they want to know.

5. Turning the lights off and showing overhead slides while reading a script.

6. Reading verbatim every word on every visual.

7. Failing to rehearse – "It'll be OK on the day!"

Planning Your Presentation – 7-Step Process

Successful presentations are scheduled and rehearsed well in advance of the event. Even the most skilled presenters rarely 'wing it' and what may appear to be an 'off the cuff' presentation is probably a well thought out and structured approach.

The following 7-step process will assist you in preparing for your presentation from beginning to end. Regardless of the nature of your presentation, this structured approach will keep you on track for success.

The steps of the Presentation Planning are as follows:

1. Know your audience
2. Set a clear objective
3. Create a content overview and gather content
4. Develop content detail and create visual aids
5. Rehearse
6. Consider co/multi presenters
7. Evaluate your presentation

STEP 1: KNOW YOUR AUDIENCE

When you have a presentation to make, its human nature to jump straight into 'content mode,' asking yourself:

- What am I going to say?
- How much information can I fit into the allotted time?
- Which visuals should I use?

As a result, you may find yourself rushing prematurely into the process of selecting material, developing an outline, creating slides, and rehearsing content.

Although these steps are essential, you risk heading off in the wrong direction unless you first consider your audience. Your audience is, in fact, the most critical aspect of your presentation.

As an effective presenter, your first step toward making a compelling, persuasive presentation is to define your audience.

Who are the listeners, and what are their needs?
To begin your presentation without this information could result in a significant waste of time and effort for both you and your audience.

By defining your audience, you lay the foundation for a successful presentation, increase the likelihood of influencing audience behavior, and getting the results you want.

Benefits of defining your audience

As a result of defining your audience, you can:

- Identify what motivates your listeners to act.
- Tailor your content to give them precisely what they want, need, and expect.
- Project an appropriate presentation style and personality.
- Increase your comfort level as a speaker.
- Obtain your objective for making the presentation.

Defining your audience means finding out who they are. This information is critical in addressing audience needs, interests, expectations, and levels of understanding. Without this knowledge, you are unable to match your message with their needs. Your ability to present from *their* perspective enables you to influence their thinking, persuade them to accept what you are suggesting, and achieve your presentation objectives.

Audience-analysis is collecting and reviewing information about the people who will be the recipients of your presentation. You should routinely analyze who the audience is and what they want to accomplish by listening to your presentation. You need this kind of information to ensure that you're designing and writing your presentation to your audience.

Having an understanding of your audience will allow your message to be pitched at the correct level. Not having this understanding may result in a presentation that is disconnected to the audience either by way of presentation style or the standard of content being presented.

By defining your audience members and tailoring your message to specifically address their reasons, wants, and needs, you can deliver a presentation that engages, informs, and persuades. By having an understanding of your audience and customizing your presentation to meet their needs they are most likely to give you their time and attention. Consider the following techniques and choose the appropriate ways for you to collect information regarding your audience:

- Speak to the participants days or weeks before the presentation.
- Send out a questionnaire or survey to the audience members.
- Speak to their co-workers or managers.
- Research audience-related issues and gather current data on their industry.
- Converse and mingle with participants at an event before your presentation or directly before the presentation itself.
- Ask questions during the presentation to gather on-the-spot feedback.
- Talk to the participants after the presentation to verify that your intended message was received and their needs met.
- Ask audience members to complete an evaluation form after your presentation.

STEP 2: SET CLEAR OBJECTIVES

What is the message you want to convey? What are your objectives in talking to your audience? What knowledge or experience do you have that can benefit people?

An effective presentation demands that you market your topic and yourself. You have to sell your ideas and yourself to the audience. Regardless of the size of the audience, whether internal or external, you are still selling a message.

A presentation will have at least one of the four aims:

1. To inform
2. To entertain
3. To touch the emotions
4. To move to action

Successful presentations will likely
include all four purposes.

Writing clear objectives

The Aim is a short sentence that starts with an action verb and defines what you want to accomplish in the presentation.

Objectives describe the specific actions that you want to occur either during or as a result of your meeting or presentation.

- What *specific desired outcomes* do I want from this event?
- What action do I want *my audience* to take as a result of my presentation?
- What must audience members know, say, or do differently when they leave my presentation?
- When are these actions required?

Case Study T - Presenting at a Meeting

Meeting aim – Develop a plan for new employed recruitment

Objectives in order to achieve the objective:

- Identify new college graduate personnel hiring needs
- Discuss/confirm colleges and universities targeted for on-campus recruiting
- Understand last year's results
- Suggest/agree adds and deletes
- Specify materials needed for advance solicitation of candidates
- Identify/assign on-campus recruiters
- Outline work plans and agree who does what by when

SAMPLE – PRESENTING TO A LARGER GROUP

Presentation aim: Jump-start quarterly sales campaign

Objectives to achieve the objective:

- Review and celebrate successes within year-to-date sales results
- Identify product lines and customer groups with below-objective year-to-date purchases and specify actions needed
- Review marketing support for the quarter
- Answer questions and listen to "What's on your mind?"
- Present "Sales Tips for the Quarter"
- Discuss and get buy-in on sales objectives for the quarter and recognize high-achievers

STEP 3: CREATE CONTENT OVERVIEW & GATHER CONTENT

The next stage of planning for your presentation is to create a high-level agenda and then collect all of the content you need to present.

Questions to ask yourself during this part of the planning are 'why,' 'what' and 'why not?' The content of your presentation will form the 'what', i.e., what are you presenting? It's important to solidify your thoughts on what you want to accomplish in your presentation. Developing an agenda will create an efficient and practical guide for your presentation.

Content Overview – The Agenda

> What key points or recommendations
> must your presentation include to
> support or develop your primary
> strategy and persuade your audience?

Using post-it notes, brainstorm the main content area of your presentation. Write one idea per post-it note. Brainstorming is all about quantity, not quality, so ensure that all of your senses are recorded. Then begin to cluster similar ideas into logical groups. These will become your topics.

Content Details – Gathering the Content

- Write each topic heading and consider how you will gather the information.
- For each topic create a list of sub-topics
- Summarize all resources you need to research the topic
- List the jargon that you'll need to define or avoid. This will help guide you when writing each part of your presentation.

A visual representation of the Virtual Presentation Flow

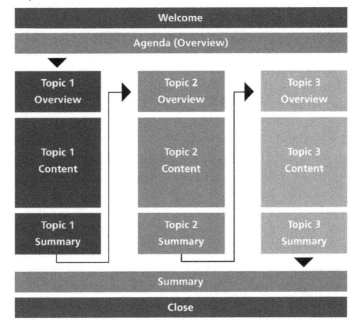

Figure 12 - Virtual Presentation Flow

STEP 4: CREATE CONTENT DETAIL & VISUAL AIDS

When creating a presentation the following must be completed:

- Consider visuals
- Write presentation – according to the Virtual Presentation Flow (above)
- Logistics and supporting materials

Using visual aids why bother with visuals?

We learn through our senses. Presentations generally use both hearing and sight. These visual aids are an essential way to increase retention of your message.

- Taste   1.0%
- Touch   1.5%
- Smell   3.5%
- Hearing   11.0%
- Sight   83%

Using visual aids for impact and message retention

- Printed visual aids with several paragraphs of text should be designed using serif fonts (typeface) for quicker readability. For virtual meetings using Zoom, or similar, use sans serif fonts, especially if the point size (letter size) is small. For example, Arial is a sans serif font, and Times New Roman is a serif font. (A serif font is one with the extra little cross-lines which finish off the strokes of the letters. Interestingly, serif fonts originated in the days of engraving, before printing, when the engraver needed an exit point from each letter).

- Extensive sections of text can be read more quickly in a serif font because the words have a horizontal flow, but serif fonts have a more old-fashioned traditional appearance than sans serif. If you need to comply with a company branding, you may not have a choice. Whatever the situation, try to select fonts and point sizes that are fit for the medium and purpose.

- Use no more than two different fonts and no more than two font variants (size/bold/italic); otherwise, your presentation will become confusing. If in doubt, simply pick an excellent, readable serif font and use it big and bold for headings, and 14-16 point size for the body text.

- Avoid uppercase (capital letters) in body text, because your audience needs to be able to read word-shapes as well as the letters. The upper case makes every word a rectangle, so it takes a long time to read. An upper case may be appropriate for a heading if you feel that it is essential.

- Create your prompts and notes to suit your presentation flow and your level of confidence. Speaker notes can be useful. However, you need to ensure that it is not a script. A simple running sheet (summary flow) that you can quickly glance at is an excellent safety-net for anything longer than 30 minutes. You can use this to monitor your timing and pace.

Designing and preparing visual material

Combining the visual with the verbal gives tremendous strength to any communication and is much more effective than when either is used alone.

However, regardless of the amount of time, effort and money you spend on visual aids, they can never prop up a poorly prepared presentation.

Using visual aids doesn't ensure a successful presentation. If a visual aid doesn't help get your message across, don't use it. A good presentation without visual aids is better than a poor visual aid demonstration.

Be selective	Determine if visual aids are necessary, then assess whether a simple aid like the flipchart is enough. If necessary, investigate other visual possibilities.
Ensure Relevance	Does it help your subject matter, or does it detract from it? Does it contain information that you will not be discussing? Is it appropriate for the level of knowledge of your audience? Will it provoke unwanted questions?
Don't overdo it	The characteristics of a good visual are closely allied to the standard principles of an effective presentation.
Be Accurate	Provide a correct interpretation of the facts.
Be Clear	Keep it neat, bold, and clearly readable by all. Translate unfamiliar terms and concepts so that people understand them. If you have an above-average knowledge of your subject, it is easy to overcomplicate your message.
Be Simple	Keep it short and to the point.
Be Direct	Focus sharply on the main idea you must get across.
Be The Right Size	Visual aids must be large enough to be seen by the whole group >24 pt is recommended.
Be Colorful	Use color wisely. Don't be too lavish. It is better to have too few colors than too many. Use red in moderation and avoid yellow unless in a highlighting capacity.
Be Imaginative	You don't have to be an artist. Remember the purpose of your vision and don't over-clutter it. There are plenty of visual design packages available.

Adding Impact - Telling Stories

Tell stories to give your presentation impact and call your audience to action. Paint word pictures that create images in the listener's minds. If they can see it, they are more likely to understand and remember the message. The best public speakers are storytellers. Use stories and anecdotes to illustrate and reinforce the main points of your presentation.

The best stories are personal. When they are your own, they are easier to remember and make your presentation unique. We listen to stories. Generally, we dislike long lectures. If you have forgotten that lesson – just ask a child. The way to find personal stories that can be used in your presentations is to write them down. Make a list of important things that have happened to you and those around you; the first time you did something, your best times, worst times, the biggest mistake, the best break, the greatest 'ah-ha', the funniest moment, the most frustrating incident, the silliest thing you did, the most embarrassing moment, etc.

The things that drive you the most make the best stories to tell in your presentations. Rehearse your stories and edit them down into a short narrative that is easy to listen to. While it may be hard for you to leave some of the details, it will be harder for your audience to listen to unnecessary information. The key to storytelling success if keeping it short, sharp, and relevant.

Handling question and answer sessions

You can better prepare for questions following your presentation if you spend some time pre-empting audience reactions. This is time well invested and will help raise your credibility and professionalism in the eyes of the audience. Suggestions for managing your question and answer session include:

- Having several statements ready. Use your answers to emphasize the main points you want to drive home.

- Accepting questions from the entire audience. Most speakers tend to favor the right or left side of the room, so be careful not to focus on a particular segment.

- Listening intently to questions. Repeat each one in your head and recite it (if it's positive) back to the questioner.

- Rephrasing negative questions. You can recast embarrassing questions by wording them differently. For example, if someone asks why our firm is "polluting the environment," you can say, "The question was about the environment and what we're doing about it."

- Addressing the entire audience. Look first at the person who asked the question, then engage everyone with eye contact.

- Being brief. Get to the point quickly. Remember: the audience has already sat through your presentation.

- If you don't know the answer, say so. But call the person a day or so later with the answer. Word will spread.

- Setting a limit on the questions. It helps to arrange a wrap-up signal with your host.

- Making your responses credible. Quote reliable outside experts. Round off statistics and other numbers to make them easy to remember. Give references to your own experience such as 'In the 15 years as a......'

- Learning to bridge. You can return to your main points by saying, 'That's important, but I think the main issue is......."

Step 5: Rehearse

Remembering your speech
'The best public speakers do not memorize their presentation.' Know the topic and the issues, and then make notes for yourself. Avoid reading your presentation, or you are at risk of boring your audience.

Instead, write keywords that remind you of the critical communication messages. Ensure your notes are easy for you to follow and that you can read them comfortably from a distance.

Rehearsing your presentation
Rehearse your presentation on your feet at least three times. It feels different when you speak standing up. Get used to the feel of delivering your presentation, and this will maximize your success on the day. You can also practice important parts of your presentation while sitting at your desk.

Editing for the ear
Unlike the reader, the listener cannot pause to reconsider a phrase or paragraph that didn't connect with them the first time through. The listener has to move right along with the speaker or risk losing even more of the presentation. In the time he or she spends reconsidering one point, two or three others may be lost. This gives the speaker a special responsibility in keeping the audience with them from the beginning of a presentation to the end.

1. **Aim for simplicity**. (Never use a long word when a short one works; use simple sentences.)

2. **Use the active voice rather than the passive voice whenever possible.** (Say 'Marketing prepared the report,' not 'the report was prepared by marketing.")

3. **Be politically correct**. Guard against using words that could turn off or offend the audience.

4. **Vary your pattern of speech**. (Guard against using words and phrases repetitively' vary sentence length and structure.)

STEP 6: CONSIDER CO/MULTI PRESENTERS

Working with team presentations

Anyone who's ever delivered a team presentation can appreciate the difficulty in synchronizing a group. Team presentations can be a fantastic way to build momentum and interest. But they can also be extremely time-consuming. If you decide to deliver a group presentation, consider the following strategies to keep the audience attention and interest.

Team leader

A good leader is critical. The team leader needs to define the strategy, set the tone, and explain the message. If the team leader simply delegates a different segment of the presentation to each team member, the result will be a 'mishmash' of styles and tone.

The team

While technical competence is a crucial component in selecting a team, individual personalities are just as important. Do you have someone who can tell stories and entertain the audience? Do you have someone good at moderating if the Q&A session gets out of hand? Do you have someone who can confidently assure audience members if they get skittish? Make sure every person on your team can contribute something to the group. This needs to be carefully considered during virtual presentations but all platforms, such as Zoom, etc., cater for multi-host presentations.

Synchronization

If your preparation time is short, you may want each team member to create her visual aids. The key is to ensure the format is standardized. The easiest way to do this is to create a master slide in your presentation software and make sure that everyone follows it to the letter. Your master slide should define the background, font, headings and subheadings, text, and graphics.

Once all the segments have been completed, assign one member with the task of putting the whole thing together and checking each slide for consistency. While visual consistency ensures a professional-looking presentation, a robust and consistent message will make your presentation stand out. Make sure everyone is clear on the aim of the presentation, the grammatical style, the acceptable amount of jargon, the level of formality, and anything else that will influence the message.

Introduction, transitions and the conclusion

As part of your preparation, make sure you've assigned one person to do the introductions and that everyone is clear how they're going to make the transition to the next speaker. Once the presentation is over, have one team member wrap up the session and thank the audience for their time.

Handling questions

Make sure you've defined your core team members' competencies before you go into the presentation. Then, when the Q&A session rolls around, you'll know exactly who should answer which type of questions. It's amazing how many people will attempt to answer questions about which a co-presenter is the expert.

Also, keep answers short and to the point. Even though it's your area of expertise, there's no need to deliver a long monologue to the detriment of the overall presentation.

STEP 7: REVIEW

Once your presentation is complete, the disciplined presenter learns from his or her presentation and conducts a formal or informal review. Even taking a few minutes to reflect on what went well during your performance and taking note of what could have worked better will prepare you for the next time you present.

In closing

Public speaking is a skill. It is not about talent. It is a set of techniques practiced, rehearsed, and delivered. You will never deliver the perfect speech. But you might provide a powerful and effective presentation.

Public speaking is both an art and a science. The more you learn and practice the presentation process, the easier the technique will work for you. You can be a powerful and effective presenter. But it will take time, practice, and energy, and those are the elements of greatness.

For success with your presentations:

- speak well
- speak effectively
- speak with confidence
- speak to make things happen

Virtual Presentations

Virtual presentations are different in some respects – however, the principles of presenting will always be helpful. You do not have the advantage of being able to engage with someone in the front row of an auditorium or receive instant banter or feedback from the audience. Or know when someone laughs at one of your comments. If you are usually an interactive presenter, this can be a little daunting until you get used to it. You will always have a slight delay between your words and written feedback.

Preparation is the key – the more prepared you are mentally and physically for the virtual presentation, the more professional you will come across to your audience, and your message will be understood.

Thirteen Deadly Virtual Presentation Mistakes

1. **Don't wear flowery patterns on your shirt or jacket.** Consider the background where you will be viewed from and wear an intense contrasting color. Avoid wearing white close to your face; it can give a very washed-out look.

2. **Don't wear clunky jewelry that makes a noise or something metallic around your neck that reflects the light and can cause a distraction.** If you are wearing either of these things, remove them before you speak. Avoid wearing low cut blouses or shirts and showing bare skin. Preferably wear a jacket for a professional look.

3. **You are failing to explain the reasons why the subject has any relevance or value to the audience.** Do your homework, know, and understand your audience. They are one click away from turning you off or browsing social media during your presentation.

4. **Don't talk for too long.** Think media sound bites. Your message needs to be short, sharp, and to the point. If you are going to tell stories, give an abridged version of an incident. Repeat the key points at list once or twice to ensure the message is clear.

5. **Don't give notes or back up slides.** Your actual presentation may last less than ten minutes. However, back it up with slides, restating the key facts plus more comprehensive notes.

These can be then forwarded at the end of your presentation, or a link is given to participants.

6. **Don't give a time frame.** Upfront, state how long the virtual presentation will go for. "In the next 8 minutes, I am going to give you an overview of the restructuring." "In the next 9 minutes, I will take you through the background of the Jason account and why we need to nurture this account."

7. **Don't read their speech.** It is such an insult to a virtual audience to read your presentation from your speaker's notes. By all means, prepare your presentation but include spots to ad-lib and adapt as you see the comments and response coming through from the participants.

8. **Don't read verbatim every word on every visual.** Respect the intelligence of the audience. They can read. You do not have to read the PowerPoint slides to them – by all means, refer to it. Remember, your slides are a visual aid to your message. Your slides should enhance your message, not distract from it.

9. **Don't take questions.** Let the virtual audience know that you have allowed time at the end for a question and answer segment and they are welcome to type and send their questions during your presentation or they may wait until the end to see if their question has already been answered. Alternatively, if you are happy for them to interrupt you (either by asking questions on the audio line, or via the chat box), say that in the beginning.

10. **Don't eat or drink during the virtual presentation.** This is a big NO-NO! If your mouth is dry by all means, take a sip of water from a glass, not a bottle. Ensure that you drink water before you start your presentation.

11. **Don't allow enough time for questions.** The upside of virtual presentations is that you have a record of people's questions, and at the end of the presentation can email responses to the individuals. Or, if you see a common theme or thread with the questions, announce that you have identified that and will respond with a general email within 24 hours to address these critical queries.

12. **Failing to rehearse – "It'll be OK on the day!"** Rehearse your presentation with someone in your office who will give you feedback on the light, the angle that you are being

viewed at and anything that may interfere with a clean, clear image.

13. **Don't move around.** If you step out of the screenshot you will lose your audience very quickly. Make sure that anything you have to refer to during your presentation is within reach. Remove any clutter from the background – it again is a distraction to your audience.

Just as face-to-face presentations, the more virtual presentations you do, the better you get. If you think of the image of a journalist reading the news or a talk show host relating a story – that is the image that you will portray with your virtual audience. Prepare, be professional, and, most of all, be authentic.

KEY POINTS SUMMARY

- The more confident you are as a presenter, the more confident you will come across as a leader.

- Use different types of presentations, for different purposes.

- Preparation = confidence = more relaxed

- Generally, you have 4 – 7 seconds in which to make a positive impact and good opening impression, so make sure you have a good, robust, and reliable introduction and rehearse it multiple times.

- Avoid the Deadly Presentation Mistakes and follow the 7-Step Process for Planning Your Presentation

HOW TO GET TO YES FASTER – VIRTUAL NEGOTIATION SKILLS

Negotiating across Multiple Locations

"Let us never negotiate out of fear.
But let us never fear to negotiate."

John Fitzgerald Kennedy

As someone in a virtual leadership role, you will be asked to negotiate everything from a salary package for yourself or one of your team, your next career move, to the purchase price of a project to be delivered by a vendor.

The classic definition of negotiation involving two parties could be defined as:

Each party has something the other
wants – and the process includes
trying to reach a mutual agreement to
exchange, through a process of
dialogue and bargaining.

In any negotiation, the key to effective negotiating is to have a game plan – your ultimate aim and a strategy for achieving it. The challenge for anyone leading geographically dispersed teams means that the classic game plan, which includes reading body language, meeting face to face, and taking time to negotiate over several meetings, also changes.

A new game plan is needed taking into consideration cultural differences, differences in time zones, attitudes, delays, and knowledge of how business is conducted globally.

Unless the negotiation is taking place with a video facility, such as Zoom, Skype, or another web conferencing platform, often, the negotiation is taking place over email with delays in responses. These new challenges make negotiating for the virtual leader, especially challenging – and then we add into the mix negotiating with other cultures.

"In order to succeed, you must fail, so
that you know what not to do the next
time."

Anthony J. D'Angelo,
The College Blue Book.

Negotiation Foundation Stone: Influence

It is an underlying fact that in any negotiation, the contributing parties try to influence each other to reach agreement on a topic, decision, or course of action. Whether negotiating over a major capital purchase or rallying to increase employee headcount, all negotiations incorporate a number of critical variables aimed at influencing the parties involved. These variables will be covered in this chapter, and they include:

1. Power

2. Time

3. Information

From a very early age, we learn either formally or informally, how to influence others to make certain decisions.

This doesn't mean that we can change a person's way of thinking, only their choice on a decision at a particular point in time.

This is the true art of negotiation; the ability to influence another party that the outcome you desire is also the best outcome for them.

Activity 23 - Negotiation Skills Assessment

Understanding the key elements of negotiation is critical in improving career success. The assessment covers the core negotiation skills required to improve both personal and business performance.

This assessment is for your personal use to help you determine your current strengths and areas of development.

For each question, rate yourself on each of the techniques.

Negotiation Skills Assessment I...	1 Never	2 Rarely	3 Sometimes	4 Most of the Time	5 Always
Can identify and explain the steps in the negotiation process					
Understand the difference between selling and negotiating					
Understand the difference between positional bargaining and principled negotiation					
Use creative techniques to uncover interests and build collaborative solutions					
Always adequately prepare for a negotiation					
Assess the other side's BATNA prior to entering a negotiation					
Use standards to ensure fairness during the negotiation process					
Can counteract dirty negotiation tactics					
Understand the various types and use of power during the negotiation process					
Always focus on maintaining the negotiation relationships					
Can identify the negotiation variables and decision-making influencers in the negotiation process					
TOTAL					

Please total your scores and list them for Never, Rarely, Sometimes, Most of the time, and Always.

All of the skills above are necessary to lead virtual teams and will be explored in this and later chapters.

Reflecting on your answers

Congratulations on all the statements that you answered, 'Most of the time' and 'Always.' Please don't worry, though, if you scored high on the 'Never,' 'Rarely,' or 'Sometimes' columns. This book will guide you through the maze of virtual leadership and give you strategies to significantly improve the skills you have identified.

This chapter discusses practical ways that managers who lead global and virtual teams can disentangle the negotiation process and provide some shortcuts on gaining a mutually beneficial outcome for both parties, without damaging global relationships!

Variable 1 – Power

When people hear the word 'power,' they typically have one of two reactions. They either fear or admire it, depending on their experience of power. A fear response generally occurs when someone has experienced an 'abuse of power.' For example, where an authority figure has used their position to bully those under their control. Conversely, an admiration for power may be brought about by an experience of 'power for the greater good.' For example, the achievements of the late Nelson Mandela and the late Mother Theresa.

Types of Power

There are many different types of power in a negotiation, and given that bargaining can be a complicated process, the skill it takes to become a successful negotiator can also be involved. The following are the various types of power that may be present in a negotiation.

Legitimate power

Legitimate power is derived from the **ability to influence based on one's position**. Legitimate power is used in many ways during a negotiation. Parties with a lot of legitimate power may use their position of authority to 'instruct' other parties to follow certain procedures. Depending on the **perceived authority of the individual**(s) involved, the other players in the negotiation could agree with whatever is decided, relying totally on the 'positional pull' of the individual in authority.

Using legitimate power as a tactic

Sometimes one party will use legitimate power as a tactic against another party by:

- Bringing in someone who has influence to make important decisions, and who has credibility with the other party, or by

- Assigning legitimate power to an individual or individuals in an opposing party so as to use the need for power and status that exists in all individuals to get major concessions from them.

This is sometimes referred to as 'ingratiation.'

Using legitimate power in a virtual leadership environment

Often those leaders leading virtual teams are not co-located with their managers. For example, a regional head may be located in Los Angeles, reporting to her manager in New York, who, in turn, reports to Head Office in London.

Remembering that power is simply the 'perceived authority of the individual' may mean that the Los Angeles leader may feel somehow inferior in negotiation to anyone in London, simply given that that person is located in the L.A. Head Office and has direct contact with the power players of the organization.

Case Study U - Jackie's challenge – Meeting #1

Jackie is a Human Resources manager for a construction company in Sydney, Australia. Jackie leads a team of six people, located in Sydney, and she has one person in Melbourne, Brisbane, and Auckland, New Zealand. The organization has a matrix model of reporting, so Jackie reports to her country head, also located in Sydney as well as to the Asia Pacific HR Manager, located in Hong Kong. The Hong Kong manager reports to head office in Rio de Janeiro, Brazil.

Since the coronavirus outbreak, Jackie and her entire team have had to reprioritize projects and are all now working from home.

Jackie was asked to submit her HR strategic plan and presented it to her Hong Kong manager. Previously, it had been signed off by her country manager, so Jackie felt confident going into the negotiation. Jackie knew she would have to negotiate for additional FTEs (full-time employees) however, she was well prepared with statistics gathered from similar size divisions of the organization worldwide.

What Jackie didn't expect was on the Zoom call her Hong Kong Manager had also invited four other HR managers from the region as well as the local HR manager from the head office in Rio de Janeiro, Maree.

Jackie was surprised that Maree was on the call as she was a lower level in the company to Jackie and the others, had fewer people on her team, less budget, and little knowledge about the Asia Pacific region.

During the call, it became evident that despite her level in the organization, when Maree spoke, everyone was quiet, and agreed with what she was saying, even when it was unfounded or incorrect.

Jackie presented her plan, which was supported by some others in the region; however, Maree was very outspoken in a negative way about the plan. As the discussion was getting heated, Jackie decided the best she could do was to stop speaking, reconvene at another time.

The perception that because Maree had a direct professional relationship with the Global Head of HR meant that everyone at the meeting bowed to what she said, even when it was misguided.

Case Study V - Jackie's challenge - Meeting #2

In between meetings, Jackie rallied the support of other regional HR managers, her country manager, and other key stakeholders who she had professional relationships within Brazil.

In the follow-up meeting, Jackie met again with her Hong Kong head. Jackie also asked her country manager to attend, who was very supportive of the plan. Maree was also in attendance. However, during the second presentation, Jackie was clear to include comments of support from Brazilian key stakeholders who were a higher rank than Maree and asked the other Regional HR Managers to give their professional critique of the plan - all of whom were supportive.

Jackie negotiated and gained the resources that she had asked for by using the perception of **legitimate power** in the second negotiation. Jackie was careful not to upset the relationship with Maree choosing in the second negotiation to acknowledge her suggestions and then immediately ask someone in the meeting with a higher degree of legitimate power to comment, who had no qualms about discounting what Maree had said.

Jackie learned a valuable lesson: during a negotiation, know precisely who will be involved and **who has the power**, perceived or otherwise.

And, based on this knowledge, **prepare for the negotiation to counter that perception** with either fact, data, or other people with a greater perception of power.

Denying legitimate power

It is essential to recognize that legitimate power can only influence if other individuals recognize it. Some negotiators may attempt to deny the other party of their legitimate power by:

- Denying them an opportunity to talk

- Ignoring prior agreements on how to proceed; or

- Denying that any one of the other parties can have any legitimate position of significance.

A negotiator may find it necessary to establish some minimal legitimate authority before proceeding and, in some cases, may be advised to refuse to continue until the other party recognizes that the authority is in place. Once a small base of legitimate power is established, a skillful negotiator can extend it.

Legitimate power in print

Legitimate power may also be attributed to any 'printed' information, which we perceive to be true simply because it exists in 'black and white.'

Most people take what is printed in the media, business reports, texts, and other types of publications to be fact. In their book "Getting to Yes," Roger Fisher, William L. Ury, and Bruce Patton (2011) refer to this as negotiating on 'standards.' This refers to the standards that may be used in the industry, researching similar situations, or providing information and data which provides the legitimate power base.

Standards could be in the form of Market value (perceived worth in the market), Precedent (tradition), Professional standards, (accepted by the industry), Product Efficiency standards (product performance/quality ratings, etc.), Product Cost, Competitor Standards, Moral Standards (socially accepted), Environmental Standards, Technological Standards, Reciprocity (mutual give-and-take) and others that relate to your role or industry.

To find the appropriate standards to present at your negotiation, answering questions like those following may assist in determining the 'right standards for the right negotiation':

- Which Standards are accepted in business today by the people at the negotiation?
- How can I apply these Standards in my negotiations?
- What information do I need to source to ensure that these Standards are objective?

However, despite our acceptance of legitimate power, we know that it isn't always valid and that the information we receive isn't always accurate. Take, for example, the media tabloids. The information we read about lifestyles of the rich and famous is mostly fictitious, yet because we see relevant photos, taglines, and quotes, we are inclined to believe it. In the absence of knowing these people ourselves and in the absence of knowing the truth, we trust the written word.

The same can be said of our beliefs during the negotiation process. When we are presented with documented or printed material in a negotiation, we tend to accept it as fact. While this information may be accurate, it is vital to question the validity of the data presented and to research the topic yourself to be adequately prepared.

When planning for a negotiation, gather as much information as you can before the meeting. By supporting your view with facts and figures, you increase your opportunity to influence the other parties in the negotiation.

Using legitimate power in print across cultures may be tricky. What may be a well-known publication in your city, state, country, or region, maybe utterly unknown in another part of the world. If you are negotiating across boundaries, ensure that you cite references both from your local area and respected references from where the others at the negotiating table are from. If not, your well prepared 'standards' may hold little weight across borders, cultures and diminish the negotiation rather than enhancing it.

Expert power

Expert power is an extension of legitimate power and relates to the degree of knowledge on the issue being negotiated. In any negotiation, the party who has the most intimate understanding of the issue at hand is in a better position to negotiate. Expertise breeds trust, and trust breeds power.

Take, for example, professions such as doctors, lawyers, and engineers. The people who occupy these positions are considered experts in their field and are automatically trusted to give us the best possible information. Even where this information may be incorrect or misleading, we are inclined to believe them because we don't know any better. They have automatic power over us because we have a knowledgeable gap.

In a negotiation, you do not necessarily have to be the expert. What is key is to **know who the experts are** and who are the people in positions of authority related to the negotiation. In his book "Influence: The Power of Persuasion," Robert Cialdini refers to this as the social influence pattern of **Authority**. This can be a powerful card to play in a negotiation as people like to be associated with those who are considered experts.

Authority	Power of "Opinion Leaders" – featuring
People who are wearing nice suits. Police officers. Firefighters. Doctors. We become zombies in the presence of such authority figures in their domains of expertise. "I'll do whatever you say..."	Consumer Reports' favorable review of your product, including an endorsement from a famous author on the back of your book. Getting a well-established accounting firm to endorse your new tax software or a TV talk show host to support your new product.

Presenting yourself as the expert

If you choose to position yourself as the expert, the #1 rule is: don't fake it. You'll be found out which makes not only what facts have been discovered as untrue to be void, but it likely to bring into question all of the facts that you present. After all, if one thing is untrue, then everything is now under the spotlight.

If you are not a legitimate expert in the topic or issue at hand, it is equally important not to come across as having too much knowledge. There is a risk that you will be 'found out', and your credibility in the negotiation process questioned.

To achieve expert power in a negotiation, research is critical. At the very least, you will ensure a level playing field and, at best, be able to influence the other parties to your point of view.

Expert power can be introduced into a negotiation in one of two ways, either in general conversation or by incorporating some deliberate phrases or keywords that signal content knowledge.

Questioning other experts

Similarly, you should also examine other parties in the negotiation who claim to be experts. Question their credentials and their knowledge and ask for specific information that supports them as an expert. This can be done in a friendly way, perhaps over coffee, or while waiting for others to join the meeting. If meeting in a virtual environment with people whom you don't know, you may reach out to them before the meeting and with an open question like, "What brings you to the meeting?" This will open up the conversation and potentially create an ally in the meeting.

> Based on my failings in the past in a
> moment of frustration during a heated
> negotiation I asked
> "What expertise do you have in this
> field?" which was seen as adversarial
> and broke down the negotiation – not
> my most exceptional negotiating
> maneuver!

Know the smart questions to ask about the issue at hand, and how they should be answered. Performing adequate amounts of research on both your topic and your opposing negotiators will better prepare you to walk away with a successful negotiation outcome.

Using expert power across cultures again may be challenging. As discussed, with legitimate power in print, it is crucial that the people with whom you are negotiating know of the experts that you are referencing.

Activity 24 -   Reflection - Power

Power can be used in many different ways and can have many different meanings. Based on your experience of power, define what power means to you by answering the following questions:

I define power as _____

I have observed or experienced an abuse of power when _____

The result of this abuse of power was _____

I have observed or experienced admiration for power when _____

The result of this admiration of power was _____

Commitment power

The power of commitment is a critical factor in any negotiation. Take, for example, the relatively simple negotiation that occurs in purchasing a new car. If there is more than one person involved in the purchase decision (as is the case with a couple and a family), you are unlikely to buy without first having agreed your needs and established a purchase limit. As a team, you commit to a buying position before approaching the dealership.

Consider, in this example, the negotiation, which is likely to occur over the price of the vehicle. During the talks, the sales manager may decrease the total cost of the car but increase the interest rate of the loan to sustain monthly sales targets. At this point, one half of the buying party may agree with the terms of the financing, while the other half is unsettled due to their prior agreement. Since the buying party is now split, the sales manager assumes the upper hand. He has influenced at least one party to consider his position in the negotiation.

The same principles are valid for more complex negotiators in the corporate world. Where more than one person represents a party in the negotiation, everyone should be 'on the same page' before the consultation begins. Having agreed on the facts of the negotiation, the relevant variables, and the tradable terms of negotiation, gives the party a position of strength by presenting a united front.

For this reason, it may be beneficial to hold preliminary discussions before the negotiation to determine what information will be presented, who will be the main contributors to the discussion, who will be secondary contributors, and who will serve as the point of reference if a conflict arises.

No matter what your role at the negotiation table, decisions and commitments should be made beforehand so that each person involved in the process knows their position and what is expected of them during the negotiation.

The power of persistence

Persistence can be a potent negotiation tool when used in a manner which the other party admires. However, there is a fine line between being persistent and simply being annoying. If the other party in the negotiation feels that they are being 'beaten into submission' by a tenacious negotiator, there is every chance that the communication process and, therefore, the negotiation process will break down. Persistence, like all other types of power in the negotiation process, needs to be managed carefully.

Being persistent may not be a characteristic that is common to all of us. However, it is something that can be developed and may be a useful skill in the negotiation process.

Purchasing a new vehicle is again, an excellent example of the power of persistence. Very rarely, when we are buying a car, do we pay the advertised price set by the seller or dealership. There will almost always be a negotiation over price, and the level of buyer persistence is crucial to the final amount paid.

Persistence is not about 'splitting the difference.' It is about seeking commitment and maximizing success on the desired outcome. If you are buying, aim low because your first stake in the sand sets the limit on your best possible outcome. There is no moving it closer to where you want to go; it will only move the other way. Your opening position also fixes the other party's minimum expectation, and the closer your start point is to the eventual finishing point the more difficult it is to give the other person concessions along the way and ultimately arrive at a win-win outcome.

It is logical that to achieve the best possible finishing position, you should, as ambitiously as you can, start without losing credibility.

Negotiation Power Words

Language plays an important part in the negotiation process. The choice of words during a negotiation can influence the other party often quite unconsciously.

The following 'power words' are known to grab the attention of a listener and assist the speaker in appearing more legitimately influential or to promote expert influence.

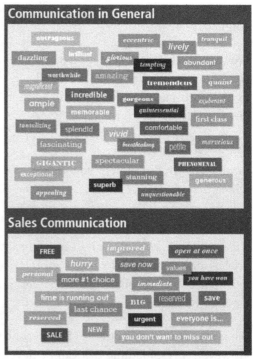

Figure 13 - Power Words

Power and risk

In any negotiation, there will always be an element of risk. The amount of risk, however, can be controlled by the negotiating parties.

Herb Cohen used this example in his book, "You Can Negotiate Anything." He offered everyone in his audience a chance to beat him on a coin toss. He stated if any audience member won the bet, he would pay them $1million. If they lost the bet, they would pay him just 10% of that, $100,000. As expected, nobody in the audience took him up on the chance.

He goes on to mention that if he had lowered the risk, more people would have taken him up on the offer. Since the odds on the bet were 10/1, it's a deal if you are a winner. But since the stakes were so high, not many are willing to bet.

The moral of the story is that when the stakes are being set, take into consideration the amount you are willing to risk on the negotiation. If you go into a negotiation without knowing what you are ready to risk, chances are you are going to either risk too much or not risk enough. By risking too much, you stand to have more to lose. However, risking too little will yield a lower return on the negotiation.

Case Study W - Working example: Occupancy Space

Vamini is based in Mumbai, India, as the Business Continuity Manager at a global bank.

Vamini is responsible for the preservation of all systems and processes to keep the bank functioning should a disaster occur. Now, with the COVID-19 virus, these plans have come to fruition and require extending.

All operations in India matrix to her in the areas of Produce Business Impact Assessments, Identify business-critical activities, Undertake Risk Assessments, Develop Business Continuity Plans, Test BC Plans plus other related activities.

Vamini is considered an expert in her field with a high performing team located across Asia. Vamini's counterpart is Nerida, based in New York City.

Vamini has established that the business unit requires third party support to maintain business-critical activities and plans on negotiating at the next global meeting to have a global vendor provide these services, based in India, and managed by her. Vamini knows that Nerida is very smart and carefully prepares a budget, implementation strategy, and negotiation.

The risk to Vamini is that the plan would work equally well if based in the US. Vamini gathers her global key stakeholders and before the negotiation presents the strategy, including the budget and implementation plan.

At the global meeting, the issue is placed on the agenda for 'discussion'. Vamini knows that this is a full-scale negotiation. Vamini has calculated all potential risks and has contingencies at hand. She has also armed herself with indicative proposals from vendors from India, USA, China, UAE, and the UK. She does not want to be seen in an India vs. USA contest. In a balanced presentation, she presents her case.

The negotiation goes to plan.

Nerida was advised that this topic was on the agenda, however has done little to prepare and only brings floor plans of another unused building in New Jersey that could be used to house the new site.

Vamini holds the power in the negotiation, presenting with confidence in an unbiased business approach. The decision is made to move forward with locating the new site in India and proceeding to the next step of evaluating global vendors with a strong presence in India.

Activity 25 - Reflection – Negotiation Situation

Reflect on a negotiation situation where you did not persist and where you agreed to an outcome that you were not entirely committed to.

What was the negotiation situation?	
What didn't you persist in this negotiation?	
What was the outcome?	
What would you do differently next time?	

Variable 2 – Time

Time will always be an important part of the negotiation process. Any commercial decision or course of action will be bound by deadlines and timeframes which must be adhered to. While deadlines provide structure and context for a negotiation, the amount of time available can significantly affect the outcome.

Where there is an appropriate timeframe allocated to the negotiation process, all parties have the opportunity to prepare, to research, and to gather relevant information before making any decisions and concessions. Where there is limited time allocated to the negotiation, one or more of the parties may be forced to decide without having time to prepare.

> "We must use time as a tool, not as a crutch."
>
> John F Kennedy

Time may be used strategically by either party to force the opposing party into a decision without adequate preparation or information. When entering into a negotiation, we don't always know the opposing party's deadline, and similarly, they may not know ours.

This can give either party the upper hand, depending on who has the most time available for making a decision or taking a course of action. When pressured by a deadline, either party may make concessions that they would not usually make if more time were available.

It's important to open the negotiation with questions that relate to time, such as:

- How much time have you allowed in your schedule for today's meeting?
- By what date are you hoping to have (this) delivered/installed/signed/authorized/etc.

Given that the negotiation process can begin weeks or even months before the actual negotiation taking place, it is essential to plan a negotiation timeline to maximize preparation time.

Activity 26 - Negotiation Timeline Planner

Using an upcoming negotiation that you have to prepare and to research relevant information before sitting down at the negotiating table.

Timeline	Preparation/research that I could undertake at this time
Day of Negotiation	
One Week Prior	
Two Weeks Prior	
One Month Prior	

Variable 3 – Information

The final critical variable is information. Information is the basis of both legitimate and expert power and is fundamental to our success in the negotiation process.

We have already discussed the importance of research in the negotiation process, whereby you investigate and collate relevant information to support your view. This information may include statistical data, product reports, industry trends, or any number of other supporting documentation. Typically these would be referred to as formal information channels and are useful in establishing legitimate and expert power.

However, informal information channels are also critical to the negotiation process. This is the information that you collect informally on your opposition and gives you crucial insight into their position in the negotiation process. Any information you can source informally allows you to prepare in advance, and to match any concessions with the perceived interests of the other party. It may also provide you with information about the negotiation styles of the other parties, or give access to their deadlines and timeframes.

Often this type of information is sourced via industry or corporate grapevine, colleagues, customers, suppliers, or any other source with whom you interact on the issue at hand. For example, a casual conversation with a supplier alerts you that one of the key players in an upcoming negotiation is scheduled to take vacation leave the following week. Knowing that it is more common to make concessions when pressed for time, planning the negotiation a few days before the opponent's vacation may favor you in any negotiation outcome.

Decision Making Influencers

People often make decisions based on three common factors; finance, time, and resources. By understanding the importance of each of these factors, we can better equip ourselves for a negotiation.

Finance

The financial position of both parties is critical to any negotiation. Finance is the broad term we use to define how much we are willing to pay, or how much we are willing to lose as a result of the negotiation. The finance available establishes the upper and lower limits for both parties and sets the boundaries for the negotiation.

While it is not always possible to know the financial position of the other parties in a negotiation, a smart negotiator will be able to determine if this is the most important element in the negotiation, or whether price/cost can be used as a concession to achieve some greater interest.

When negotiating with an external company to your own, research their website and other publicly accessible information sources, such as stock exchange reports, annual reports, and brochures, and so on.

Time

We have already discussed the issue of time in some detail. If time is critical to either party in a negotiation, then it is likely that concessions in cost or resources may be made to achieve an immediate outcome. A skilled negotiator must determine how important time is in the negotiation process and how significant an impact this will have on the result of the negotiation.

Resources

The resources available during a negotiation can often be the ruling factor in a negotiation outcome.

Resources is not about the number of people at the negotiation table, but the amount of human and capital resources available to complete the project or tasks being negotiated. When one party has greater access to resources, they have increased power in influencing the outcome of the negotiation.

Prioritizing the three factors

When entering the negotiations, we should always prioritize these three factors – finance, time, and resources, and identify which is most important.

By prioritizing our decision making influencers, we are better able to control the negotiation and know where we can and can't make concessions. Where possible, it is also useful to know the priorities and interests of our opponents so we can predict where they, too, will be more open to making concessions.

Activity 27 - Decision Making Influencers

Using the same negotiation situation as previously identified, list the three decision making influencers according to their perceived level of importance. Identify why you have ranked them in this order.

Decision Making influence	Ranking	Reasoning
Finances	1----2----3	
Time	1----2----3	
Resources	1----2----3	

Now try to determine how your opponent might rate each of these factors and identify where they may make some concessions in their negotiation.

Decision Making influence	Ranking	Reasoning
Finances	1----2----3	
Time	1----2----3	
Resources	1----2----3	

"He who has learned to disagree
without being disagreeable has
discovered the most valuable secret of
a diplomat."

Robert Estabrook

Dealing with Negotiating Tactics

In recent times, negotiation has aimed to focus on creative collaboration and principled negotiation, rather than traditional confrontation, or winner–takes-all result.

The new and ideal aim of negotiations is for those involved in the negotiation process **to seek and develop new ways of arriving at a better collaborative outcome** by thinking creatively and working in cooperation with the other side. Negotiating should develop a 'partnership' approach – not an adversarial one.

Every negotiation, when viewed creatively, entrepreneurially, and collaboratively, **provides an excellent opportunity to develop and improve synergies between and benefiting both sides**, within the negotiated outcome. That said, it is still essential to understand and to master the traditional techniques and principles of negotiation, if only to provide a defense and strategy where the other side is firmly committed to an old-style confrontational approach.

When the other party is more powerful

Often negotiators will establish a "bottom line" in an attempt to protect themselves against a poor agreement. The bottom line is what the party anticipates as the worst acceptable outcome. Negotiators decide in advance of actual negotiations to reject any proposal below that line. Because the bottom line outcome is decided upon in advance of discussions, the outcome may be arbitrary or unrealistic.

Having already committed oneself to a rigid bottom line also inhibits inventiveness in generating options. Having a "bottom line" isn't the best option and should rarely be used in negotiations.

Instead, the weaker party should concentrate on assessing their **Best Alternative to a Negotiated Agreement (BATNA).** The whole reason we negotiate a deal is to obtain a better outcome than what we would typically receive. The weaker party should always reject agreements that would leave them worse off than their BATNA.

BATNA is the acronym for "Best
Alternative To a Negotiated
Agreement" and was coined by Roger
Fisher, Bill Ury and Bruce Patton in the
book Getting To Yes

Without a clear idea of their BATNA, a party negotiates blindly. The BATNA is also the key to making the most of existing assets. Power in a negotiation comes from the ability to walk away from the negotiations. Thus the party with the best BATNA is the more powerful party in the talks.

Developing your BATNA will give you a clear idea of what your least possible productive outcome is and will minimize unwanted concessions.

When the other party won't use principled negotiation

Principled negotiation is when the principles surrounding the negotiation are determined and agreed upon. These are the ground rules of the negotiation and are established and committed to by each party before the negotiation taking place. A principle negotiation is more likely to result in a win/win outcome.

Positional bargaining occurs when the negotiating parties "stick to their guns" and only listen to facts that benefit their position. This is an emotional method of negotiating and looks only at each party's perception of the issues, not their real interests in achieving a mutually acceptable outcome. It is counter-productive 'them versus us' mentality.

Approaches to deal with positional bargaining

There are three approaches to dealing with an opponent who refuses to participate in principled negotiation.

1. Continue to adhere to the principled approach

Continue to use the principled approach no matter how persistent the other party is in pursuing positional bargaining. Continuing to use the principled approach is somewhat contagious. After a while, the opposing party will transition its approach from the positional to the principled approach.

Persistence is one of the keys in negotiations, and often the most persistent opponent wins. Of course, the 'win' is only if a favorable outcome is agreed on by both parties.

2. Negotiation Jujitsu

The principle party may use 'negotiation jujitsu' to bring the other party in line. The key to this technique is to refuse to respond to a positional attack and to deflect such attacks by continuing to address the issues at hand.

For example, calmly asking questions and exploring the reasons behind their position, inviting constructive feedback, and seeking advice where necessary. Personal attacks should be recast as attacks on the problem. Generally, the principled party should use questions and strategic silences to draw the other party out. By utilizing questions to your benefit, you are not only gaining more information but diffusing the personal attacks.

3. One-text approach

In this approach, a third party is brought in to conciliate and to determine what the underlying interests of each party are. The third party then assembles a list of benefits and asks each side for their comments and criticisms of the list. Those comments are then taken and analyzed, and a proposal is created. The plan is given to the parties for comment, redrafted, and returned for further input. This process continues until the third party feels that no further improvements can be made. At that point, the parties must decide whether to accept the refined proposal or to abandon negotiations.

When the other party uses unfair negotiation tactics

Sometimes parties will use unethical or unpleasant tricks in an attempt to gain an advantage in a negotiation. Such tactics include the good guy/bad guy routine, creating an uncomfortable negotiating environment, leaks to a media, or a deliberate deception about the facts, their authority, or their intentions.

The best way to protect against this tactic is to seek clarification of the other side's claims. It may help to ask them for further evidence or to put the request in writing.

Another common tactic is personal attacks. However, personal attacks can be made less effective by merely recognizing them for what they are.

Explicitly identifying them to the offending party often puts an end to such attacks. The principle negotiator should ignore them where possible or undertake principled negotiations on the use of threats in the proceedings.

Activity 28 - Strategies for Combating Negotiation Tactics

For each of the negotiation tactics listed below, identify how you would manage this tactic in a real-life negotiation.

Negotiation Tactic	Strategy For Managing This Tactic
Positional bargaining	
Misrepresentation of facts	
Psychological warfare	
Threats	

> "If you don't get what you want, it's a sign either that you did not seriously want it, or that you tried to bargain over the price."
>
> Rudyard Kipling

Maintaining the Negotiation Relationship

Fighting fires without burning bridges

Negotiation is not a competitive sport, and unless the parties collaborate to reach an agreement, even short term solutions may fall apart. Good negotiating isn't about winning, and it isn't about someone else losing. Good consulting is about both sides leaving feeling they got what they wanted, or at least better off than when they went in.

Unsuccessful negotiating is when either side feels they've compromised too much, given way when they didn't want to, felt undue pressure, felt threatened, made sacrifices they didn't want to. In those situations, the other party might believe they've won and go away feeling good about themselves; but this is not genuinely successful negotiating. They may have won in the short-term, but the other party will never trust them again and may not want to repeat the experience. As the cliché says, "they may have won the battle, but they won't have won the war."

Effective negotiations occur when each party understands the other's interests, and through collaboration, both parties reach a mutually acceptable solution. Cooperation, not competitiveness, accommodation, or compromise is the key to building long term relationships and optimizing results. It is important to remember that negotiation is often a series of episodes, which means that considering your counterpart as a partner or a collaborator is the foundation of trusting and fruitful – and ongoing – negotiation, how the game is played matters more than who wins.

> Treating one's counterparts as an opponent rather than a partner in a collaborative process decreases the likelihood of reaching an agreement that contains the fundamental element of commitment.

When you accept that almost every negotiation is an episode in an ongoing relationship, you also recognize that, while a party may get better results in the first instance, he or she may not get more the next time the two of you negotiate. You don't always negotiate with the very same individuals or organizations. However, a substantial proportion of your negotiation partners are "repeaters," and ongoing success of the negotiation process is dependent on the history and status of your relationship.

> "The most basic of all human needs is the need to understand and be understood. The best way to understand people is to listen to them."
>
> Ralph Nichols

Creative ways to achieve win/win

The challenge is to find creative ways to satisfy both you and your opponent and to make the ultimate win/win outcome. The following are some helpful tips to assist you in building effective negotiating relationships.

Differentiate between positions and interests

If you can figure out why you want something – and why others want something – then you are looking at interests. Interests are building blocks of lasting agreements and relationships.

Be creative

Anyone can do things the same old way. Using brainstorming techniques, listening to outlandish proposals, and opening up to unanticipated possibilities, expand agreement opportunities. If you respond with new ideas and do the unexpected, you can open doors to far more significant gains that when you behave predictably. Creativity can make everyone look good.

Be fair

If people feel a process is fair, they are more likely to make real commitments and less likely to walk away, planning ways to wriggle out of the agreement. Sometimes things are helped when a neutral, external authority (Standards) are used to measure fairness – a dictionary, a lab test, or an academic article, for instance.

Be prepared to commit

You shouldn't commit unless you can fulfill it. Your commitment isn't worth much unless the parties to the negotiation are Drop-Dead Decision-Makers. Moreover, commitment is not likely to result unless all parties feel the process has been fair.

Be an active listener

Communication takes place when information passes from a source to a receiver. If you spend all of your listening time planning how to respond to the other party, then, when they finally stop talking, you haven't heard them. Focus on what others say, both on their words and their underlying meaning. This will help you understand the interests upon which agreement can be based. When your response makes it clear that you've really been listening (and after the other party gets over the initial shock), they, too, maybe more prepared to listen. Active listening can change the rules of the game and raise the level of civility in the negotiation.

Be conscious of the importance of the relationship
Most of your negotiation is with repeaters (people you run across time after time, such as your spouse and children). If you understand the relative priority of the relationship, it can be easier to know when giving in on a particular point may yield short term cost but long term gains.

Separate the people from the problem
Religion teaches us to hate the sin, not the sinner. If we view the problem as that which needs to be resolved rather than seeing someone holding a contrary viewpoint as a person to be defeated, the odds of a successful collaboration increase.

Only one person can get angry at a time
This is yet another means to help individuals keep a cool head and pay attention to the process and the strategy, as well as the substance of the negotiation. If it's not your 'turn' to be angry, the activity of restraint can be turned into a positive opportunity to observe what is going on with a clear eye. No less important, yelling at each other is not negotiation; it is confrontation. In those situations, there may be a 'winner,' but it is even more likely there will be a 'loser.'

Activity 29 - Negotiation Reflection

Identify a person/party that you negotiate with on a regular basis and answer the following questions:

Negotiation Reflection	Notes
Identify how your current relationship helps or hinders the negotiation process i.e., how you interact and communicate.	
Identify how your current relationship helps or hinders the negotiation outcome i.e. the result of the negotiation.	
Identify how you could improve the negotiation relationship to better serve both parties.	

Case Study X - Collaborative Negotiation

There is a classic scene in the famous award-winning film Erin Brokovich when the unemployed single mother who becomes a legal assistant almost single-handedly brings down a California Power Company accused of polluting a city's water supply.

When the PG & E lawyers come to Ed Masry's office to negotiate a settlement for the people affected by the polluted water, four PG & E lawyers walk into the board room.

To equal the numbers, Ed Masry and Erin Brokovich recruit the receptionist and the mail boy to join their team and even the numbers in the board room.

They are poised for a classic David and Goliath fight, that they believe they have no hope of winning. Although there is serious evidence to show the water supply is severely polluted.

You may recall this classic line:

> Erin Brokovich giving a glass of water to the PG & E lawyers, Ms. Sanchez: "By the way, we had that water brought in especially for you folks. Came from a well in Hinkley."

> Ms. Sanchez: [Puts down the glass, without drinking] I think this meeting is over.

> Ed Masry: Damn right it is.

What Erin Brokovich knew was in high stakes negotiation, creating your team to equal the size of your opposition team makes good sense.

With global virtual teams, it may not always be possible to physically have your specific people on the ground for the physical negotiations. However, a strategy you may use within your organization is to recruit a group of allies in the particular negotiation process.

Case Study Y - Big Contract

Let's assume that you are negotiating a big contract for your organization, and there are four or five components to this significant deal. Play to your strengths.

By selecting people on the ground that are very knowledgeable in these four or five areas and can answer tough questions in their specific fields, you are increasing your chances of fielding all questions and presenting a professional team effort; without you necessarily needing to know everything about the five components.

Obviously, you will need to bring your group of people together for role-playing before the negotiation meeting. And you will need to be very specific about the likely issues that the 'opposition' may have. Each team member is then allocated one key area of expertise, and any questions that are asked about that specific area will be deferred to that expert.

If by chance, a question is asked outside of those areas, you would then have your assistant (who is sitting beside you) makes a note of the issue and advise that a response would be given later that day. With everyone agreeing on their roles, and the more significant objective of winning the contract, growing the organization as well as securing everyone's job for the future, a team effort would be presented at the meeting - this is your game plan.

During the meeting, as questions are asked, you defer to the expert in that specific area. This is collaboration at its best. When the deal is won, be sure to acknowledge the part your 'crack team' played in the success of the negotiations.

There may also be times with your virtual teams where the agreement needs to be reached where you expect the negotiations to be controversial. Remember how the game is played matters more than who wins. If you are a new leader, your counterparts will be observing how you manage these negotiations. We know as a leader that there will be times when you have to make tough, unpopular decisions. Allow all parties a chance to present their case.

Your best strategy pre-meeting is preparation. Know exactly who will be involved and who has the power, perceived or otherwise. And, based on this knowledge prepare for the negotiation to counter that perception with either facts or data, or other people with a greater perception of power. Do your homework. You must know before you go into the meeting who has your back and who is undecided and, most of all, who is totally against your decision or need for change.

You do not want any surprises in a negotiation situation. Far better to be over-prepared than under-prepared. As you progress your career, observe strategies when you are part of negotiations and not leading them yourself. Watch how people respond to positive, influential leaders with a vision. What can you learn from these situations?

Whether you intend to collaborate across continents or from one side of the city to another, you will need to be very clear on why you will work and what you want to achieve. Our lives are filled with informal collaborations and alliances e.g., going to a doctor, hairdresser, restaurant, dentist, attending a course, or booking a holiday. We base our decisions on trust in the service provider either from prior contact or referrals. This is sometimes referred to as the trilogy of trust – the belief that one person has in another that is passed on to the third party. For example, John has worked with you before, knows, likes and trusts you and knows you can complete a project on time, within budget, and without any major dramas.

When new projects come up, your name is often top of mind with John. And as you progress your career, you will have a shortlist of people from your virtual teams who you trust as much as John believes you. Many times throughout your job, you will come to crossroads, where it is impossible to complete a project by yourself. You will need to collaborate to complete the project and achieve the desired outcomes.

Again preparation is everything when it comes to collaborations though the effort is well worth it.

Benefits of Collaboration

When collaboration is used to address multiparty problems, several advantages are possible.

- Broad, comprehensive analysis of the problem domain improves the quality of solutions
- Response capability is more diversified
- It is useful for reopening deadlocked negotiations
- The risk of the impasse is minimized
- The process ensures that each stakeholder's interest are considered in any agreement
- Parties retain ownership of the solution
- Parties more familiar with the problem, not their agents, invent the solutions
- Participation enhances acceptance of the solution and willingness to implement it
- The potential to discover novel, innovative solutions are enhanced
- Relations between the stakeholders improve
- Costs associated with other methods are avoided
- Mechanisms for coordinating future actions among the stakeholders can be established.

Collaboration and Control

The process of collaborating builds in certain guarantees that each party's interests will be protected. It does so by continually remanding ownership of the process and any decisions reached to the parties themselves. Parties often assume that by collaborating, they will lose any individual leverage they have over the problem. This concern about the loss of control is deceptive. It is rare in any multiparty conflict that any party satisfies 100% of their interests and incurs no costs while the other parties gain nothing. Collaborative processes protect each party's interest by guaranteeing that they are heard and understood. Also, the methods are structured to ensure that ownership of the solution remains with the participants since agreement hinges on their reaching agreement among themselves.

> Instead of trying to restrict participation, a common tactic, the professional manager gains more control over the situation by ensuring that all the necessary parties are there at the table, recognizing that parties in a dispute often engage in adversarial behavior because no other approach is available to protect their interests. [Carpenter and Kennedy, 1988[20]]

Parties retain control during collaboration precisely because they must be the ones to adopt or reject the final agreement.

Realities of Collaboration

There are many circumstances in which stakeholders are unable or unwilling to engage each other in this way. Collaboration is not always an appropriate alternative. For example, when one party has unchallenged power to influence a domain, partnership does not make sense. Nor is collaboration an idealistic panacea. Realistically, collaboration involves difficult issues that have often used simple solutions in the past. Many multiparty problems are political because they include "distributional" effects. In distributional disputes, the stakeholders are concerned about the allocation of funds, the setting of standards, or facilities.

---

[20] Carpenter, S.L. and W.J.D. Kennedy (1988), Managing Public Disputes: A Practical Guide to Handling Conflict and Reaching Agreements, Jossey-Bass, San Francisco and London.

Stages of the Collaborative Problem Solving Process

A typical collaborative process has three well-defined stages, each containing many steps, tasks or objectives

Problem Solving Process - Overview

Getting Started (Stage One) Pre Deliberation

- Initiate the process – assess issues and stakeholders

- Design a strategy

- Set up a program

Searching for Agreement (Stage Two) Deliberation

- Establish procedures

- Educate each other and specify needed information

- Define the problem

- Generate options

- Develop evaluation criteria

- Evaluate and select options

- Develop a plan

After the Agreement (Stage Three) Post-Deliberation

- Ratify the agreement

- Integrate agreement into formal processes

- Implement the agreement

- Keep avenues open for renegotiation

Problem Solving Process – In Detail

Stage 1: Getting Started: The Pre-Deliberation Phase

A stakeholder or a trusted outsider raises the possibility of collaboration and initiates the process. Following initiation, the pre-deliberation, or planning stage, should be carried out with a group of stakeholders who are knowledgeable about, and committed to the issue and are willing to participate in the process from the beginning. During this stage, the objectives of the collaborative process are to:

- Initiate the process – assess issues and stakeholders

    - Identify conditions for collaboration.

    - Develop a clear description of the issues that need to be addressed.

- Frame the problem as a joint search for resolution of the issue: "How can we...?"

- Identify Stakeholders

    - Determine what (or whose) interests are at stake.

    - Identify who can affect - and who is affected by - the issue

    - Contact stakeholders and determine their needs for participating in a collaborative process.

- Design a strategy

    - Consider the most productive format: committee, negotiating team, or conference format.

    - Agree on process steps.

    - Identify roles and who might fill them: chairperson, facilitator, recorder, technical resources, meeting logistics, etc.

    - Plan your time frame.

- Set up a program

    - Decide on logistical details: where and when to meet, agenda, etc.

    - Draft the meeting ground rules and protocols (also called a group charter, meeting plan, or convening document).

Stage 2: Searching for Agreement: The Deliberation Stage

Once all the stakeholders have been contacted, the first meeting convened, and the protocols ratified, the participants can begin to deliberate the substantive issues.

- Establish procedures

    - With the whole group, ratify the meeting ground rules and protocols drafted in the planning phase. Make changes where necessary.

- Educate each other

    - Share concerns related to the topic.

    - Identify what is given.

    - Identify what is understood.

    - Identify sub-issues.

    - Identify and share interests -- reasons, needs, concerns and motivations underlying participants' positions --rather than assert positions.

- Define the problem

    - Define the present situation.

    - Define the desired future.

- Specify information needs

- Identify technical background information that is pertinent to the issue.
- Identify the information that is available and information that is needed.
- Agree on methods for generating answers to relevant technical questions, or a path to follow even if no technical consensus exists.

- Educate each other (again, and whenever it is needed)
    - Field trips.
    - Collecting data/soliciting reports.
    - Briefings.
    - Interviews.

- Generate options
    - Use task forces for larger groups.
    - Bring in the public.
    - Brainstorm.
    - Use expert opinion.

- Develop criteria for option evaluation
    - Feasibility
    - Fairness
    - Efficiency

- Evaluate options
    - Priority matrix
    - Goal achievement.

- Reach agreements
    - Building block
    - Single text
    - Agreement in principle

- Develop a written plan
    - Document areas of agreement to ensure a common understanding of the participants' accord.
    - Develop a plan of action: what, how, when, where, who.

Stage 3: After the Agreement is reached: The Post-Deliberation Phase

Once an acceptable solution has been identified, it must be approved and implemented by all responsible parties. During Stage 3, the objectives of the collaborative process are to:

- Ratify the agreement

    - Parties get support for the plan from organizations that have a role in carrying it out.

    - Each organization follows its internal procedures as it reviews and adopts the plan.

- Integrate the agreement into the public decision-making process

    - Governing bodies and agencies not directly included in the process have been kept informed during earlier phases of the process.

    - The plan is considered and acted upon by the relevant agencies and governing bodies for implementation.

    - Implement the agreement

    - Maintain communication and collaboration as the plan is carried out.

    - Monitor your results.

    - Renegotiate, if necessary.

    - Celebrate your success

Negotiating Checklist for Success

> "I'm not upset that you lied to me; I'm upset that from now on, I can't believe you."
>
> Friedrich Nietzsche

- It's important that both the issue (the task at hand) and the relationship (the desire to do business again) are in balance.

- If the balance is right, there will be an emotional commitment to the deal and its implementation

- Tactfully question

- Observe carefully

- Ensure mutual understanding

- Be empathic and assertive

- Another side are people just like you

- Focus on the issue, not the person
- Usually, if people do not feel good about how they performed, they will not feel committed to the deal
- Balance emotion with reason
- Actively listen
- Don't buy the relationship
    - Always represent your organization – keep true to the organizational values
    - 10/10 is not always the optimal outcome
    - Understand Positions
    - Be Flexible
    - Hold onto the big points and Plan!

Key Points Summary

- By understanding our negotiation opponent, we are more likely to walk away from negotiations with the majority of what we set out to accomplish.

- The three crucial variables of power, time, and information will always be an asset to our negotiation toolbox. The knowledge of the types of power and how each one will benefit us, as well as our opponent going into negotiations, is knowledge most opponents are familiar with.

- Remembering that negotiations begin far in advance of the day, everyone sits at the table is a crucial element to a successful negotiation. Gather as much information on your opponent as possible. What seems to be a casual conversation may yield essential facts.

- We all have negotiations with individuals and other business units who we can't afford to sever relationships. Now that you are prepared with the tools to help you keep those relationships intact, you will be a more formidable negotiator when the time comes.

PART 7
LOOKING AFTER YOU
AND YOUR VIRTUAL
LEADERSHIP CAREER

Are you the VIP in your life?

Are you the Virtual VIP in your life?

Virtual Leaders are too often experts at emotionally putting themselves down. And during the COVID-19 crisis working from the comfort of their home, self-doubt can creep into their lives/minds at the most inconvenient times. Just when they are about to chair an important meeting or present their report to senior management or attempt something for the first time, that niggling doubt can take over. Your self-talk might sound something like this:

- "What if I can't do this, what if they laugh at me and tell me my report is hogwash?"

- "This is it; they (management) are going to realize I have no clue what I am doing. My secret will be out. I will be fired today!"

- "I know I am going to forget what I am talking about during my presentation or someone will ask me a question I don't know the answer to, what will I do?"

- "I'm not as valuable as my counterparts. Since coronavirus, management will see through this, and I'll be stood down."

Rest assured, you are not alone. Most of us experience these moments of doubts regularly. Believe it or not, most people's self-worth goes up and down all day every day. Yet very few of them talk about it.

This book would not be complete without addressing this critical issue. Self-esteem is also an issue for everyone as well, and they possibly have different strategies for dealing with their self-doubt.

Why this is essential for the Virtual leaders?

Once we have assessed the areas that need work, we will then give you some strategies to work on this. However, we must stress that building your self-worth is a journey, NOT a destination. Even with working on these individual areas, you still may find now and then, that niggling self-esteem doubt voice does come back. However, the strategies we discuss in this chapter will allow you to continually turn the volume down on your self-doubt voice.

Activity 30 -   Personal Power Assessment

Understanding how to identify when you are putting yourself down, handling the put-downs from others, and undermining your confidence and choosing to discontinue this habit is critical for you to step into your leadership role. This assessment looks at identifying your confidence and self-esteem building skill needs to improve your ability to lead virtual teams confidently without self-doubt.

This assessment is for your personal use to help you determine your current strengths and areas of development.

For each question, rate yourself on each of the techniques.

Personal Power Assessment	1 Never	2 Rarely	3 Sometimes	4 Most of the Time	5 Always
I am always confident in public forums or social events.					
I am good at accepting compliments from my peers.					
I always know I am competent enough to do my job.					
I am grateful that I have been given this leadership role.					
I know I have the respect of my peers and management.					
My confidence is always 10/10.					
I am on track to achieving all the career goals I wish to complete.					
I know I have the ability to complete any task I am given in my current job.					
I am a strong communicator.					
I know I am a great leader. I believe in myself.					
I am very clear what success means to me.					
I am well organized.					
TOTAL					

Please total your scores and list them for Never, Rarely, Sometimes, Most of the time, and Always. All of the skills above are necessary to lead virtual teams and will be explored in this and later chapters.

Reflecting on your answers

Congratulations on all the statements that you answered, 'Most of the time' and 'Always.' Please don't worry, though, if you scored high on the 'Never,' 'Rarely,' or 'Sometimes' columns. This book will guide you through the maze of virtual leadership and give you strategies to significantly improve the skills you have identified.

Based on the self-esteem and confidence assessment, we have listed each skill assessed and included tips and strategies for you to improve your skill in this area.

Confidence – the foundation of Virtual Leadership

Confidence is an inside job. No amount of anyone telling you that you are a great leader, brilliant manager, or a particular person can make a difference. Until you believe in yourself, your self-confidence will not improve.

> "We're told that 20,000 times a day
> we speak to ourselves and 19,000
> times a day it's negative."
>
> A recipe for dreaming,
> Bryce Courtenay.

If we compare our confidence and self-esteem to a glass of water full to the brim, then every time we put ourselves down, we lose an amount of liquid from the glass. If we are really having a bad day and continually putting ourselves down, then by the end of the day, there is not much water left in the glass. Plus, our confidence will be close to rock bottom.

Often our posture reflects that feeling of low self-worth. Our shoulders are hunched, our head is slumped, our voice is flat – overall, we are feeling very ordinary.

To have been given the opportunity to lead your virtual team, senior management definitely believes in you. They looked at your resume and saw you're potential. Often great leaders see other people's potential long before the individual does. As a result, sometimes, you are given a promotion or career move that is a stretch.

But until you start believing in you, no one else will believe in you either.

Activity 31 - Personal Skills Analysis

I invite you to complete a personal skills analysis. It's time to look in the mirror – at all the things you like about yourself and the areas you'd like to improve. By being blatantly honest, you'll be able to celebrate the things you want, and decide if you'd like to start a plan to improve on your areas for development.

10 things you like about you:

1.

2.

3.

4.

5.

6.

7.

8.

9.

10.

10 things you would like to improve about you:

1.

2.

3.

4.

5.

6.

7.

8.

9.

10.

Without putting yourself under more pressure, what are three things you can work on in the next 60 days to improve yourself?

1.

2.

3.

Please note these activities are not intended to stress you or create more pressure for you. They are designed to highlight your excellence and the gifts and skills you already have. The more you value you, and the contributions and skills you have, the higher your confidence will be.

List 10 things that you are good at (no matter how small or insignificant you think that skills are):

1.

2.

3.

4.

5.

6.

7.

8.

9.

10.

Daily Reflection

A daily habit that we would encourage you to introduce is a brief reflection at the end of the day:

WHAT WAS MY WIN FOR THE DAY?

What worked well for me today? What challenges did I overcome? Did I avoid over-reacting to a situation? Am I proud of the way I resolved something today?

The more you acknowledge what you do well, the higher your self-esteem will grow. So developing this daily habit – is a straightforward and quick tool to assist this process.

Accepting Compliments

Many managers are masters at dismissing compliments. You might identify with these examples:

1. "Yuan, that was an excellent report, you crunched the numbers and highlighted where we have been going wrong."

"I've always been good with numbers, and the report was nothing."

Just because you are great with numbers, does not mean that you should dismiss the compliment. Far better to respond:

"Thanks John yes I was really pleased with my report too."

2. "Gina that color suits you. You look fantastic today. "

"This outfit is ancient; really, I have had it for years."

Yes, your outfit may not be new, but that does not mean that you don't look fantastic. Far better to respond:

"Thanks, John, it's one of my favorites."

3. "Juanita, congratulations on your promotion. I am delighted that you got the position."

"Thanks, John, I was sure Susan would get the job, she is so much better than me."

Even if that is your opinion, you are only undermining your reputation, responding in that fashion. Far better to respond:

"Thanks, John, I am looking forward to putting my stamp on the position."

> Most of the time THANK YOU is all that
> you need to say when you receive a
> compliment.

Being Competent to do your Job

Leaders are regularly stretched beyond their comfort zone. Often because their potential is observed and nurtured by their managers and leaders. Stepping up is part of accepting a promotion. Very few people apply for career moves where the position is a backward career move. Though few people are selected for jobs that they cannot do.

The bottom line, you would not have applied for the job if you did not think you could do it.

START BELIEVING IN YOU, STOP
DOUBTING YOURSELF!

If you have identified a couple of skills deficits, then up-skill via a course or webinar or on-line learning. Or ask someone very skilled in that specific area to spend some time with you and coach you. Everything can be learned, and the more you work at something, the better you will become at that skill.

Gratitude in a Virtual Leadership role

One of the quickest ways we can start to improve your self-esteem and self-confidence is by developing a gratitude attitude. Start to acknowledge the things in your world that you are grateful for.

Activity 32 - ACHIEVE LIST

Let's start with an **AM-CAN-HAVE** gratitude list today:

I am grateful that I am:

1.

2.

3.

I am grateful that I can:

1.

2.

3.

I am grateful that I have:

1.

2.

3.

Be aware though, a gratitude attitude does not revolve around possessions! The latest car or biggest house does not necessarily make you a better or happier person.

THINGS CANNOT MAKE YOU HAPPY –

ONLY YOU CAN MAKE YOU TRULY
HAPPY

Writing a Gratitude Journal

A simple activity you may introduce daily is at the end of the day to write down ten things you are grateful for. Start each sentence with the phrase – "I am grateful that…." or "I am grateful for…"

If there is anything troubling, take the time to write a page about that problem. Writing helps you to clarify the situation.

This is also a great system to share with your virtual team. Even when there are problems and challenges, being grateful for those learning opportunities is a great way of getting things into perspective.

Ideas for implementing this might be to include this activity into virtual team meetings, discussion boards, chat etc.

Respect of Peers and Management

Leadership is NOT a popularity contest. If you want everyone to like you and accept all the decisions you make without question, you are in the wrong role. It is futile and a waste of energy that you would expect everyone to like you. Many times throughout your career, you will have to make decisions that will be unpopular with your virtual team. People may not like you; however, they will respect you for standing up for what you believe in, making tough decisions, and being fair to all.

Respect of peers and management is earned not given. Remember, people may not like you, but they will respect you.

- Practice what you preach – you need to meet the same standards consistently
- Be authentic and trustworthy
- Do what you say and say what you do
- Take responsibility for your own decisions and actions
- Do not blame others for your mistakes
- Demonstrate integrity and encourage and value it in others
- Establish consequences of not meeting your expectations
- Using this list as a guide is guaranteed to earn you respect from your peers and management.

You are not your job!

Always remember you are not your job — you are a person currently working or employed as a _____

Your self-esteem does not need to be linked to your work — in fact, many readers, in addition to their paid or unpaid work are:

Mothers, fathers, sisters, brothers, daughters, sons, cousins, aunts, uncles, grandmothers, grandfathers, lovers, partners, girlfriends, boyfriends, soul mates, neighbors, friends, volunteers, helpers, carers, chauffeurs, teachers checking homework, teachers home-schooling, bookkeepers balancing the family budget, cleaners, books, ironers, home-makers, builders, painters, and the list goes on.

What other roles do you currently do, that are not included in your paid work?

Phew, no wonder some days you are exhausted.

Remember, you are
NOT your job.

10/10 Confidence

What would a 10/10 day look like to you?

A 10/10 day might not include winning the lottery or having a significant windfall. However, until you know what a 10/10 day looks like to you, it's hard to imagine everything going to plan in your life.

The reality is that no one has a 10/10 day every day. Many of the things that happen in our life are out of our control. Major clients change their product range, affecting our supply chain. International natural disasters impact and devastate cities and towns — totally beyond our control.

CEOs, General Managers, and other key stakeholders make decisions that impact your team and even your position — again, something that is out of your control.

Would you believe that every day could be a 10/10 day in your life – if you want it to be? This does not mean you have to settle for less, purely appreciate what it is that you have.[21]

Activity 33 - Plotting Self-Confidence

On a scale of 1 to 10, where is your self-confidence today? (0 being depleted of any self-confidence, 10 being having the feeling that you can conquer any challenges that come your way)

0_____5_____10

So what has contributed to that score today?

1.

2.

3.

Out of the 3 things you have listed, how many of these things did you really have any control over?

What would have to happen for you to feel 8/10 or even 9/10 on a regularly basis – 80% of the time?

1.

2.

3.

Remember confidence and self esteem are inside jobs. Only YOU can raise or increase your self esteem and your confidence.

If you knew you could not fail what would you like to achieve:

In the next 12 months

In the next 2 years

In the next 5 years

In the next 10 years

---

[21] Adapted from Dare to Dream – self-esteem and confidence building for busy women by Robyn Henderson

The Superwoman / Superman Syndrome is alive and well and often takes hold of our "to-do lists" on any one day.

Questions to help…..

- Am I realistic about the number of tasks I intend to complete in any one day?

- How are my tasks on my to-do list, contributing to my bigger picture?

- What are the things that I'm doing each week, or two weeks, am I investing in every one of my roles?

- For my neglected roles, what can I do today that is simple and quick to reinvigorate these relationships?

- For each of my virtual team members, what am I doing on a daily or every second day to keep them of paramount importance to my business success?

- Have I set a weekly or fortnightly time with each of my virtual team members, when they know I will connect with them for 10-15 minutes and focus on any queries or challenges they may be having? Knowing this allows them not to sweat the small stuff daily.

- If I feel I am in overload today, what can I do in the next 24 hours to relieve this pressure?

- If one of my virtual teams are in overload and are sending distinct signals of this, how can I assist them to reduce this pressure?

- Is it time to have an "I would like to get to know you better" phone call with a number of my visual team members, whom I know have more potential than they are currently using?

- Have I expressed to my virtual team that this current staff shortage is a temporary situation, and within a month, we will have new staff on board, and the pressure will ease?

- Sometimes we have to slow down to speed up particularly when we are working across different time zones.

Strong Communication Skills

We have covered communication skills extensively in earlier chapters. However, we would like to make one addition to that section

Say No without Feeling Guilty

"No" is a sentence – it does not need extra words or reasons attached.

However, if you are not strong enough at times to say no outright, to unreasonable requests, you may like to use one of the following:

- No, I am not available – but thanks for thinking of me.
- No, I have other commitments at that time.
- No, that time is not available.

As your self worth and confidence grows, you will find that NO becomes a sentence for you also, and you stop thinking that you have to give a reason for saying NO.

Often we want to make the other person feel better about our rejection. Frequently making them feel better, makes us feel worse.

Often we will say –

- "I'll try if I can......."
- "I might......"
- "I'll see if I can...."

Forget it, stop trying to please everyone, just say NO!

Some words you might consider removing from your language:

But	replace with	And
Just a	replace with	I am
I have to	replace with	I choose to
I can't	replace with	I won't
I'll try	replace with	I will

Believing in You as a Virtual Leader

If you don't believe in you, how can you expect others to believe in you?

Energy follows thought. What you think about is what you create in your life. If you see yourself as a leader, that is exactly how others will see you. If you continue to doubt yourself and your ability, you will never gain the respect and recognition you deserve.

Activity 34 -   Believing in yourself

If you are still unsure, ask yourself, what 3 things would have to happen for you to see yourself as a leader – the leader that your bosses know you are capable of being?

1.

2.

3.

THE ME THAT YOU SEE IS THE ME
THAT YOU WILL BE

Defining Virtual Leadership Success

When you are clear what success means in your life, you will know precisely when you achieve it. One of the negative habits many of us have is to dismiss their accomplishments.

- They win awards, are congratulated a month later, and may say, "Thanks, yes, that was last month. Now I am busy doing....."

- "Well done, you achieved your targets for the quarter!"

- "Thanks, yes, I am not sure how I will go for the year though."

Activity 35 - Success Snapshot

So let's take a snapshot of your success to date. This activity may take a little time, take as long as you like.

List 10 of the proudest moments in your life to date:

1

2

3

4

5

6

7

8

9

10

Can you define success in your world in under 30 words:

Do you think you are worthy of success?

If you answered yes, congratulations!

If you answered no, what three things would have to happen for you to be worthy of success?

1   .

2

3

Being Organized – Personal Productivity

In a nutshell, always work with a to-do list and highlight tasks completed as you go. At the end of each day, take ten minutes to create a to-do list for the next day and number the top 5 priority tasks.

The next day work through your top 5 priority tasks before you start other tasks on your to-do. Realistically, you may not complete your to-do list every day. However, most of us have a to-do list with 15 hours of tasks on it and only 8-9 hours to complete the job.

Stay focused, complete one task at a time, and be flexible. If something significant unexpectedly happens, ask yourself, what are the repercussions if this situation is not resolved immediately? If there are no significant repercussions, add the solution to your list and complete the current tasks you are working on.

Share your system with your team so that everyone stays on task as much as possible. The trap we often fall into is continually checking emails – as you know, you can waste/invest an entire day checking emails and complete nothing on your to-do list.

Be the change you want to see in others. Remember –

THE ME THAT YOU SEE IS THE ME
THAT YOU WILL BE

KEY POINTS SUMMARY

- As we progress up the virtual leadership ladder self-doubt can creep into their lives/minds at the most inconvenient times.

- Self-esteem is also an issue for everyone as well, and they possibly have different strategies for dealing with their self-doubt.

- Confidence is an inside job. No amount of anyone telling you that you are a great leader, brilliant manager, or a particular person can make a difference.

- Everything can be learned, and the more you work at something, the better you will become at that skill.

- Practice gratitude. Start to acknowledge the things in your world that you are grateful for.

- The reality is that no one has a 10/10 day every day. Many of the things that happen in our life are out of our control.

- As your self worth and confidence grows, you will find that NO becomes a sentence for you also, and you stop thinking that you have to give a reason for saying NO.

- When you are clear what success means in your life, you will know precisely when you achieve it.

- Stay focused, complete one task at a time, and be flexible.

How to use social media to develop your on-line presence

Why is Social Media Essential for Virtual Leaders?

Social media includes various online technology tools that enable people to communicate easily via the internet. It is used predominantly to share information and resources and is an essential tool for virtual leaders.

Whether you are personally connected via social media, or not, be assured that your virtual team members are. If you are already active in social media, we present this chapter as a refresher and hopefully a spark for some further ideas.

Across most industries the use of social media is accepted, used and enjoyed by both leaders and team members. The main benefits include:

- The ability to network with people in a variety of geographic locations that match team member's locations.
- Knowing what is happening in your team member's locations (new, prominent people, sport results, local events).
- Having a great tool to assist in building your team dynamics across cities and countries.
- Tapping into an instant way of overcoming cultural boundaries.
- Assessing your peers on a national and international basis.
- Building an on-line presence relatively quickly.

Social Media – the definition

According to Wikipedia, 'Six Degrees Of Separation' refers to the idea that everyone is on average approximately six steps away, by way of introduction, from any other person on Earth, so that a chain of "a friend of a friend" statements can be made, on average, to connect any two people in six steps or fewer. It was originally set out by Frigyes Karinthy and popularized by a play written by John Guare.

Thanks now to our wired world of the internet, LinkedIn, Instagram, Facebook and Google; we are generally only two degrees of separation from anyone we want to meet. Creating an online presence is vital as a virtual leader and has never been easier.

Activity 36 - Social Media Online Presence Skills Assessment

Knowing you have limited time available we have created ideas for your social media online presence strategy. Firstly we would encourage you to complete a social media assessment to identify where your weakest links are.

This assessment looks at the key skills in managing your social media online presence in order to improve your leadership profile.

This assessment is for your personal use to help you determine your current strengths and areas of development.

For each question, rate yourself on each of the techniques.

Social Media Online Presence Skills Assessment	1	2	3	4	5
	Never	Rarely	Sometimes	Most of the Time	Always
I have a LinkedIn profile.					
I have spent at least 30 minutes building a comprehensive profile on LinkedIn.					
I have a premium account with LinkedIn and realize the benefits of upgrading my account.					
I regularly publish articles and post to social media.					
I have a professional photograph and use this on my social media profiles.					
I have set up Google and other news alerts, so I keep abreast of daily happenings affecting my profession/industry.					
I use social media to keep up to date with events and news from the geographic locations of each of my virtual team members.					
When speaking with my virtual team members, I can converse about local events and news that is where they are from.					
I use social media to connect with prominent people in the geographic areas where my virtual team is located.					
I have Googled myself in the last 3 months.					
I have a Facebook account.					
I have an Instagram account					
I am meticulous what information I put on Facebook and Instagram as I realize that it is my online resume.					
I follow key leaders in my industry via Twitter/their blog/other outlets.					
Totals					

Please total your scores and list them for Never, Rarely, Sometimes, Most of the time, and Always. All of the skills above are necessary to lead virtual teams and will be explored in this chapters.

Reflecting on your answers

Congratulations on all the statements that you answered, 'Most of the time' and 'Always.' Please don't worry, though, if you scored high on the 'Never,' 'Rarely,' or 'Sometimes' columns. This book will guide you through the maze of virtual leadership and give you strategies to significantly improve the skills you have identified.

Social media for career development

Today, LinkedIn is by far, the best social media career-building profile currently available. Some experts say that Facebook and Instagram are your social profile, and LinkedIn is your career and business profile.

LinkedIn is used regularly by recruiters to find new talent for organizations. Human resources and recruitment firms certainly scan Facebook and Instagram profiles as a standard part of their resume checking these days. So be warned anything that is on your Facebook pages is extensive history for your current employer as well as future employers. Facebook generally stays with you for a lifetime.

Essentials of social media in virtual leadership

The checklist of social media and online news that virtual leaders should have will continue to change as new sites evolve. Sky News and Al Jazeera and other global news networks will give a summary of world news events. Google search with keywords can feed you a regular stream of information about the regions in your virtual team's locations. A Twitter feed can be a continual stream of information.

Virtual leaders can become consumed with keeping up with what is happening on a global or national basis. And we can be bombarded with information 24/7. So everything in moderation.

Reality is that EVERYTHING is public, and virtual team members don't see their virtual manager and leader daily. However, they do have the ability to tune into social media and news sites looking for information on their virtual leaders to get a better understanding of the type of person their manager is.

Expanding your social media and news footprint

So, where do you start?

> You are responsible for your own
> career. You are brand YOU!

When you use social media, ask yourself:

- Is it building your reputation and profile?
- Is it increasing your industry expert status?

Aim to:

- Actively manage your profile.
- Understand that the world revolves around relationships.
- Think about the connections you need to make to achieve your career goals.
- Share exciting, valuable information about your industry.

The point of social media is to remain high on your industry's radar.

Social media allows you to listen, learn, share, research, establish credibility, job search, and create meaningful dialogue with people in your industry.

Recruitment experts predict that social media will become the foundation of all hiring strategies, and for many companies it is already. Many application forms include fields for candidates to enter their social media links. Social-media savvy job seekers who can think like a search engine are most likely to succeed in the future world of job hunting, say recruitment experts.

A new generation of software tools that can trawl the web – including social media sites - for job candidates will completely transform the hiring process.

> In the future, you won't be sending off
> a resume. Your professional profile will
> be online, and you will expect to be
> found.

"Recruitment is heading the way of 'big data' and everything online will be used to not only find you, but to assess you as a candidate for a role that you have never applied for in a company you have never heard of and, maybe, in a town, city or country you have never visited", said recruitment trainer Ross Clennett.

"Big data" refers to all of that unstructured public information – such as that found in social media sites – and it has captured the attention of business commentators.

In a recent blog, US recruitment commentator Kevin Wheeler wrote about the big analytical systems currently in development by large software firms like Oracle, IBM, HP, EMC and SAS.

"We have an increasing ability to learn more and more about people by gleaning bits of information about someone from scraping or extracting data from websites/public information/social networks and from information about the products or services someone buys or uses, and from their interests extracted from comments, Tweets, locations, and so forth," he wrote.

Wheeler also recently told delegates at the Australian Talent Conference that social media would become the foundation of all recruiting.

Clennett said job seekers also stood to gain from the trend. It won't make recruitment more impersonal or robotic, he said. Instead, it will "result in the placement of more people, more frequently and quickly, into jobs that are well matched to their capabilities and aspirations."

This has some implications for the way we use social media, however. For instance, it may stifle the more frivolous side of our interactions.

It's worth pondering, especially considering nine out of ten US companies already use social media to screen potential job candidates, according to a survey by Reppler, a California-based social media reputation management service."

Your On-Line Personal Profile is what
people say about you when you are
not around

Using LinkedIn for Virtual leaders

LinkedIn is your shopfront - your
profile is your store

Build your LinkedIn profile

Just in case you have not had a LinkedIn profile before, one of the first
things you need to consider is if you want an open or closed profile. An
open profile means that when your connections go to your profile page,
they will also be able to look through your connections list. If they
locate any mutual connections, they will be able to send them an
invitation to connect with them personally. They will also be able to
learn more about you by looking through your connections and reading
through your profile.

If you have a closed profile, the only information that can be read by
someone you connect with is the information that appears on your
profile page. They cannot access your connections. We recommend that
you have an open profile. In this way, you gain considerably from being
an active LinkedIn member.

In December 2019, LinkedIn had 660 million users, the majority of
which have open profiles. 260 million Linkedin users are logging in each
month and 40 and of monthly active users use LinkedIn daily. 61
million LinkedIn users are senior-level influencers, and 40 million are in
decision-making positions. These users realize LinkedIn is a powerful
global networking tool.

There are two schools of thought with LinkedIn – some believe it is
better to have a limited quality number of connections, and the other
school says to build an extensive connection network. The choice is
yours. However, we would recommend that you have both a small
group of reliable connections whose relationship you nurture. Plus, a
larger group of contacts who can connect you with a broader network.

Premium account

We recommend that you upgrade to the premium account – there are
lots more benefits and features, and the monthly cost is minimal. With
LinkedIn being the preferred career-building profile of choice, it makes
sense to utilize it to its full capacity.

One of the main benefits that you will continually use will be your ability to send an "inmail." Inmail, an internal LinkedIn mail system allows you to send an email message to anyone in the entire LinkedIn network. Plus, you can have a much more detailed personal profile, which enables you to build your online presence faster and more professionally.

Invest in your profile

Take time to complete your profile - initially spend at least 20-30 minutes completing the various segments of the profile. You can go back anytime and edit the profile – but the adage, the more you tell, the more you sell, certainly applies here. The more facts you give about your work history, the more linkages LinkedIn can suggest for you. Include a professional photo with your profile.

If you are unsure what to include in your profile, review the profiles of other senior managers in your organization, your peers working for different organizations in similar roles, and your mentors. Also, be prepared to review your profile every 3-4 months as your duties and functions increase, and you upgrade specific skills.

Remember all your virtual team, your senior management, and your future employer will also be reading this profile

Rejections

90% of the people you invite to be one of your professional business connections say yes. And the 10% that don't—that's okay too.

Time allocation

Spend at least 15 minutes per day, if possible, on LinkedIn. One of the great things about LinkedIn is that it's a 24/7 platform so it can be accessed at any time of day.

Tracking

You will find companies you have worked with and their employees who you have worked with previously, school friends, relatives, current clients, team. All sorts of connections, many of whom you would have lost track of over the years. And it's effortless to reconnect with them.

Visibility - polls

Visibility is the key with LinkedIn – so the more active you are, the better. Polls are another great LinkedIn tool. You can run polls asking opinions on research, community or social issues, etc. You may also find viewing the results of polls you answer very interesting , and often people make contact after your responses. Plus, you can gain invaluable research from your marketplace by asking opinions and slanting the polls for your specific marketplace needs.

Special interests

Knowing that we are not our jobs, nor the title on the business card, we do have a life outside of the business. LinkedIn again allows you to connect with special interest groups throughout their network. There is a big directory of these groups (including the criteria to join), some more business than social.

Plus, listing your interests on your profile gives more insight into your whole life, not just your workplace.

Group participation

Active participation in groups is also another great way to expand your connections and build your online presence. Depending on your industry/professional sector, you can join a group-specific in that sector. Aim to be an active member of the groups you are part of, whether it is just keeping track of the current conversations and discussions or starting discussions yourself.

LinkedIn also recommends groups that you may be interested in. Plus, all groups have lists of members, and again, you will be able to identify key players in your industry whom you wish to connect with.

Recommended LinkedIn Group: TED

For Virtual leaders, a group that we recommend joining is the TED group – Technology, Education, and Design – based on the www.ted.com website. The group discussions are often thought-provoking, challenging, and innovative.

With a global reach, TED is a nonprofit organization devoted to Ideas worth spreading. It started (in 1984) as a conference bringing together people from three worlds: **Technology, Entertainment, and Design.**

Since then its scope has become ever broader. Along with annual meetings, the award-winning TED Talks video site, the Open Translation Project and TED Conversations, the inspiring TED Fellows and TEDx programs, and the annual TED Prize. There are now TED groups located globally and are worth seeking out.

TED's mission – "We believe passionately in the power of ideas to change attitudes, lives and ultimately, the world. So we're building here a clearinghouse that offers free knowledge and inspiration from the world's most inspired thinkers, and also a community of curious souls to engage with ideas and each other".

Instant updates

Your connections regularly update their profiles as their situations change, they gain recognition, or they change jobs. These are all excellent reasons for you to reconnect with them. And the perfect time to send a congratulations message.

Update your profile regularly

Spending time on your profile page is also a valuable use of time. You just don't know who is clicking on your profile and where that may lead to. Again LinkedIn has a great system where it shows you how much of the profile you have completed. Aim for 100% profile completion within the first few weeks of joining LinkedIn.

Recommendations

LinkedIn has a great tool where you can recommend someone you know. You might aim to send testimonials/endorsements regularly to your connections or individuals you have worked with or known. When you write a recommendation, some people write one or two lines, others approximately 250 words. Make it sincere, descriptive, and genuine. Don't be surprised if you receive a recommendation/ testimonial in response.

Be aware that when you recommend others, that recommendation also appears on your LinkedIn page.

Invitation Wording

Just a word of advice when sending invitations to connect with people you know or would like to know. Those who want to build their network quickly often send the standard – 'I'd like you to join my professional network.' It is good to vary your invitation style, and these may include:

- For people who you knew years ago, you may write
  - A blast from the past – great to find you on LI, hope all is well in your world. All the best for the year. I would like to add you to my professional network.
- For people who are part of a group, you are a member of.
  - We are both members of XYZ. I have checked out your profile, and find we have X number of connections in common. Would you be interested in joining my network?
- For people, you have met at a recent conference
  - We met at the recent XXX conference after the plenary session on innovation. All the best with your XXX (whatever you discussed with them), I would like to invite you to join my network.
- For people, you went to university with or have met while you were studying
  - We met at XX University when I was completing my MBA. At the time, we worked on the VV project. May I invite you to join my network?

LinkedIn also has the option of classifying people as friends. We have researched people's responses when they receive an invitation to connect with someone they describe as "friend" – A significant point is that LinkedIn is NOT Facebook. If you don't know someone or you have only vaguely met them – don't click "friend." In your world, friends are probably people who you speak to regularly, usually call at least once every couple of weeks, and see once a month. So just be careful with your classifications and, if in doubt, don't.

Reactivating Connections

An example of a vast industry is the meetings and events industry, a multi-million dollar industry with networks of people who have been in the industry for many years. It is easy to lose track of where they move to in this global marketplace – so again, LinkedIn is a tremendous reactivating connection tool. Seth Godin is well known for his "build your tribe" theory. The stronger you grow your connections, and the more you expand your links, the closer you bring the world to your doorstep. The more people know you, the more potential career opportunities will come your way. Be direct; on LinkedIn don't waste people's time[22].

Virtual Leadership and Twitter

Twitter is messaging, known as a Tweet, in multiples of 140 characters. If there people or organizations you want to connect with – follow them on Twitter. Start a conversation and connect with people who can influence your career.

PERSONALITY + PERSON = TWITTER

On Twitter:

- Add value

- Have conversations

- Ensure you are conversational on Twitter

Twitter is beneficial when attending virtual or real-time conferences, and summits as the Twitter feed is often used as a running commentary of what is being said from the podium, the atmosphere of the event, and any significant incidents during the conference. And the benefits of a Twitter feed if you are unable to attend the event, is that you have a record of the conference tweets to review at your leisure.

Twitter for Virtual leaders

As a leader in a socially connected world, consider filling your Twitter feeds with inspirational thoughts and quotes. Your virtual team may naturally follow you, or perhaps in meetings open with one of your quotes or inspirational ideas, mentioning that you post these on Twitter.

Learning is a crucial benefit of Twitter. By following people and organizations that are important, you links become available to you. Sharing links from articles or ideas that you have are quick and easy via Twitter. Networking via Twitter with people in your industry is easy and fast via Twitter and doesn't require the more formal 'invitation' that LinkedIn requires.

---

[22] Adapted from eBook, why I love LinkedIn and how I went from zero to 2500+ connections in 12 months by Robyn Henderson

You may also invest some time in following influential leaders that inspire you, topical feeds, and thought-provoking Twitter discussions. Remember, who you follow provides a picture to those looking at your Twitter profile of who you are, what you care about, and what you are interested in. Follow your friends, experts, favorite celebrities, world leaders and breaking news, or a mixture of these that suit you. Most importantly, ensure that the people or organizations that you follow the matter to you and provide an accurate reflection of you.

Facebook and Virtual Leadership

Facebook is a social networking service and website launched in February 2004, owned and operated by Facebook, Inc. As of 2019, Facebook has over 2.5 billion monthly active users. Users must register before using the site, after which they may create a personal profile, add other users as friends, and exchange messages, including automatic notifications when they update their profile.

Additionally, users may join common-interest user groups, organized by workplace, school or college, or other characteristics, and categorize their friends into lists such as "People from Work" or "Close Friends."

A decision for the virtual team leader is whether your virtual team will be on Facebook.

It is straightforward for your virtual team to set up a private Facebook group page. Working from home during the coronavirus pandemic, can be stressful. Setting up a private Facebook Group Page is a way of creating a social community, build better relationships, and build a close-knit virtual team. Consider the benefits of a private Facebook Group as opposed to a separate Slack Channel (or similar platform) dedicated to social sharing.

Martha is a senior manager at a large manufacturing organization in New York. She is a fun, vibrant, and charismatic leader who used to travel every month to one of the locations where she has virtual team members: Los Angeles, Singapore, London, Paris, Sydney.

Since COVID-19 she's working from home.

Martha meets with her team weekly, which means late night and early meetings. Martha has added her entire team to her Facebook account, and they 'tune into' where she is and what she's doing. Being an effervescent personality, Martha's posts are personal with photos of where she is and what she's doing.

Photos of family events, social gatherings, new outfits, concerts and holidays, taken both at home, have always been on her Facebook account. Her team members make the occasional comment, but not often. In business, Martha is known for not returning emails promptly and has poor decision-making skills saying, "I'll get to that later and come back to you," often not getting back to them at all.

Meantime, her Facebook comments flow freely. She now shares her feelings about coronavirus, the latest newsfeeds and reminisces with old photos of her fun past. Her team has become constantly frustrated and sees Martha now has prioritized her social life rather than her work life. Whether this is true or not is not the point. **Their perception is their reality.** They work in isolated places from home, waiting for decisions and meetings with Martha, which are often not forthcoming.

Since relocating to home offices during the pandemic, they have turned to 'doing their own thing' and making their own decisions, preferring to work around Martha. Martha intended that having her team members as friends on Facebook would build a unified team and healthier relationships. Martha is blind to the fact that her team views her frivolous and boastful on what she's doing.

Remember: perception is reality, and in the world of social media, you are often not in control of:

- who reads what you've posted
- how they will perceive what you have posted.

KEY POINTS SUMMARY

- Social media is undoubtedly here to stay, and who knows what innovative social media tools will be introduced in the next decade.

- Virtual leaders must ensure that they are clear on their social media policy for their virtual teams and continually remind their virtual teams that Facebook is their resume. Be careful what they include on the Facebook pages, their tweets, and their LinkedIn profiles.

- Once something is online, it is virtually there for life – regardless of whether it is positive or negative.

Be seen, get known, move ahead – Building your networks.

Activity 37 - Classic Networking Skills Assessment

This assessment looks at the key skills in creating classic face-to-face networks from scratch, growing and maintaining your networks. Then, how you can transition your regular face-to-face networking skills to the virtual world. Networking is a key leadership skill. This assessment is for your personal use to help you determine your current strengths and areas of development.

For each question, rate yourself on each of the techniques.

Classic Networking Skills Assessment	1 Never	2 Rarely	3 Sometimes	4 Most of the Time	5 Always
I can confidently enter a room full of strangers at a networking event.					
I am currently a financial member of my industry or professional association.					
I have a follow up/keep in touch system in place when I meet new people.					
I know the names and special interests of each of my team.					
I have a business card with all of my contact details clearly and legibly included.					
I send thank you notes and cards regularly, either by mail or email, to show appreciation to those who help me					
I regularly mentor others who are building their careers around me.					

Virtual Networking Skills Assessment	1 Never	2 Rarely	3 Sometimes	4 Most of the Time	5 Always
As a virtual leader I have a system in place where I record and acknowledge my wins and accomplishments every day.					
I network with people 'virtually' using the internet to attend events, online webinars, seminars and other events.					
After online events I follow up with people, either personally, via email or LinkedIn or in other ways to build my network.					
I seek out virtual networking opportunities with special interest groups, where I can build my profile.					
I have a list of company leaders, whom I would like to get to know well and follow them via LinkedIn, so that I can participate in any webinars, virtual presentations they may be doing.					
When I find interesting virtual events, I share them with my virtual team.					
TOTALS					

All of the above skills are necessary to lead virtual teams.

Please total your scores and list them for Never, Rarely, Sometimes, Most of the time, and Always.

All of the skills above are necessary to lead virtual teams and will be discussed in this and later chapters.

Reflecting on your answers

Congratulations on all the statements that you answered, 'Most of the time' and 'Always.' Please don't worry, though, if you scored high on the 'Never,' 'Rarely' or 'Sometimes' columns. This book will guide you through the maze of virtual leadership and give you strategies to significantly improve the skills you have identified.

Reflect on your answers regarding your Classic Networking Skills. How can you transition these skills to the virtual environment?

> "To go fast - go alone, to go far
> - go together"
>
> African proverb

Professional Networking: The Vital Commitment

Effective virtual leaders usually develop and utilize their strong networking skills, and there is a direct correlation between strong leadership and strong networking skills. As a virtual leader, you have the opportunity to have substantial influence in your networks, communities, face to face, and virtual workplaces.

Let's define networking and then look at traits of master networkers and see how closely they link to strong and effective leadership and the ability to lead and influence others.

Living Networking – Not a Chore!

The biggest mistake that we make with networking is seeing that it is something that they DO, rather than something that they LIVE. Influential Virtual leaders understand that networking is a life-skill – not just something that you do when you want something.

Virtual Networking 24/7

The same principles apply to virtual networking. Successful Leaders know that:

- You network 24/7 – this does not mean you don't sleep. It means that your virtual team knows that they can connect with you any time of day, and you will respond in a timely and predetermined manner.

- You realize that your virtual team is made up of a group of people who have lives outside of their work. Every conversation that you have with your virtual team is NOT necessarily work-related.

- You make regular contact with your virtual team, never just when you want something from them.

If you only make contact when you want something, you risk developing a virtual team attitude of "Oh, here's Olga, what does she want this time? She only connects when she wants something. It's the only time I hear from her. I can go weeks without contact."

Virtual leaders understand that networking includes:

- **Doing something for someone**, not because you gain from doing it, but because you want to help someone achieve their goal. It might be something small; one of your virtual team members mentions they have an assignment to do with their external studies, and you send them several articles you have read recently on the assignment topic. You share the materials without an expectation of receiving anything in return.

- **Believing that there are plenty of opportunities for everyone** – even if the market is tight and very competitive, especially during the coronavirus pandemic. There is always an abundance of opportunities for everyone, even if sometimes those opportunities appear to be hidden.

- **Knowing that if you are generous and helpful, other people will be generous and helpful for you too**. Not everyone will believe this, and you will often find people who are takers. However, the belief that there is good in everyone and if you are a helpful person when the time comes and you need help – there will always be someone there to help you.

One of the essential networking skills that leaders tap into is their ability to be present and mindful when they are communicating with a person. This means that they are not multi-tasking while they are on the phone or Zoom call with you, for example, checking emails while they are half-listening to you. They stop what they are doing and are actively listening to you. The reality is this is a great time management tool because when you actively engage with someone, you listen to everything they say to you, you recall more information and you can have a constructive and meaningful conversation.

Not surprisingly, this conversation usually takes half the time that it would if you were multi-tasking while the conversation is happening.

Virtual Networking Ladder Of Loyalty

Stranger, Contac, Acquaintance,
Enthusiast, Client/Mentor, Advocate

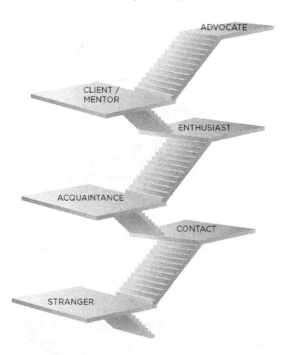

Figure 14 - Virtual Networking Ladder Of Loyalty

From Stranger to Contact: Social Media for Initiating Connections

In previous chapters, we have explored using LinkedIn direct invitations, LinkedIn Groups, Facebook Groups, Instagram, and other social networks to connect with others in your industry.

Identifying potential contacts has never been easier. Engage in collaborative conversations after someone accepts a LinkedIn invitation, or responds to one of your posts.

Case Study Z -   How Eric's landscape business was saved by his Facebook followers

Eric is self-employed and has a small team of landscape architects doing award winning garden designs across Australia.

Eric has always shared his time from his home studio and his inner city Melbourne office. While Eric has been agile to work remotely, his team is challenged.

While many of the systems Eric's team used are cloud based, they were ill-equipped to handle the immediate shutdown of their office as the coronavirus took hold.

Eric has had to navigate the 'new normal'

His immediate response was to ensure that everything that was on their central office computer system, moved to a cloud-based system.

He used his extensive network of Facebook followers to call for IT professionals, and others who could quickly assist him and his team move to a remote working environment.

The response was immediate. People who had visited his home garden on open days rallied to assist. Ideas flooded in, so he set up a group Zoom call as an idea sharing forum.

Usually, a private person, during the call, Eric was open about his businesses short-comings. Ideas flowed and solutions followed.

The win:win outcome resulted in Eric recruiting independent contractors and other small businesses who came to the forum and thereby giving them work at their most challenging times.

Within two-weeks his landscaping business was operating completely remotely.

Eric had previously considered social media, his followers, the number of 'likes' on a post as business fluff. By tapping into his network, he maintained business continuity and provided income for other small businesses.

Consider your own existing network and how they can assist you.

From Contact to Acquaintance, then onto Enthusiast: Get Visible

While LinkedIn is the obvious choice for connecting with professionals and industry groups, follow Industry Leaders, and comment on their posts or updates professionally. Retweeting and sharing of posts is quick and easy. Answering questions, responding to polls, and sharing thoughtful responses is one key is visibility and consistency.

Think long-term about the value that you can bring to your network and engage in small ways every week. The goal is to make your name familiar so that when the moment is right, you can meet them by way of a Zoom call, or phone call.

Virtual networking helps you to build and maintain relationships with critical contacts globally.

Enthusiasts will follow your social media accounts, commenting, liking, and will be openly sharing your posts. In line with your visibility, you'll see that your number of LinkedIn Connection requests increase.

Your team as part of your virtual network

When working with new team members, whom you have not met before or know nothing about, they are virtual strangers. Through communication and building trust, sharing a few ideas, maybe a few things about our day, our work history, or our life, we can quickly jump from Stranger to Acquaintance.

Some team members never move beyond the acquaintance level, and that is perfectly okay. However, to step up as a virtual leader, it is vital for you as a leader to move to advocate status quickly and comfortably.

Building Trust is the Key to Moving up

Building Trust Through the Virtual Networking Ladder Of Loyalty

So how do you build trust? Previously, we listed the following under the heading – **Skills to become a successful virtual leader.** Guess what? These same skills and habits are also needed to move through the networking ladder of loyalty. Developing as many of these skills as possible will build trust quickly and effortlessly between you, your team, and your networks.

You have a responsibility as a virtual leader to establish expectations and consequences of not meeting these expectations. Remember, practice what you preach – you also need to meet the same standards consistently. In short:

- Be authentic and trustworthy
- Be genuine
- Do what you say and say what you do
- Take responsibility for your own decisions and actions
- Do not blame others for your mistakes
- Be honest
- Be considerate to others
- Do the right thing
- Demonstrate integrity and encourage and value it in others
- Establish expectations
- Establish consequences of not meeting your expectations
- Be consistent
- Staying calm and unemotional are the keys to successfully managing conflict and highly emotional situations.
- When everyone else is stressed, angry, and frustrated, it takes just one person remaining calm and being the voice of reason to bring everyone else back to resembling normal, healthy team members.

During the coronavirus pandemic, cohesion and leadership are vital. The speed and agility with which virtual leaders and their teams react can be the difference between maintaining business, income, and reducing company exposure.

The more trust we build with our team, the faster we move from 'stranger' to 'acquaintance' through to Enthusiast. Don't be concerned by the word 'Enthusiast' – we are not talking about the friend whom you go to dinner every Friday night. Not at all, and Enthusiast is someone knows, likes, respects, and trusts you and will go the extra mile to deliver, especially during these difficult times of the pandemic. Trust is the key here; you know you can trust them.

And as trust continues to grow in that network, they move to advocacy level. You know that you have set them many tasks, and they have performed all of them well. You totally trust them, and as more projects come online, you know just the person for the role. They have proved their worth to you.

Now let's reverse the situation – what do your virtual team members think of you? Throughout your virtual team, you will have varying levels of trust. The more you do what you say and work your way through the list (see the previous chapter), the faster you will reach advocacy status with your team.

These suggestions do not mean that your virtual team will immediately put you on the "best manager I have ever worked with" list. And that is not your intention, your ego might like that, but as we know from previous chapters, virtual leadership is not a popularity contest. You will probably always find team members who may find fault with you.

When you inherit or create a new team, the people whom you have worked with before will trust you. Those who know little about you will look for evidence that you can be trusted. This trust is built by doing what you say you will do, by being consistent with your behavior and through actively listening to these individuals.

Before you know it, you will have a highly functioning team that trusts you.

Memorable Virtual Leaders and Master
Networkers Are Strong
Communicators

Communication Influence

Master networkers and successful leaders are strong communicators – they always make heart-to-heart connections with the people they are speaking to. This means that they are present and in the moment for the length of that conversation. They give the person in front of them or the person at the end of the phone or conference call total focus – they listen with their heart as well as their ears. The conversation may, in fact, last for only seconds or minutes, but the recipient knows that they have been heard.

Master virtual networkers are also not afraid to ask questions to clarify details, and they are always ready to admit that they may not understand something. They do not see this admission as a weakness, but rather the opportunity to learn something new, and give the other person an opportunity to share their knowledge.

Strong networkers continuously work on improving their listening skills by looking beyond the words and observing the tone, inference, and body language of everyone in the group. Obviously, with virtual teams, you may not see the whole body, but the facial expressions will tell you a lot about the person's disposition and response to your comments.

Networking Communication for Virtual leaders

Influential virtual leaders realize that communication doesn't start and stop at the employment doorstep. Weaving networking and regular communication throughout your life, you embrace these skills 24/7. And you also see these listening, speaking and understanding skills as a work in progress or a journey. Realizing that no matter how much we know, there is always more to learn, and other people have the information we need. You purely need to know where and how to make contact with these knowledge keepers. And if you don't know where to find them, someone you know will know where to find them.

Using a person's first or full name in conversations is a potent tool. The bonus of having strong listening skills is that you can remember more about previous conversations you may have had with this person. Having the ability to recall some of those highlights, at the appropriate time is invaluable in building more trust with that person. For example, you remember the name of their child or partner or the fact that they had been unwell, traveling back home during the challenging coronavirus travel restrictions, studying, renovating a home – anything that shows that person that you have been listening to them.

Picture a house being built brick by brick; imagine trust being built in the same way – conversation-by-conversation, contact-by-contact. The more contact you make, the stronger your connection becomes. You also acknowledge that some people may not like you, and the more they get to know you, the less they like you. Remember, virtual leadership is

NOT a popularity contest. Some people may never like you, and that is okay too.

However, the large potential for influence is when you have built a strong connection with someone, and they do trust and like you. The natural flow is for them to speak highly of you within their networks, so you do, in fact, have the potential to influence total strangers – either positively or negatively, purely based on the connection you make with the original connector.

Nobody is a nobody

Master networkers know that nobody is a nobody – everyone is connected to other people and everyone is a somebody, somewhere. Everyone has an interesting life journey if you care to ask. So, when you leave a poor impression with someone, you never know whom that person knows and whom he or she may share that poor impression or opinion with. You will never know what was said when your name came up in conversation, somewhere down the track, but you can imagine it was not a positive image.

Time Management For Effective Networking

We recommend that influential leaders work at their networking skills for at least 15 minutes per day. Whether it's a phone call, text message, email, thank you note, a small gift, or good morning to a total stranger, fellow worker or neighbor, giving a recommendation or LinkedIn or connecting one of your network with someone else – it is all part of networking.

Finding 15 proactive networking minutes in your busy day

Can't spare 15 minutes per day? Don't worry – this does not have to be a solid 15 minute block. There may be many opportunities for stolen minutes, for example:

- When you are waiting for a teleconference call to start and you use that time to network.
    - You might scan a report and highlight the key ideas for one of your virtual team.
    - Or you may write a quick thank you note to a virtual team member who has worked extra hard completing a report.

- Alternately a welcome back note to a virtual team member who has just returned from sick leave.

- When you are waiting for a 1:1 meeting to begin
    - You might write a 'well deserved note to someone in your network congratulating them on their promotion
    - Scan your LinkedIn profile for connection suggestions

- When you are waiting for a personal appointment, on hold waiting for a customer service person, anytime you are waiting!
    - Update your LinkedIn profile
    - Send a tweet via Twitter

Gail: I used to use my flight time to 'virtual' network. I calculated approximately 15 hours a week was spent transiting from one office to another.

Since the pandemic has stopped all of my business travel I realize that I'm now doing more work at home and not prioritizing networking.

I've put in a new workday schedule. After a break for lunch, I spend 10-15 minutes reaching out to my LinkedIn Connections and colleagues with a friendly non-work-related message.

If I calculated all the wasted time going through airport security, waiting to board a plane, and in transit to hotels and business meetings, my 10-15 minutes of virtual networking each day would never total that amount of time.

I send emails to people that I haven't connected with for a while. A simple 'how are you?' or 'thinking of you' message is enough to re-spark connection. By only focusing on this type of email (rather than getting into answering day to day emails in my inbox), focuses me on reconnecting with those with who I'm out of touch.

Also, it gives me an opportunity of telling them what I've been doing (without being verbose). I usually set a time for this task – usually no more than 15 minutes.

What's great, is the responses and improved connections. From there, I sometimes suggest a 'virtual coffee' to continue the conversation.

Working from home, alone, during this crazy coronavirus lockdown, is more enjoyable. 'Isolation with connection'…it starts with me reaching out!

Proactive virtual leaders often suggest a quick coffee break with people they want to get to know better. Or if this is not possible, what about a virtual-coffee? A virtual-coffee is a planned conversation with someone with a specific agenda but more relaxed than an official meeting. It is an excellent use of your time and helps build virtual relationships as well.

If your virtual team members know that they have a set time to have a weekly phone appointment with you – then they can save up all their small inquiries for you and discuss them at one time – at their virtual-coffee with you. This virtual -coffee would have a set time frame, and it would be wise to cancel it only under extenuating circumstances.

Remember, building trust with your virtual team is doing what you say you will do. If your team members don't know from one week to the next when they are going to have your undivided attention, this can add to their isolation and silo-like workplace. And something that appears a small trivial problem in the morning can build up to be a large and significant problem within a couple of days.

The Power of Giving Recognition
Most leaders are aware that more than 80% of the marketplace does not get recognition on the job. They work for organizations that often take their staff and virtual teams for granted, treat them poorly, have no systems in place to recognize achievement or progress, and can be accused often of complacency – both with their team and their customers. These often are also organizations with high staff turnover, low morale, erratic profits, and poor names in the marketplace. Yes, they influence the market but usually in a negative manner.

Acknowledging someone's effort and contribution can be easily recognized on a daily, weekly, or monthly basis, depending on the logistics of the company. Sometimes, this is lost in a virtual working environment.

Especially during the COVID-19 pandemic, it is important to recognize also that the desire for recognition is vital in small teams (under five employees) as well as large global organizations with thousands of employees. The upset to every team member's work and home life is evident, and the changes and agility that people have utilized is nothing short of amazing.

Long-term team members are often perceived as a liability because of their job entitlements, long service leave, sabbatical requirements, retirement funding and so on. Yet when the decision to cut these team members is made, rarely is their knowledge bank considered. Rarely are they recognized for giving so much of their life to the organization.

One of the traps with sales incentives for the business development teams is that the "factory" or the "engine room" are often neglected when the rewards are given out. The back office makes the salesperson look good by completing the delivery on time every time – yet they are often forgotten when the bonuses are given. The master networkers within organizations realize the influence a word of thanks and show of appreciation to the engine room can have on their future results. Smart organizations again have systems built in to acknowledge the behind the scenes workers, when sales results are announced and targets exceeded and have quickly adapted these systems for working with an entire distance workforce or a split workforce between on-site and virtual.

These may include such simple things as – relaxing worktimes for those with children at home, being flexible on project deadlines, giving a paid afternoon early mark to celebrate results, certificates of appreciation, or paid membership to online entertainment services, such as Netflix, etc., or an acknowledgement in company newsletters.

Previously, we discussed Herzberg's Motivation Theory, so ensure that your rewards are real motivators, not your perception of what might motivate. Another word of caution here, whatever is introduced, must be continued for the pre-agreed time frame. If you give recognition once and forget it the next time, morale often drops lower than it was before the acknowledging started.

Great virtual leaders know that the most essential words in the English language are a person's name, and the second most important are the words THANK YOU. These words are the basis of any recognition and should be part of the company culture. Thanks for doing a great job, staying online to complete the project, covering for someone when they were delayed, and doing that extra something that made a great difference can be a boost in motivation for even the least motivated team member on your virtual team.

In the fast-paced virtual world, there is no substitution for a handwritten thank you card. If you look at your virtual team member's workspaces, you'll see what's important to them. What is valued by one virtual team may not be appreciated by another virtual team in a different country. If you are stuck for motivating ideas, you might write a note to the person or a whole group advising them that you have a budget for a certain amount of money to acknowledge their recent contribution. Then invite the person or team to nominate how they would like to spend their money. You won't please everyone, but you will please the majority.

Terri: I was meeting 1:1 of my virtual team members who works from her home. Like many people who work from home Molly has a family and she has a fantastic desk in her lounge room that by day is her home office, and each evening closes to become a neat cupboard.

Molly's 'real estate' in her home office is limited – with just a small bookshelf desk with a tiny pinboard for precious things and post-it notes of essentials. During our last call she twisted her webcam around to show me her pinboard.

What was interesting to me was the of all of the things Molly could have on her pinboard, she chose to keep the handwritten cards that I had sent to her and cards that she had received from clients.

I asked her about them, and she said that when she's overloaded with work, she looks at those notes with pride, knowing that she's appreciated.

Also, she said that when she receives a thank you card, she proudly shows her two children with a "look what I got today?" - just like she does when they get school awards that she puts on the refrigerator. She laughed, "Perhaps I'm just a kid at heart, but it keeps me going!"

By contrast, I had also sent Molly many thank you emails, and I know that clients have as well. Those weren't printed and not visibly displayed. It was a great lesson for me as a virtual manager.

As a virtual manager, it's often easy to go weeks with the greatest of the intent of doing these things but nothing in reality. So, at the end of each week, I think about who I can write a card to. I have a box of cards in my desk drawer and make it a habit each Friday to do this as my final task of the week. It only takes me a few minutes to write one or two. I then pop them in my purse, and when I'm going on essential errands to the pharmacy or grocery store, I post them using the oldest method of 'snail mail.' I know that this most old fashioned form of recognition still resonates with most of us!

MASTER NETWORKERS AND STRONG
LEADERS MAKE RECOGNITION
GIVING JUST ANOTHER PART OF
THEIR DAY

Finding Role Models

We are regularly told through a variety of media formats that we cannot change anyone – only ourselves. And change starts from within, not outside of us. With this in mind, how can we influence people by being role models?

Good leaders watch what other successful networkers do and do the same – that's how they become masters at what they do. Tradespeople, engineers, professionals, teachers, designers do much the same thing. They look to people they admire and want to be like and copy what they do without becoming their clones or stealing their ideas and concepts.

Master networkers are often called 'Spheres of Influence,' and that influence is more effective when coupled with ethics and morals. Each city in the world has a daily newspaper. Often when you are faced with a decision, you may be undecided. It's the "Will I, won't I?" test – "Is this a good business move, or might it come back to bite me." In order to decide on your path you might ask yourself the "National Newspaper Test" that is, if this incident or situation appeared on the front page of the national newspaper, would you be embarrassed in anyway and would you need to do some serious explaining to your family and friends? If the answer is yes, don't do it.

In today's world of social media, Twitter, Facebook, etc. – you only have to watch media reports on any day and see how celebrities, as well as everyday people's careers, are destroyed when photos are released showing inappropriate behavior.

Be sure to warn your virtual teams that Facebook forms part of an employee's resumes today. And encourage them to avoid putting inappropriate photos on their social media profiles.

It takes years and years to build your reputation and good name, whether you are an employee or an employer – why risk your good name on anything that might remotely be or be perceived as unethical, illegal, or lacking integrity? Many corporate high flyers have had their reputations destroyed by greed, mismanagement, and unaccountability for their actions. Sometimes it appears they see themselves as bulletproof. Unfortunately, they are mistaken.

As a virtual leader, you will know when you have authentic influence over others when you become a role model for many. There is no set timeline on how long this takes – sometimes, it seems like months and other times years. And I don't think it is something you can force; it is something that happens as a result of what you do.

The people that you have as role models may all share the following:

- They are passionate about the work they do.
- They believe in themselves, even when others don't.
- The buck stops here – is their motto – let's fix it rather than find a scapegoat.
- They always stand by their team as long as they have the total truth told to them.
- They look for the good in others, even when it's hard to find.
- They make the heart to heart connections when they speak to you.
- They are fun to be around.
- They often laugh.
- They don't overindulge.
- They don't hold grudges

> MASTER NETWORKERS AND GREAT
> LEADERS BECOME A LIGHT FOR
> THOSE WHO ARE LIVING IN
> DARKNESS

Self Networking Tracker

To have a significant impact as a virtual leader, you need to do small things consistently. Networking is a skill filled with doing little things always. Successful virtual leaders are organized, particularly when it comes to creating and monitoring networking opportunities.

Activity 38 - Monthly Networking Tracker

Use the following Monthly Networking Tracker to plan and monitor your networking activity. Ensure that you add your intentions to your calendar or another reminder so that during the busiest times, networking is prioritized.

At the start of each month	
Month	
How you plan to network during this month?	
List three networking activities you intend to do	

At the end of each month	
Month	
List the networking activity you completed during the month	
List three people you met or made a new connection with	
How you plan to network next month?	

What you may find is that the three things you initially intended to do are not the three things that you ended up doing.

In your virtual leadership role, often you are given unexpected networking activities, for example:

- One of your global managers invites you to be part of a teleconference connecting you with some key managers you may not have met before.

- One of your senior managers from another state is meeting one of your managers on a virtual meeting, and you are invited to attend the meeting meet this manager.

- You may unexpectedly be given a ticket to attend a national or international online conference relevant to your industry.

- You are invited to join a teleconference of leaders, one level above you, to participate in a 'round table' discussion.

- You are invited to join a virtual training course in another city or country.

These examples give you access to key players in your network or organization, with whom you would typically not have an opportunity to meet.

One of the keys to being part of these networking opportunities is making sure that you always follow up with the people that you meet.

Catherine (Author): I'd like to share a story from many years ago. It was pre- the coronavirus pandemic when we were still attending in-person networking events! Oh, they were the days!

I was at a Women's Executive Leadership networking event in America, and throughout the entire evening, it struck me how adept American women are at the 'flattery approach.' All evening, conversations were started with a compliment about my shoes, my suit, my handbag, the color of my hair, in fact, any way to begin a conversation. I thought I'd start this approach as a little 'test case' to see if it worked when I did it. Yes! Success! It was so easy to bring another person into a group of women talking by saying, "I like your purse," or "what a great dress." It was an instant icebreaker. Perhaps it's a women-to-women thing. I've haven't tried it with men, and I'm not sure that I'd feel confident in saying "great suit" or "great tie." I don't know. But, with women in America, wow, it worked fantastically!

As an Australian, I decided to see if the 'flattery approach' worked here, as well as in America. I was invited to afternoon tea at the Governor General's residence in Sydney, the Queen's representative in Australia, and the highest Office in the country. It was a daunting scene, but an excellent networking opportunity with 50 other professional women. The Australian Governor-General at that time was a woman, and I wondered if this approach would work with her and with the other highly admired professional women at the event. Being candid, Quentin Bryce, is a formidable and inspirational woman, not to mention impeccably dressed with perfect grooming top to toe and always seen to be in total control of every situation from political events to being a guest at William and Kate's wedding! During the afternoon tea event, a woman that I was standing next to used the 'flattery approach,' complementing Mrs. Bryce on her beautiful dress that she was wearing. Instantly, I saw the essence of the woman with so much power in Australia, melt, and glow from the compliment. From that moment, she engaged with our group in a very natural way enquiring about what we all did professionally.

As a woman leading a virtual team, ever since this event, I know that the 'flattery approach' works with my virtual team to break the ice at the beginning of Zoom meetings, Skype video calls, virtual training sessions and at other times when meeting virtually.

However, I also know that fabricated flattery doesn't work, and I make sure that my compliments are genuine and down-to-earth.

Virtual Conversation Starters

Something happens to some of us when they attend networking events. We become tongue-tied and mumble and stumble our way through conversations. Often mentally beating ourselves up along the way. Yet, when they are speaking to our workmates or friends, conversation flows.

A simple virtual conversation model that you may use is:

- Past

- Present

- Future

With this model, you are aiming to put people at ease by asking them questions that you know they know the answer to. This might sound strange, but there is a reason. Many people who attend networking events are not leaders, they are team members sent there by their bosses, and they are totally out of their comfort zone – just like you used to be.

PAST

Questions about the past – are good to use with team members from all levels of the organization. Often, they appear to be out of their comfort zone. Questions might include:

- "Jane, you say you have been at XYZ for 10 years, that's a long time. What would be the biggest change to XYZ in the last few years?" You will observe that Jane thinks for a minute, realizes she knows the answer, and then answers.
- "Jane, you work at XYZ, have you always worked in the xxx industry?"

Your conversation aims to put the person at ease and be remembered positively.

PRESENT

Questions about the present are helpful to use for middle management, supervisors, and aspiring managers.

Questions might include:

- "Jill you are with AAC Company, how are you finding staff retention these days?"
- "Jill you are with AAC Company, are staffing levels as low as the media is portraying?"
- "Jill, what impact do you think xyz will have on your company?"

FUTURE

Questions about the future are useful for senior managers, CEOs, CFO's, GMs, etc.

Questions might include:

- "Ash, what trends do you think will be impacting your industry in the next twelve months?"
- "Ash, with the growth in your marketplace, do you have any expansion plans?"

- "Ash, what are your thoughts about............?"

Golden Rules for Communicating at networking events

The following list is certainly not complete but serves as some guidelines for every networking event that you attend.

- Listen, listen, listen

- Be friendly

- Make eye contact

- Smile

- Be interested – remember everyone has an interesting life story if you choose to ask

- Ask open-ended questions and listen to the answers (open questions typically start with who, what, how, which, or where)

- Remember the heart to heart connections! Listen with your heart as well as your ears!

- Don't fear pauses (most people dislike pauses and will jump in with conversation to fill the silence)

- Be positive

- Observe body language, crossed arms, lack of eye contact, etc

- Play safe on hot topics: What's your opinion of...(climate change, politics etc.) See which camp they are in before you start preaching your opinion

- Don't focus on negative topics – turn negatives into positives. What was the highlight of your day? Your weekend? Last week?

Business Card Use – in person and virtually

We have discussed building your online profile in a previous chapter.

It is unwise to go to a face-to-face networking event without a business card. Why make it so hard for people to contact you? Ensure that you are networking in a virtual setting that you share your contact details early in the conversation. Don't log-off and regret that you didn't get the details of the person that you were speaking with. Generally, be the first to share your details and the other person will respond in kind.

Ken: At a recent virtual networking event, we had to all introduce ourselves. It was uncomfortable for many people there, but one man made an impression – in the wrong way.

He said, "Hello, my name is David, and I'm into hunting, fishing, and drinking. I don't have a LinkedIn Profile, so don't ask me. I never answer my cell phone, so I'm not going to give you my number. And, I don't have that social media stuff. I'm a consultant in sales coaching, so if you want that, let me know, and I'll email you a brochure." Everyone laughed….at him.

I noticed that throughout the event, people were talking about David, and having a laugh. I was watching him on the video, and he was laughing along.

Coincidentally I was in a project meeting the following week, and who should be there? David.

At the end of the project meeting, I asked him how he enjoyed the virtual networking event the previous week.

He said, "what a waste of time these things are….I never get any business from them, despite showing up to every event!"

I simply smiled, said, 'bye for now' and logged off.

What do you take to a virtual networking event?

This diagram represents what you take to a networking event and what you have to offer the strangers whom you meet.

The intersection of passions & special interest, current & past roles, your life experiences, wisdom & networks makes for an interesting combination for people whom you meet.

Passions & special interests

Current & past roles

Your life experiences, wisdom & networks

Figure 15 – What you take to a virtual networking event

You arrive with a combination of:

- Your special interests
- Your wisdom
- Your connections
- Your life experiences
- Your current job
- Your past jobs
- Your network

Just because you don't know anyone, does not mean that you do not have a lot to offer to every conversation that you have and every connection that you make.

Attending Internal Virtual Events

When you attend an internal networking event – the same principles apply – you intend to network with people whom you do not know well or at all. Take the initiative to meet new people, introduce yourself to senior management, and make new team members welcome. Remember – act like the host, not the guest.

Before attending an internal event – make sure that you prepare a couple of questions that you feel comfortable asking and answering. If you are new to the organization and not familiar with all the senior management, make a note of their names from your internal directory and locate a headshot of them either on your organization's website or on LinkedIn. You do not want to be asking one of the senior partners who they are, that would be a career-limiting move.

Roger: A client invited me to a lunch where I would be able to meet a group of managers. This moved online via Zoom because of everyone working from home. I wondered how it would ever be able to work.

My client told me that it was an excellent opportunity to be introduced and network. What a brilliant opportunity, I thought. When I arrived all of the participants were chatting to their known peers, via the chat box, and not networking with others all!

As soon as everyone was online, my client did a fantastic job of facilitating the online networking forum. She had a series of structured activities and questions for people to answer via chat and break-out rooms.

We were all asked to ensure that our video cameras were on, and microphones were working to introduce ourselves to the group. Usually, this is very dull, with people droning on about their experience, but this was structured. We had to answer four simple questions:

1. What's your name & job title?

2. Where are you working from now?

3. What's the biggest challenge that you have faced today?

4. What is the best thing that's happened this week?

People's responses were candid, open, thought-provoking, funny, and heartbreaking, all rolled into one simple activity. She then asked different groups to break-out into Zoom Rooms to have a discussion on other topics.

I met more people in this 75-minute virtual meeting than I usually do in a conference facility in a day! It was great. Because my client had prepared the interaction, it was organized and valuable.

Be Prepared to Move Out of Your Comfort Zone

Networking is a life skill, and it can open any door in the world for you. The most critical aspect of networking is to accept yourself, be yourself, be authentic, and know that some of the best contacts you will ever make will be accidental meetings.

If you are prepared to move out of your comfort zone, engage with people, you will not only become a great virtual leader, you will also have a much more exciting life.

> Remember, every best friend was once
> a perfect stranger.

Professional Follow-up

If you neglect to follow up with the connections you have made, you will have wasted your time, money, and effort during this virtual networking event.

Your choice of follow up may include:

- An email
- An invitation to connect on LinkedIn – making sure that you mention the virtual networking event and something that happened during that event
- A phone call
- Snail mail with some information you discussed during the virtual event
- Setting up or joining a LinkedIn Group as a result of the event and ensuring that you become an active group member
- If there were points raised and interesting discussions throughout the event, you may follow up with them either with a question on LinkedIn or a poll question to expand your knowledge in this area. And you may find that once you receive the results of your poll and questions, you will be able to share them with the participants of the virtual networking event.
- Be sure to thank the organizer and chair of the virtual event.

> "Networking is a lot like watching
> sunrises; if you don't show up (virtually
> or face to face), you will never know
> what you missed." Robyn Henderson

Professional Follow-Up within 24 hours

After every networking event, you attend, within 24 hours, it's a great idea to take five minutes to debrief the event. As you a leaving the event, ask yourself:

- What worked well?
- What were the highlights?
- What didn't work?
- What would you change the next time you attend a similar event?
- What was the most significant learning from the event?
- Which people are expecting to be followed up immediately?
- Would you make this network a regular event?
- What did you notice about the good networkers?
- When are you going to your next networking event?

As a virtual leader, aim to continually improve your networking skills by evaluating your results. Small improvements at each networking event will make you a much better networker long term.

As you meet new people, note the place you met them, the date of the event and something you remember about them. The 'something' might be the non-work related thing you spoke about, what their interest was outside of work or a chance comment about something they were doing, plus any action needed. Using the notes facility in Microsoft Outlook Contacts (or similar) allows for this to be stored electronically.

If you have connected with this stranger and mentioned that you would send them an eBook, website connection, or specific piece of information, make sure you do that within 48 hours. A straightforward follow-up system is to connect with someone on LinkedIn.

Be sure though to send your LinkedIn message to connect with a message e.g., "Hi Jane great to meet you at the Institute's virtual lunch today. All the best with your promotion. I would like to connect with you on LinkedIn." When your invitation is accepted, you may then put Jane into a particular group in your LinkedIn account. And you can follow up as regularly as you like.

Follow-up Frequency

How often do you want to make contact with this new connection? Well, that depends entirely on your reason for reconnecting. A lot of keep in touch activity is spontaneous:

- You may see them at the next event
- You may email them and ask if they are attending
- You may send a promised article etc.
- You may phone them
- You may enter them in your organization's distribution list

If you want to do business with them, you may indicate that when you initially follow up. Remember, though, that sometimes when you make a new connection – they are a 10/10 prospect in your world. But in their world, you are a 6/10 – one day, I will purchase/need that. Without pestering them, you want to keep in touch but not harass them or be too pushy.

HONESTY is the best policy. "Jane, you mentioned XXX. On reflection, I think our XX line may be appropriate for your organization. When would it be convenient to discuss this with you?" and if Jane's answer is "Not right now." That's fine; you can still find reasons to follow up with Jane down the track.

Ideally, every 30 days, you want to make some form of RELEVANT contact. These days it is effortless to stay in touch with the variety of tweets, e-ezines, blogs, social media information that may pass your inbox every day.

Remember, though, quality, not quantity. You are better to send something very relevant, than something just for the sake of making contact.

KEY POINTS SUMMARY

- As a virtual leader, you have the opportunity to have substantial influence in your networks, communities, face to face, and virtual workplaces.

- One of the essential networking skills that leaders tap into is their ability to be present and mindful when they are communicating with a person.

- Use the Virtual Networking Ladder of Loyalty to determine how your network of business relationships is advancing.

- Trust is built by doing what you say you will do, by being consistent with your behavior and through actively listening to these individuals.

- Influential leaders work at their networking skills for at least 15 minutes per day

- Proactive virtual leaders often suggest a quick coffee break with people they want to get to know better.

- Acknowledging someone's effort and contribution can be easily recognized on a daily, weekly, or monthly basis, depending on the logistics of the company. Sometimes, this is lost in a virtual working environment.

- Use the Past, Present, Future conversation structure for meeting new people at virtual networking events.

- The intersection of passions & special interest, current & past roles, your life experiences, wisdom & networks makes for an interesting combination for people whom you meet.

- Ideally, every 30 days, you want to make some form of RELEVANT contact.

Planning your Virtual Career Development

As you build your reputation as a Successful Virtual leader, not only will you be noticed by your organization but also by those in your profession. It is essential though, that you clearly understand the difference between management and leadership.

> "A leader takes people where they
> want to go. A great leader takes
> people where they don't necessarily
> want to go, but ought to be."
>
> Rosalynn Carter

Leadership is the process of directing the behavior of others towards the accomplishment of some common objectives. Leadership is influencing people to get things done willingly, and to a standard and quality above the norm. When you combine leadership qualities and skills in a virtual environment this is a powerful and sought-after competency.

As an element in virtual social interaction, virtual leadership is a complex activity involving influence, striving for the achievement of goals, team commitment and the reinforcement or changing of organizational culture.

The pandemic of coronavirus is providing leaders with significant challenges at all levels of organizations. Leaders who are agile to adapt in a mode of crisis leadership, managing their virtual teams remotely, while building self-resilience will be able to navigate these disruptive and uncertain times. It is those leaders, who will be highly sought after on the other side of COVID-19.

While most leaders are focused on the current crisis and keeping their incomes, I believe it will be the leaders who shine in the future will be those who work, **during** the pandemic, on their future careers.

For virtual leaders, it's important to differentiate between virtual management tasks and virtual leadership tasks.

Virtual Management vs. Virtual Leadership

Virtual Management = day to day
operational tasks

Virtual Leadership = influencing for
long-term goal achievement

Virtual Management and Virtual Leadership are often thought of as one and the same thing however, there is an important distinction between the two. In essence, leadership is a broader concept than management.

Management is the managing of day-to-day operational tasks, for example, managing projects, finance, staff, administration and so on.

Leadership occurs whenever one person attempts to influence the behavior of an individual or group, regardless of the reason. It may be for one's own goals or for the goals of others and these goals should be congruent with organizational goals.

So, when adding the word virtual or remote into the mix, management and leadership take on new levels of complexity.

"Virtual managers manage things,
virtual leaders manage people."
Catherine Mattiske

Activity 39 - Your Management vs Your Leadership Role

In the table below, list your management responsibilities and your leadership initiatives over the last 12 months. (If you are new to your organization, consider previous leadership roles.)

Management Responsibilities	Leadership Initiatives – the past 12 months

Now, reflect on what you have writte, and and think about what's changed since the global outbreak of coronavirus. Note which tasks have been decreased, increased or altered.

"To lead people, walk beside them. As for the best leaders, the people do not notice their existence. The next best, the people honor and praise. The next, the people fear; And the next, the people hate.... When the best leader's work is done the people say, "We did it ourselves!"

Lao-tsu

"Leaders must be close enough to relate to others, but far enough ahead to motivate them." John Maxwell

Activity 40 - The COVID-19 Impact: Your Career

Reflect on the previous activity and think about what's changed since the global outbreak of coronavirus.

Prompting Question	What's changed since COVID-19 for you as a manager & leader
Where you were five years ago?	
On a rating of 1 to 10 how happy are you with your current position/ level/ organization/ role? (10 very happy, 1 unhappy)	
Where do you want to be?	
What steps can you take to get there?	
How have your peers changed since the outbreak of coronavirus?	
Your future...Post-coronavirus pandemic	What can you put in place during the pandemic to set you up for future success
Who can help you move to your next level?	
What study/courses can you help to increase your skills to facilitate your next level?	
What networking activities can you start/stop/continue to facilitate your future?	
How can you share your expertise/ gain visibility / become known as an expert / etc in order to help lay the pathway for your future?	
What would you do if you knew that you could not fail? 10 years from now. 5 years from now. 2 years from now. 1 year from now:	What can you put in place during the pandemic to set you up for future success
What steps can you take, this week, this month, during the next 6 months to start?	

One of the sabotaging habits that leaders often have is that they talk themselves out of promotions and career opportunities. For example, "I would love to work in the United States. But I know that will never happen."

"It would be great to work a four day week to allow for my external studies. But I know that won't happen as the company frowns on people doing short weeks."

From today on, I recommend that you treat your career as if it was your own small business. Just as you would invest in your business, you also invest in your career. What would this look like?

Regardless of whether your employer pays for it or not, here are some examples of career building activities:

- Attending a national or international conference for your industry or profession
- Joining and attending your industry institute or association's seminars and events
- Writing articles for your industry; journals or blogs
- Converting your expertise to an on-line training program
- Attending in-house events
- Speaking at your industry annual conferences
- Interviewing industry experts and sharing the results
- Talking to one extra team member/stranger every day, aiming to have a quality conversation that lasts for at least two minutes – a great way of expanding your connections
- Identifying the key players in your industry and connecting with them via LinkedIn. Make a list of questions that you would like to ask these key players and work towards creating that opportunity.
- Reconnecting with your university alumni

What specifically can you do to build your career? All of these suggestions can easily be done remotely, working from home. Remember, it will be those that do this that will forge ahead on the other side of the COVID-19 crisis.

Activity 41 - Identifying Your Peers

Who are your peers in similar leadership positions nationally and internationally?

How well do you know your peers?

Why not make a list of the peers you do not know well and take action to connect with them and see if you can arrange a virtual meeting? Be prepared and plan to be very specific when you make the initial contact. Busy people hate time wasters – the more organized you are the more chance you have of your peers agreeing to meet you.

Name 3 peers whom you would like to connect with this year?

1.

2.

3.

How soon will you connect with these peers?

How did you get from where you were five years ago to where you are now?

Virtual leaders are sometimes very good at dismissing their successes and not always good at appreciating their achievements. In this activity, make a list of 10 things that you did in the last 5 years to take you from where you were to where you are now.

1.

2.

3,

4.

5,

6.

7.

8.

9.

10.

Would any of the items listed above be strategies that you could use NOW or in the near future to move you towards your next career achievement?

Knowing your Advocates

In the old days, it was said that there are six degrees of separation between you and the person you would like to meet. These days, via social media opportunities it's said there are only two degrees of separation.

So let's look at the people who are your advocates – e.g. old bosses, current leaders, industry professionals, etc. These advocates may well be able to connect you with key players, introduce you to their networks and boost your career. It is important that you nurture connections with your advocates. These are the people who speak highly of you, know you are professional, usually have personal contact with you either on the job, volunteering or a special interest group or study.

Activity 42 - List 5 of your advocates

In the table, list your top five advocates. People who publicly support you, your work, your business, a cause that you are involved with, your thoughts.

Who are they connected to? e.g. boards, politics, industry bodies etc.

Advocate's Name	People/Networks they can connect you with
1.	
2.	
3.	
4.	
5.	

Remember networking is a two-step process. What you give out comes back tenfold.

One of the most important lessons for virtual leaders today is to:

ASK FOR HELP BEFORE YOU NEED
IT!

KEY POINTS SUMMARY

- As you build your reputation as a Successful Virtual leader, not only will you be noticed by your organization but also by those in your profession.

- While most leaders are focused on the current crisis and keeping their incomes, I believe it will be the leaders who shine in the future will be those who work, during the pandemic, on their future careers.

- Regardless of whether your employer pays for it or not, here invest your time and effort in career building activities.

- Your advocates may well be able to connect you with key players, introduce you to their networks and boost your career.

References and Suggested Reading
– Articles and Books

Key Words

Virtual training, Virtual management, Leadership, Management skills, Emotional intelligence, Workplace prejudice, Local/Face to Face vs Virtual training, Team culture, Corporate culture, Team dynamics, Virtual projects, Business communication skills, Workplace motivation, Collaborative workplace, Audio and Video conferencing, Corporate and team trust, Managing globally, Language, Managing diverse teams, Power words, Business social media, Online networking.

Articles

Azarnov, D., Chubarov, A., Samsonovich, A. (2018) **Virtual Actor with Social-Emotional Intelligence**: 8th Annual International Conference on Biologically Inspired Cognitive Architectures, BICA 2017

Caulat, G. (2006) **Virtual Leadership: 360° The Ashridge Journal**: Virtual leadership

Chandra, S., Srivastava, S., Theng, YL. (2012) **Cognitive Absorption and Trust for Workplace Collaboration in Virtual Worlds**: An Information Processing Decision Making Perspective: Journal of the Association for Information Systems, Volume 13, Special Issue, pp. 797-835, October 2012

Ferrazzi, K. (2012) **How to Build Trust in a Virtual Workplace**: Harvard Business Review October 08, 2012

Ferrazzi, K. (2014) **Getting Virtual Teams Right**: Harvard Business Review, December, 2014

Furst, S., Blackburn, R., Rosen, B (1999) **Virtual team effectiveness: a proposed research agenda**: Info Systems Journal (1999) Issue 9, pp. 249-269

Gilson, L., M. Travis Maynard, T., Jones Young, N., Vartiainen, M., Hakonen, M. (2014) **Virtual Teams Research: 10 Years, 10 Themes, and 10 Opportunities**: Journal of Management Vol. XX No. X, pp. 1–25

Grech, M. (2019) **Video Conferencing in 2019: Will it Ever Become The Norm?**: Blog Post, GetVoip: Cloud Communication Advisor 2019

Hardin, A., A, Fuller, M., Davison, R. (2007) **I Know I Can, But Can We?: Culture and Efficacy Beliefs in Global Virtual Teams**: Sage Journal, Small Group Research

Harvard Extension School, Professional Development (2020) **Challenges to Managing Virtual Teams and How to Overcome Them**: Blog

Henderson, R. (2013) **What I Learned from Creating 6000+ LinkedIn Connections**: Connect with Robyn via Facebook, LinkedIn or email @ www.networkingtowin.com.au

Henttonen, K., Blomqvist, K., (2005) **Managing distance in a global virtual team: the evolution of trust through technology-mediated relational communication:** Wiley Online Library, Volume 14, Issue 2: Special Issue: Trust and Strategic Change, March/April 2005, pp. 59-119

Hertel, G., Geister, S., Konradt, U. (2005) **Managing virtual teams: A review of current empirical research.** Human Resource Management Review Volume 15, Issue 1, March 2005, pp. 69-95

Johnston, K., Rosin, K. (2011) Global **Virtual Teams: How to Manage Them:** 2011 International Conference on Computer and Management, CAMAN 2011. 10.1109/CAMAN.2011.5778849.

Kankanhalli, A., Tan, Bernard C.Y., Wei, Kwok-Kee. (2006) **Conflict and Performance in Global Virtual Teams,** Journal of Management Information Systems, 23:3, pp. 237-274

Martin, N. (2012) **Diversity and the Virtual Workplace** – Performance Identity and Shifting Boundaries of Workplace Engagement: Seattle University School of Law Digital Commons. 16 Lewis and Clark L. Rev.605 (2012).

Maznevski, M., Chudoba, K. (2000) **Bridging Space Over Time: Global Virtual Team Dynamics and Effectiveness:** ORGANIZATION SCIENCE, 2000 INFORMS Vol. 11, No. 5, September–October 2000, pp. 473–492

Millham, M., Atkin, D. (2016) **Managing the virtual boundaries: Online social networks, disclosure, and privacy behaviors:** Sage Journal, New Media and Society research article, June 27, 2016

Natrajan, N. (2016) **Use of social media as a communication tool in virtual teams for software development project:** A paradigm shift: ResearchGate Blog

Pauleen, D., Yoong, P. (2001). **"Facilitating virtual team relationships via internet and conventional communication channels."** Internet research: Electronic networking applications and policies 11(3), pp. 190-202

Piccoli, G., Ahmad, R., Ives, B. (2001). **Web-Based Virtual Learning Environments:** A Research Framework and a Preliminary Assessment of Effectiveness in Basic IT Skills Training. *MIS Quarterly, 25*(4), pp. 401-426

Precup, L., O'Sullivan, D., Cormican, K. and Dooley, L. (2006) **'Virtual team environment for collaborative research projects'.** International Journal of Innovation and Learning, 3 (1) pp. 77-93.

Rose, F., Attree, E., Brooks, B., Parslow, D., Penn. P. (2000) **Training in virtual environments: transfer to real world tasks and equivalence to real task training,** Ergonomics, 43:4, pp. 494-511

Schmidt, G. (2016) **Virtual Leadership: An Important Leadership Context:** Industrial and Organisational Psychology, Indiana University Purdue University Fort Wayne

Smith, M. K. (2005). 'Bruce W. Tuckman – **forming, storming, norming and performing in groups,** *The encyclopedia of pedagogy and informal education.* [https://infed.org/mobi/bruce-w-tuckman-forming-storming-norming-and-performing-in-groups/.

Tuckman, B. (1965) 'Developmental sequence in small groups', *Psychological Bulletin*, 63, 384-399. The article was reprinted in *Group Facilitation: A Research and Applications Journal*. Number 3, Spring 2001 and is available as a Word document: http://dennislearningcenter.osu.edu/references/GROUP%20DEV%20ARTI CLE.doc. Accessed January 14, 2005.

Warkentin, M., Beranek, P. (1999) **Training to improve virtual team communication**: Info Systems Journal (1999) Issue 9, pp. 271-289

Završnik, B. (2015) Exploring the Role of Business Social Networking for Organisations: Innovative Issues and Approaches in Social Sciences, Vol. 8, No. 1

Ziek, P. and Smulowitz, S. (2014), "**The impact of emergent virtual leadership competencies on team effectiveness**", Leadership & Organization Development Journal, Vol. 35 No. 2, pp. 106-120

Books

Amini, R. (2019) **Virtual Training - The Threshold for the High-Powered Managers**: Amazon Digital Services LLC - Kdp Print Us. ISBN: 978-1-79349-863-2

Brake, T. (2008). **Where In The World Is My Team?** - Making a Success of Your Virtual Global Workplace: John Wiley & Sons (UK). ISBN: 978-0-470-71429-4

Brookshire, R., Lybarger, K., Keane, L. (2011) **Virtual Workplace Learning: Promises Met?**: Chapter 24, page 331: Sage Publications Ltd, 1 Oliver's Yard, 55 City Road, London. ISBN: 978-1-84787-589-1

Brown, M., Huettner, B., James-Tanny, C. (2010) **Managing virtual teams - Getting the Most from Wikis, Blogs, and Other Collaborative Tools**: Getting the Most from Wikis, Blogs and Other Collaborative Tools: Jones & Bartlett Learning; 1 edition (October 22, 2010). ISBN: 1598220284

Editors: Carayannis, E., Kwak, Y., Anbari, F. (2005) **The story of managing projects - an interdisciplinary approach**: Praeger Publishers, 88 Post Road West, Westport, CT, USA. ISBN 1-56720-506-2

Caulat, G., Pedler, M. (2012) **Virtual Leadership, Learning to Lead Differently**: Independent Publishers Group. ISBN: 978-190747-150-6

Fried, J., Hansson, D (2013) **Remote – Office Not Required**: Crown Publishing Group, a division of Random House LLC, a Penguin Random House Company, New York. ISBN 978-0-8041-3750-8

Garton, C., Wegryn, K. (2006) **Managing Without Walls: Maximize Success with Virtual, Global, and Cross-cultural Teams**: MC Press, Corporate Office – 125 North Woodland Trail, Lewiville, TX, USA. ISBN 1-58347-062-X

Godar, S., Ferris, S. (2004) **Virtual and Collaborative Teams: Process, Technologies and Practice**: Idea Group Publishing (an imprint of Idea Group Inc.) 3 Henrietta Street Covent Garden London. ISBN 1-59140-204-2

Henderson, R. (2007) Dare to Dream – Self-esteem and confidence building for Busy Women: Sea Change Publishing, Kingscliff, N.S.W. (at time of publishing ISBN was unavailable)

Huggett, C. (2013) **The Virtual Training Guidebook, How to Design, Deliver and implement Live Online Learning:** ASTD Press, 1640 King Street, Box 1443, Alexandria VA, USA. ISBN-13 978-1-56286-861-1

Lojeski, K., Reilly. R. (2008). **Uniting the Virtual Workforce: Transforming Leadership and Innovation in the Globally Integrated Enterprise (Microsoft Executive Leadership Series):** John Wiley and Sons. Inc, Hoboken New Jersey, USA. ISBN 978-0-470-19395-2

Lojeski, K., Reilly, R. (2009) **Leading the Virtual Workforce - How Great Leaders Transform Organizations in the 21st Century (Microsoft Executive Leadership Series).** John Wiley & Sons Inc (US). ISBN: 9780470422809

Meister, J., Willyerd, K., (2010) The 2020 **Workplace: How Innovative Companies Attract, Develop, and Keep Tomorrow's Employees Today:** HarperCollins Special Markets Department, HarperCollins Publishers, 10 East 53rd Street, New York. ISBN 978-0-06-176327-4

Review, Harvard Business (2016) **Leading Virtual Teams:** The Virtual Manager Collection - Hold People Accountable, Build Trust, Encourage Collaboration (3 Books) HBR 20-Minute Manager Series: ISBN 978-1-633-69237-4

Runion, M., Mcdermott, L. (2012) **Perfect Phrases for Virtual Teamwork: Hundreds of Ready-to-use Phrases for Fostering Collaboration at a Distance:** McGraw-Hill Education – Europe ISBN: 9780071783842

Settle-Murphy, N. (2012) **Leading Effective Virtual Teams - Overcoming Time and Distance to Achieve Exceptional Results:** Taylor & Francis Ltd. ISBN: 9781466557864

Stahl, G., Björkman, I. (2006) **Handbook of Research in International Human Resource Management:** Chapter 19, pp. 364 -384: Published by Edward Elgar Publishing Limited Glensanda House Montpellier Parade Cheltenham Glos GL50 1UA UK. ISBN-13: 978 1 84542 128 1

CPSIA information can be obtained
at www.ICGtesting.com
Printed in the USA
LVHW081146231020
669506LV00012B/53/J

9 781921 547997